The Church's Other Half

The Church's Other Half

Women's Ministry

Trevor Beeson

scm press

Published in 2011 by SCM Press
Editorial office
13–17 Long Lane,
London EC1A 9PN, UK

SCM Press is an imprint of Hymns Ancient & Modern Ltd (a registered charity)
13A Hellesdon Park Road
Norwich NR6 5DR, UK

www.scmpress.co.uk

British Library Cataloguing in Publication data

A catalogue record for this book is available
from the British Library

978-0-334-04382-9
Kindle edition 978-0-334-04455-0

Typeset by Church Times
Printed and bound by
CPI Group (UK) Ltd, Croydon, CR0 4YY

Contents

Preface

Women, who have always constituted half, and often more, of the Church's membership, were for almost 2,000 years excluded from a significant part in its leadership – at every level. Since 1994, however, over 5,000 have been ordained to the priesthood of the Church of England, a few are now deans and archdeacons, and some will soon become bishops.

The implications of this have yet to be fully realized, but they are bound to be of fundamental importance, comparable only to those that resulted from the decision of the first-century Council at Jerusalem that Gentiles as well as Jews were to be admitted to the embryonic universal Church.

The consecration of women to the episcopate, completing a movement that started modestly in the 1930s and did not make much progress until the 1970s, will call for expressions of joyful thanksgiving that were largely denied by fearful male church leaders when the decision to ordain women priests was made by the General Synod in 1992. It is now possible to look forward to the realization of wholeness within the Church's corporate life.

Such celebrations will, nonetheless, need to be tempered by acknow-ledgement that the process of liberating women for leadership in the Church has been inordinately slow – much slower even than that which has taken place in virtually every other aspect of society, though much remains to be achieved there. Leaving aside those contextual constraints that for most of recorded history condemned women to an inferior place in patriarchal societies, it seems that only a high degree of spiritual blindness can explain why the prayer of Jesus that his followers 'might be one' was interpreted during the twentieth century only in terms of uniting separated churches, and not as an imperative to unite the roles of men and women within churches.

Recognition will also be needed of the truth expressed in the prayer attributed to Sir Francis Drake in 1588, 'It is not the beginning, but the continuing of the same, until it be thoroughly finished, which yieldeth the true glory.' The long haul that has enabled the ordained ministry to be opened to women is no more than the first stage in a wider process of bringing the feminine perspective to bear on every aspect of the Church's life. There is still a long way to go.

This book offers in a brief space an outline of how women have fared in the Church's life since its earliest days. The first part is historical, tracing the key points and ending with a more detailed account of the recent movement which has brought radical change. The main part, however, consists of short biographies of some exceptional women who, although not ordained and generally opposed to the idea of women clergy, exercised lay ministries of the greatest importance and often of heroic proportions. These provide an indication of the immense gifts that have always been available to the Church, and they must be remembered not only for the particular achievements of those who exercised them, but also for their contribution to the change in social consciousness essential to the liberation of women in every sphere of modern life.

Also to be remembered and celebrated are the lives and labours of several notable women who, although not themselves called to the priesthood, devoted insight, time, energy and skill to leadership of the movement that now enables others to respond to God's call. Those who seek to bring serious change to the life of so conservative a body as the Church of England are never likely to leave the battlefield unscathed, and in this case the issue was emotive enough to release unchristian reactions that were often hurtful and sometimes distressing to their recipients. The whole Church has reason to be profoundly grateful for the courage and perseverance of these reformers.

Some of the early fruits of their labours are represented in a chapter devoted to a number of women priests who are already making a distinctive and significant contribution to the Church's ministry. And an all too brief examination of feminist theology indicates some of the directions this is taking and the importance of it in the never-ending quest for truth. I have ventured to conclude with some suggestions concerning those areas of the Church's life which seem to me to be in special need of a feminine approach to renewal.

I am fortunate enough to have numbered among my friends several who were deeply involved in the post-1970 movement, and I am grateful to Margaret Webster also for her help and encouragement with this book. Once again, my thanks go to Fiona Mather for assisting with the research, and to Kathleen James for her remarkable skill in turning my increasingly indecipherable handwriting into a text that my editor, Dr Natalie Watson, can read and improve.

TB
Romsey

1

The First Millennium

That Mary the mother of Jesus was a key figure in the origination of the Christian faith has never been questioned, though there have been several interpretations of the significance of her role. The New Testament Gospels, which are the sole source of information, also portray her in different lights.

Luke's introduction to her could hardly be more dramatic. Happily betrothed to a man named Joseph in the Galilean village of Nazareth, her tranquillity is disturbed by the vision of an angel who tells her that she is to be the mother of 'the Son of the Most High', who will be given 'the throne of his father David, and will reign over the house of Jacob for ever'. Naturally bewildered, not least because still unmarried, the angel assured her that she would be in the hands of the Holy Spirit and possessed by 'the power of the Most High'. Mary responded submissively. 'Behold I am the handmaid of the Lord; let it be to me according to your word.' These few words were subsequently used by men, and accepted by too many women, to reinforce the belief that the role of Christian women must always be humble submission.

Luke goes on, however, to suggest something more assertive. In the course of a joyful conversation with her cousin Elizabeth, who was also pregnant, Mary declared that God

> 'Has shown strength with his arm,
> he has scattered the proud in the
>   imagination of their hearts,
> he has put down the mighty from their thrones,
> and exalted those of low degree;
> he has filled the hungry with good things,
> and the rich he has sent empty away.'

Across the Christian centuries these words have been a sign of hope and a rallying call to the multitudes of the oppressed, including many women, who have longed for liberation. Mary herself would before long become a refugee in Egypt when her infant son's life was threatened by a tyrannical ruler; and, when she was free to return home and with Joseph presented Jesus in the Temple at Jerusalem, an old man, said to be inspired by the Holy Spirit, warned her that her son would one day arouse great opposition to his prophetic work and that she, too, would have a sword pierce through her heart.

On the next reported visit to the Temple, when Jesus was 12 and taken there on a pilgrimage, his remaining behind to talk with the teacher earned a rebuke from Mary – 'Son, why have you treated us so? Your father and I have been looking for you anxiously.' It seems from this that she was not now especially conscious of her divine vocation, a point confirmed by the response of Jesus, 'How is it that you seek me? Did you not know that I must be in my Father's house?'

Again, later, at the wedding in Cana when the wine ran out and Mary drew the attention of Jesus to this, he rounded on her, hurtfully it might be supposed, 'What have you to do with me? My hour is not yet come.' Apparently unperturbed, she nevertheless instructed the servants to 'Do whatever he tells you', thus preparing the way for a miracle.

This apparent distancing of himself from Mary was demonstrated yet again when he was preaching to a crowd, and his attention was drawn to the presence of his mother and his brothers who asked to speak to him. His response must have puzzled everyone present. 'Who are my mother and my brothers?' and, turning to the crowd, he added, 'Here are my mother and my brothers! Whoever does the will of God is my brother and sister, and mother.' In other words, his spiritual relationship with his new family of disciples, women and men, was now more significant than his biological relationship with the family into which he had been born. It seems now an unfeeling way to make such a point, and on this and many other occasions during his public ministry, Mary may well have recalled the prophecy made in the Temple that a sword would pierce through her soul. Never more so than when she was present at the crucifixion of Jesus – one of the most hideously cruel and prolonged forms of execution. His men disciples had at this point 'forsaken him and fled', apart from John to whom he was specially close. Recognizing the plight of Mary and also a relationship with her that had never actually been severed, Jesus entrusted her to John in a new mother/son relationship.

There were many other women present – 'standing at a distance' – on that critical day in human history, and among these are named Mary of Magdala, Mary the mother of James the younger, and Salome. The order of these names is important, since Mary of Magdala is portrayed throughout the Gospels as the leader of the women disciples. Too often mistakenly portrayed by later preachers and writers as a reformed prostitute, Mary's discipleship began after she had been healed by Jesus of an unspecified disease.

This discipleship took her to the scene of the crucifixion and on to the burial of Jesus in the tomb offered by Joseph of Arimathea. After a pause to observe the Sabbath, Mary and her companions returned to the tomb to anoint his body with spices and, as it turned out, to experience a supernatural event that could only be described in symbol. The Gospel attempts to do this vary slightly, but are clear that it was Mary of Magdala to whom Jesus entrusted the task of telling the rest of the apostolic community of his resurrection. This crucial role has led to Mary being sometimes described as 'the apostle to the apostles', but nothing more was recorded about her in the New Testament writings.

Neither was there more recorded about the other women who were as much involved as were the men disciples in the ministry of Jesus, and later suggestions that they were only involved in domestic duties were mistaken – possibly in what turned out to be a highly successful attempt to play down the significance of their role. Even among the Gospel writers there appears to have been a reluctance on the part of Matthew and Luke to recognize the true significance of the story told by Mark concerning a woman who anointed the head of Jesus as he sat in the house of Simon the leper. This provoked anger among the men disciples who protested that the cost of the expensive ointment would have been better used for the relief of the poor. But Jesus would have none of this and rebuked the protesters, pointing out to them (and it was only three days before his crucifixion) that the woman had done a beautiful thing in anointing his body in preparation for burial – so important an action that Jesus predicted it would for ever be associated with the preaching of his message.

That this anointing should have taken place in the house of a leper is also significant. Modern readers of the Gospels do not always realize the extent to which Jesus flouted religious and social norms by associating with lepers, Samaritans, prostitutes, beggars and others who were deemed to be outside the boundaries of orthodox faith and behaviour. His free and sometimes close association with women was also highly unusual in a religious leader and cast doubt on the validity of his claims. Since the Gospels have a theological, rather than a biographical or historical purpose, it is always important not to try to claim too much for the detail of their content, but the evidence that Jesus regarded both women and men as his disciples and agents of his message of love is overwhelming.

It is not surprising therefore that in the communities of faith formed to continue and extend the preaching of his message after his death and resurrection women should continue to have an important role. The earliest account of the development of the Christian mission continued in the Acts of the Apostles (also the work of Luke) shows clearly that men and women were members of an inclusive embryonic Church.

Immediately after the ascension of Jesus when the apostles gathered in an upper room in Jerusalem in order to devote themselves to prayer, they were joined by 'the women and Mary the mother of Jesus'. Soon afterwards, after the outpouring of the Holy Spirit at Pentecost, Peter, the acknowledged leader of the community at this stage, addressed those present and quoted the prophet Joel who had heard God say, 'I will pour out my spirit upon all flesh, and your sons and your daughters shall prophesy.'

As the Church began to expand, 'believers, both of men and women were added to the Lord', and before long their numbers were large enough to provoke Saul, a devout Jewish businessman (later to become the Christian Paul), to 'drag off men and women and commit them to prison'. Women were evidently not passive defectors from Judaism. The first European convert to Christianity was Lydia, a businesswoman who dealt in precious purple fabric, who lived in the Greek city Thyatira but chanced to be in Philippi when the converted Paul was preaching there. Subsequently he accepted a pressing invitation to stay in her house which seems to have become a Christian centre, or house church, in Thyatira. Lydia was in fact just one of a number of women, variously described as being 'leading' or 'of high standing' who were attracted to Christianity and led house churches.

Of special interest is Prisca (sometimes known as Priscilla). She and her husband Aquila formed an often overlooked missionary partnership. They were active before Paul and among the founders of the Church in Rome. Having been expelled from there by the Emperor Claudius in AD 49, they settled in the Greek seaport of Corinth where they pursued their trade as tentmakers and established a house church. To this Paul was welcomed when he arrived in Corinth on the second of his missionary expeditions. When he left for Syria, they accompanied him as far as Ephesus where they established another Christian base. While there, they took in Apollos, a learned and eloquent wandering preacher who had a sound knowledge of the scriptures but only an imperfect understanding of the Gospel of Jesus. Prisca and Aquila instructed him further, then sent him on his way to Achaia where he was welcomed by the Christian community and preached powerfully to the Jews. In his first letter to the Corinthians, Paul mentions the church in the house of Prisca and Aquila, and in his letter to the Romans, by which time they had apparently returned there, Paul acknowledges them as his fellow workers in Christ Jesus and also expresses his gratitude to them for 'risking their necks for my sake'.

In the closing chapter of the same letter, Paul mentions 'our sister' Phoebe, a deaconess in the church at Cenchrea – 'a helper of many and of myself as well'. She was probably the bearer of the letter to Rome. A woman named Mary is acknowledged to 'have worked hard among you', as also have Tryphaena, Tryphosa and 'beloved' Persis. Junias, who was until recently believed to have been a man, but now thought by most scholars to have been a woman, is described as a relative, a fellow prisoner, a Christian before Paul himself was converted and 'of note among the apostles'. It seems that in the earliest years this title was not restricted to the Twelve, but included others who were sent out on missions.

The picture presented of those heroic, pioneering days is greatly inspiring and illustrative of verses 27 and 28 in the third chapter of Paul's letter to the Galatians (in modern Turkey): having reminded his readers that they had been liberated by faith from the constraints of the Jewish law, Paul goes on – 'For as many of you have been baptized into Christ have put on Christ. There is neither Jew nor Gentile, neither slave nor free, there is neither male nor female; for you are all one in Christ Jesus.'

No stronger statement has ever been made about the basis of Christian freedom and unity – a glorious consequence of faith. It was, in fact, probably a pre-Pauline baptismal confession which he used in this letter when he was particularly concerned to reconcile divided Jewish and Gentile members of the Church.

If, however – and it is a very big if – the later letters to the Colossians, Ephesians and Timothy are authentically Pauline, it is hard to avoid the conclusion that this great Christian teacher performed a *volte-face*. Even in the earlier and undoubtedly authentic first letter to the Corinthians there are ominous signs of change. In its eleventh chapter, readers are informed that 'Man is made in the image of God, while woman is the glory of man. Neither was man created for woman, but woman for man.' This is by way of explaining why 'women praying and prophesying must wear a veil'. Three chapters later, when Paul is dealing with various matters relating to church order, he takes several steps backwards:

> As in all the churches of the saints the woman should keep silence in the churches. For they are not permitted to speak, but should be subordinate, as the law says. If there is anything they desire to know let them ask their husbands at home. For it is shameful for a woman to speak in church.

In her groundbreaking book *In Memory of Her* (1983) the German–American feminist theologian Elisabeth Schüssler Fiorenza suggested that Paul was here trying to accommodate the Church's life to its surrounding Graeco–Roman culture in which the subordination of women to men was part of the law. At the same time he may have been attempting to distance the Church from certain secret oriental cults in which the participation of women was seen by the wider public as an offence against decency and order. Unfortunately, there is no evidence as to how Paul's admonitions were received – were they accepted obediently, or were they challenged fiercely?

In Colossians, Paul attempts to Christianize the previously patriarchal order of subordination – God, man, woman, child, slave – each owing obedience to the one above. Lest anyone be in doubt as to what this might involve in the life of the Church, the second chapter of the first letter to Timothy offers a simple clarification:

> Let a woman learn in silence with all submissiveness. I permit no woman to teach or have authority over men; she is to keep silent. For Adam was formed first, then Eve; and Adam was not deceived

but the woman was deceived and became a transgressor. Yet she will be saved through bearing children if she continues in faith and love and holiness, with modesty.

Nearly twenty centuries later it is impossible to calculate the immense harm these few sentences have done to the life of the developing Church and to the dignity of women. This first suggestion that women are responsible for the introduction of sin into the world led to the development of a corpus of theological reflection, all the work of men, which at worst crossed the borders of obscenity, and at best reinforced a move in the wrong direction. The consequences of this have yet to be fully remedied.

The conversion of Augustine of Hippo (354–430) from Neo-Platonist philosophy to the Christian faith was triggered finally by his chance reading of the thirteenth chapter of Paul's letter to the Romans. The consequences of this were in many ways disastrous. It caused Augustine to reject a way of life which included the keeping of a mistress for 15 years to one of extreme asceticism, a dominant feature of which was repression of sexual desire. This involved for him a high level of self-hatred, related to what he regarded as his previous appalling moral failure, and in order to alleviate this he found it helpful to turn to Paul's teaching that through Eve women are the catalysts of temptation and sin. This led him to wonder why God had ever made women in the first place and, having concluded that they were necessary to procreation, advised men to love their wives but only in the same sense that they were required to love their enemies. Had Augustine been no more than a somewhat eccentric member of an obscure sect, his outlandish beliefs on these matters would have been derided and allowed to vanish. But through his other writings, notably his *Confessions* and *The City of God*, his influence shaped the whole of Christian theology down to the thirteenth century and remains one of the foundation stones of theology even today. This has not assisted the emancipation of the Church's women members.

Neither was Augustine an isolated figure. One of his contemporaries, Jerome (342–420), is most remembered as a biblical scholar and the first translator of the Bible into Latin. Although he appears to have enjoyed the company of ascetic women who preserved their virginity, his hatred of women in general knew no bounds: 'The love of a woman is accursed; it is always insatiable ... It makes a manly soul effeminate and allows him to think of nothing but his obsession . . . Woman is classed among the greatest of evils.'

Active at the same time, Ambrose of Milan (339–97), who was pressed to accept the bishopric of Milan before he had been baptized, played some part in the conversion of Augustine. He, too, believed that women carried in their bodies the weakness of Eve, from which they could only escape by the life of virginity. It was from the reading of Ambrose that the doctrine of virginity as the highest of womanly virtues was developed. Inseparable from this was the presentation of Mary, the mother of Jesus, as the model of the virgin life. Thus the wife of the Nazareth carpenter, who had been beside both the cradle and the cross of their son, was raised on a pedestal that led quickly to beliefs that were a denial of her humanity. Not only was she 'ever-virgin', her own birth was the result of an immaculate conception, and she was herself a mediator of divine grace to whom prayer should be addressed. The title *Theotokos* (God-bearer) had become common much earlier and was officially recognized by the Church at the Councils of Ephesus (43) and Chalcedon (451). While devotion to Mary provided a feminine focus in a masculine-dominated faith, it had a deleterious influence on attitudes to sex and marriage which, again, still threatens true Christian understandings. Augustine, Jerome and Ambrose were all canonized as saints and are regarded as 'Doctors of the Western Church'. Augustine's immense influence on theology was not seriously challenged until the thirteenth century, when Thomas Aquinas became the towering figure, though his arrival did nothing to change attitudes to women. In spite of the Church's negative attitude there appeared, however, between the sixth and eighth centuries, a very large number of remarkable women who exercised Christian ministries of the greatest importance without the benefit of holy orders.

This book is concerned only with England, but it is necessary to begin in what is now France. There Princess Clotilde (471–545) moved from Burgundy to Rheims to marry Clovis, a pagan and king of the Franks. Through her influence he was converted to Christianity and thereafter ruled as a Christian monarch. He was subsequently credited with having made France 'the eldest daughter of the Catholic Church'. He had a real grand-daughter, Princess Bertha (539–612) who crossed the Channel to England to marry the pagan King Ethelbert of Kent. She came on the understanding that she could continue to practise her Christian faith and brought with her Liudhard, her chaplain. Ethelbert gave her a church outside Canterbury's city walls dating from the Roman era. Restored and dedicated to Saint Martin of Tours, this became her private chapel.

The mission of Saint Augustine (not to be confused with the theologian) to Kent in 597 is now believed to have been the result of a response by Pope Gregory to a request from Queen Bertha for assistance with the task of evangelizing the English, rather than to his sight in Rome of fair-headed Angles. Either way, Augustine and his party of monks were warmly received on their arrival, and among the many Christian converts during the early stages of their mission was King Ethelbert. As a consequence of this, the whole of Kent and some other parts of south-east England became Christian. Bertha and Ethelbert, standing between Augustine and Liudhard, are now portrayed in one of the nave windows of Canterbury Cathedral.

Ethelburga (585–633) was a daughter of King Ethelbert and Queen Bertha and went with her chaplain, Paulinus, to marry Edwin, the pagan King of Northumbria. Two years later, on Easter Eve 627, he was baptized by Paulinus at York. He then began, but never completed because of an attack from Mercia, the building of a church in York, with Paulinus as its Bishop. For several years Edwin was the most powerful monarch in England, and much of the north became Christian. The Pope expressed his pleasure by sending Ethelburga a silver mirror and an ivory comb, while Edwin was rewarded with fine gold-embroidered robes. He was, however, killed in battle in 633, and, his kingdom having been divided, Ethelburga returned to Kent. There the king provided her with a ruined Roman villa at Lyminge which she converted into an abbey for both men and women, and over which she ruled until her death.

Another woman of enormous influence was Hilda of Whitby (614–80), who was King Edwin's great niece. Although baptized by Paulinus on the same day as her great-uncle, she was influenced much more by Aidan, the leader of the Celtic missionary movement, who had been sent from Iona to Lindisfarne to convert northern England. It was while she was travelling to Paris in 649 to join her sister in a convent that she was recalled by Aidan to become Abbess of a religious house in Hartlepool. Eight years later, Aidan created a monastery for monks and nuns at Whitby and appointed Hilda as its Abbess.

In his *Historia Ecclesiastica* Bede recorded that, in accordance with the Celtic tradition, Hilda used the scriptures of the monastic life and the living out of their call to embrace poverty, humility and service. With a strong emphasis on scholarship and learning, as well as on spiritual depth, the abbey attracted kings, princes and scholars from all over England. Hilda built up a huge library and did most of the teaching herself. She eventually numbered at least five bishops and innumerable scholars among her pupils. She also encouraged Caedmon, the first English poet, who was a cowherd on the abbey's farm.

In 664 her abbey was chosen as the place for what turned out to be the historic Synod of Whitby. The purpose of the synod was to determine whether the Celtic or the Roman traditions concerning such matters as the date of Easter and the tonsure on monks' heads should be adopted throughout England. Hilda supported the Celtic position in the debate but afterwards she readily accepted the majority decision. The significance of the change was the consequential alliance of the English Church with continental Catholicism.

Hilda's abbey was destroyed by Danish invaders in 867 almost two centuries after her death. During its existence it provided a strong and stable Christian base in turbulent times when the influence of kings and bishops waxed and waned. The abbey, which stood high on Whitby's cliffs, was rebuilt in the twelfth century but fell into ruin again after the dissolution of the monasteries in the sixteenth century. The substantial remains offer today a constant reminder of one of the important figures in the early history of Christianity in England. Many churches in the north-east are dedicated in her saintly honour, as well as colleges in Oxford and Durham.

It was not long after Hilda's death that in south-west England another women's monastic community embarked on a great mission that, in partnership with monks, led to the conversion to the Christian faith of the German people. The leader of this mission was Boniface, a Benedictine monk of Nursling, near Southampton, who is still honoured as 'the Apostle of Germany'. A wise missionary strategist as well as a great preacher, he decided early in his campaign that it was important to establish strong bases in key locations rather than allow small new Christian communities to be spread thinly. Monasteries were needed, and these required nuns as well as monks.

For nuns he turned to the great abbey at Wimborne in Dorset. Founded by sisters of the King of the West Saxons, this had adopted the Benedictine rule and under Mother Tetta had grown to include 500 nuns. Among these was Leoba (710–82), who had been born in Wessex and was a distant cousin of Boniface. She had been sent to Wimborne when very young, and 20 years later Boniface called her to join him in Germany. She went, accompanied by 20 other nuns, and for a time accompanied Boniface on his missionary travels, benefitting him, as he put it, from her holiness and example.

When, however, he established a convent at Tauberbischofsheim, he appointed Leoba as its abbess and also made her responsible for the oversight of all the nuns working in Germany. When he went north to extend the mission to Frisia, he gave her his monastic cowl to indicate that she was his delegate. During his absence she founded two more convents and, being a woman of considerable learning as well as holiness, was frequently consulted by bishop and abbots.

This took her sometimes, and with a degree of reluctance, to the court of Pippin, the Christian King of the Franks, who collaborated with Boniface in the Christianizing of his country. Leoba was needed as a court counsellor, and this led to a friendship with Hildegard, the wife of the Emperor Charlemagne. Her later years were spent, with a few other nuns, on an estate near Mainz given to her by Charlemagne. Boniface said that when she died he wished her to be buried in his own tomb at Fulda, but when the time for this came, the Abbot of Fulda refused to allow this, and she was buried nearby. She was later declared to be a saint.

Among those who accompanied Leoba to Germany was Walburga (710–79). Born in Devon and the daughter of a West Saxon chieftain and a niece of Boniface, she had also been sent to be educated at Wimborne. Furthermore, she was a sister of Willibald and Wunibald, both monks, who were closely involved with Boniface in Germany. On completion of her education at Wimborne she remained to become a nun and, after spending her first two years in Germany in a convent at Bischofsheim, became Abbess of Heidenheim. This was a double monastery, where Wunibald was the Abbot, but on his death Walburga became Superior of both. Walburga is said to have had considerable healing powers and the ability to tame wolves. Her stilling of a storm when crossing from England to Germany led to her becoming a patron saint of sailors. Her bones lie in the small church of the Holy Cross at Eichstätt, where her other brother was the bishop.

One more relative was Hugebore, who became Abbess of the double monastery at Hildesheim. She is best remembered as one of the earliest woman writers and as the author of the first German-language travel book. This contained accounts of her brother Willibald's pilgrimages to the Holy Land, as narrated to her by him, and also an account of his missionary life. Only the preface has survived, but this indicates an author endowed with an acute and perceptive mind.

It is clear that during the seventh and eighth centuries the Church in northern Europe paid scant regard to the teaching of Saint Paul and the major theologians who followed him in the matter of women's place in the life of the Church. It is true that none was ordained to the priesthood, but far from occupying positions of subordination, a significant number were given positions of leadership, sometimes of a quasi-episcopal order, which involved the leadership of men as well as women. Overall, it appears that in the great work of bringing the people of England and Germany to faith, women and men worked together in fruitful partnership. A high proportion of the clergy who were not monks, including some bishops, were married.

It would not always be so. By the year 1000 most of Europe had become Christian. At the highest level the Church was still under lay control inasmuch as the lands from which its income was derived were owned by kings, princes, barons and other, lower ranks of the aristocracy. On the principle that those who pay the piper are entitled to call the tune he plays, these landowners exercised the right of patronage over appointments among the clergy. After some centuries of this arrangement it had become part of the tradition. With the passage of time, however, the popes and the bishops became increasingly unhappy at this disposal of power. In practical terms it could often hamper effective leadership in the Church, and it was an affront to those understandings of the value of the Church which saw it as a divinely created institution, entrusted with a spiritual purpose and led by those whom God had chosen and commissioned.

2

Glimmers of Light in Dark Places

The arrival of a new millennium provided a good opportunity to reassert clerical claims and to break the yoke of lay control. A series of radical reforms led to increasing centralization of the Church's life and the rise of papal power. This process was deemed to require celibacy in the clergy, allegedly to free them to exercise their ministries unimpeded by family responsibilities, but in fact to bring them more easily under the control of the hierarchy. The overall effect of the reforms was to clericalize the Church, so that the laity, men as well as women, were reduced to passivity, and in the eyes of some bishops their existence was a bit of a nuisance. Churches of the Catholic tradition, including the Church of England, have not yet fully changed this.

As is often the case, theological factors were produced to provide compelling 'spiritual' reasons for imposing the change. The teachings of Augustine, Ambrose, Jerome and other venerated scholars of an earlier era on the dangers of association with women were re-introduced and re-emphasized. Thus Peter Damian (1007–72), a leading eleventh-century reformer who was later canonized as a saint and declared to be a 'Doctor of the Church', could write of women:

> I speak to you, O charmers of the clergy, appetizing flesh of the devil, that castaway from paradise, poison of the minds, death of souls, companions of the very stuff of sin, the cause of your ruin. You, I say, I exhort you women of the ancient enemy, you bitches, sows, screech-owls, night-owls, blood suckers, she-wolves – come now, hear me, harlots, prostitutes, with your lascivious kisses, you wallowing places for fat pigs, couches for lean spirits.

An hysterical outburst of this sort has to be assessed in psychological rather than theological categories. Nonetheless it was expressive, albeit in an extreme form, of an attitude to women that came to dominate the life of the medieval Church. This extended far beyond the matter of clerical celibacy to include marriage, sex and the status of women in the human race.

The massive achievement of Thomas Aquinas (1225–74) was to interpret Christian truth in terms of the prevailing thought forms of his time, which happened to be Aristotelian philosophy. So successfully did he accomplish this that his teaching became the controlling influence in the outlook of the medieval Church, extending until comparatively recently to the modern Roman Catholic Church.

It was unfortunate therefore that Aristotle did not have a high view of women. He saw them as distinctly inferior to men, and so, of necessity, subordinate to men. Thomas applied this to the institution of marriage, arguing that because the husband was more reasonable, more just and capable of greater virtue, he was deserving of more love. Consequently, the wife, being naturally inferior, morally, was deserving only of a lesser kind of love. This opened the floodgates to massive exploitation of wives by their husbands, and Thomas pointed the way by asserting that wives should display sacrificial love of their husbands and be obedient to them. The task of maintaining the stability of the family was hers alone. At a time when the life expectancy of a woman was about 40 years, and she was likely to be pregnant for half of those years, the difference between marriage and slavery could for her have been only slight.

Despite the permeation of the medieval Church by this cruel, dehumanizing way of thinking and consequent acting, there were throughout Europe many shining examples of women who, usually from within the confines of the monastic life, offered to the Church new insights into God's loving will and purpose for all his people (women as well as men) that in the twenty-first century continue to illuminate and inspire. Chief among these in continental Europe were Hildegard of Bingen (1098–1179), Clare of Assisi (1194–1253), Mechthild of Magdeburg (*c.* 1207–94), Gertrude of Helfta (1256–1302), Marguerite Porete (d. 1310), Catherine of Siena (1347–80), Joan of Arc (1412–31) and Catherine of Genoa (1447–1510), whose lives spanned over four centuries. There were many more.

In England also there were outstanding women among the nuns, abbesses, recluses and visionaries, who sought to temper the harsh cruelty of their times, both within and without the Church, with a reaffirmation of the compassionate love lived and taught by Jesus. Deprived normally of much education, they expressed their faith through vision and mysticism, rather than the complexities of traditional theology. This was a major contribution to the Christian understanding of the ways of God, though unfortunately it was never received and absorbed by the medieval Church. Had it been so absorbed, the content of Christian witness would have been very different.

Although Christina of Markyate (*c.* 1096–1160) was not allocated a place in the otherwise remarkably comprehensive *Oxford Dictionary of the Christian Church,* there is a life of her in the *Oxford World Classics,* and she deserves to be better known. Born of wealthy, influential parents and named Theodora, she went aged 13 to St Alban's Abbey. There she felt called to make a vow of chastity and changed her name to Christina. This was obviously not compatible with her parents' wish that she should marry a well-placed local young man, Burthred, to whom, without her knowing, they had betrothed her.

When this was eventually disclosed to her, she steadfastly refused to accept the possibility of marriage to anyone. The response was a campaign of persuasion involving many influential people and unbelievable cruelty on the part of her parents. Considerable details of this were recorded in a Life written by a monk of St Albans, and, when full account is taken of the exaggerations which often characterize medieval material produced for edification, it is evident that Christina's upholding of her vow involved considerable pain. In the end Christina was obliged to accept marriage to Burthred but immediately and, it was said, on the advice of the Archbishop of Canterbury, made her escape, clad in men's clothing and on horseback. Having been sheltered for a time by friends, she found a place of refuge with an anchoress, Alfwen, 30 miles away at Flamstead in Hertfordshire. She next moved to Markyate to occupy part of a hut which housed Roger, a hermit and a deacon of St Albans. It was apparently a squalid existence but they established a close spiritual relationship, and she learned a great deal from him about the life of the Spirit. After four years Burthred arrived to release her from her marriage vows, and, following Roger's death, she occupied the entire hut and began to experience visions of Jesus and the Virgin Mary. In the end, she is said to have had 42 of these. When news of them spread, other women joined her and, with financial support from Abbot Geoffrey of St Albans, a more substantial building was erected, and Christina became the first Abbess of a community which survived until the dissolution of the monasteries in the sixteenth century.

She is now to be seen as a bridge between the Church of the Anglo-Saxon world and the new, very different order that gradually came from Europe as a consequence of the Norman Conquest. Although her ministry was exercised from within the confines of a convent, she worked in partnership with and enjoyed the friendship of a number of men who were also committed to the monastic life. The most important of these, Abbott Geoffrey, came to regard her as his teacher, and she was his spiritual director. Her monk biographer wrote, 'He had a deep respect for the maiden and saw in her something divine and extraordinary.' He added, 'She had the true gaze of one with spiritual eyes.'

The same could well have been said of Julian of Norwich (c. 1342–1420), who lived in one of the most turbulent periods in English history. Beset by war, the Black Death, social unrest, a divided papacy and a failed crusade, this was a time of constant and often severe human suffering, for which Julian, perhaps the most potent spiritual power of the Middle Ages, appears to have been totally unconcerned.

Hardly anything is actually known about her life – not even her name, since Julian was acquired from the name of the Norwich church to which her anchorhold was attached. Women entering into this form of the religious life were normally drawn from the upper echelon of society and, although she professed to be unlettered, her *Revelations of the Divine Love* (now a spiritual classic) displays an acute mind and one of considerable learning.

Early in life she prayed for three blessings – an experience of Christ's passion such as Mary Magdalene had been granted near the cross; a severe illness that would enable her to experience something of his passion in her own body; and a gift of compassing contrition and longing for God. The second of these came to her on 8 May 1373 when she fell seriously ill and was believed to be near death. On that day she experienced, over a period of five hours, 15 showings or revelations, followed by another on the next day. Having recovered from the illness, she wrote a short account of these 'showings'. This was enlarged some twenty years later to include her own profound reflections on their significance. The fact that she took considerable trouble over this suggests that she had a compelling need to share her experiences and faith with others, as 600 years later *Revelations of the Divine Love* continue to do, more widely than ever before.

The anchorhold in Norwich which she entered was one of about fifty such places in that city recorded between the thirteenth century and the Reformation. Usually attached to a parish church, they enabled women (anchoresses) and men (anchorites) to withdraw from the world in order to develop their spiritual lives more fully. They were locked in and remained until their death. This symbolized an early burial and the gifts of new resurrection life in the spirit.

It was not, however, quite as austere and isolated a life as might be supposed. The anchorhold would usually consist of two or three rooms, one of which was occupied by servants who were responsible for the housekeeping, shopping and cooking. Julian evidently had two women and a boy, and probably a cat to deal with any vermin. One of the windows of her room would open into the church so that she could share, though not verbally, in the daily worship. The other would open to the city street to enable her to communicate with those, and eventually they were many, including Margery Kempe (1373–1478), who came for spiritual advice or healing. Most of her time, however, was devoted to prayer and the ascetic life, without resorting to extremes of fasting and mortification.

Before entering an anchorhold, it was necessary to convince the local bishop or his representative that this was a genuine calling, and once accepted, entry was marked by a solemn ceremony involving the sprinkling of dust over the anchoress and the formal locking of the door. Just when Julian entered the Norwich anchorhold is unclear and the subject of much speculation. It is just impossible to tell and is in any case not significant.

The dominant theme of the *Revelations* is the primacy of love in the relationship with God and with each other:

And from the time it was revealed, I desired many times to know what was our Lord's meaning. After fifteen years and more, I was answered in spiritual understanding, and it was said: What, do you wish to know your Lord's meaning in this thing? Know it well, love was his meaning. Who reveals it to you? Love. What did he reveal to you? Love. Why does he reveal it to you? For love. Remain in this, and you will know more of the same. But you will never know different, without end.

This love is disclosed in God's creation. One of Julian's most memorable visions was that of 'something small, no bigger than a hazel-nut lying in the palm of my hand'. This signified 'everything that is made' and it will last for ever 'because God loves it; and everything has been through the love of God'. God also reveals his love through the redemptive death of his son Jesus on the cross, and through the relationship within the Holy Trinity. Julian had a special devotion to Jesus and wrote of

> Christ our true mother, for a mother's caring is the closest, nearest and surest, (yet) our own mother bore us only unto pain and dying. But our true mother, Jesus, bears us unto joy and endless loving . . . A mother feeds her child with milk, but our beloved mother, Jesus, feeds us with himself.

In common with many other thoughtful Christians before and since her time, Julian could not avoid facing the problem of the existence of sin, suffering and pain within the economy of a God of love. This could be understood only in the light of the Crucifixion, and she was drawn to conclude that 'all shall be well and all manner of things shall be well'. Her emphasis on God's all-embracing love was in marked contrast with the cruel world around her and with much in the life and teaching of the Church of her time. The late twentieth century brought a renewal of interest in her spirituality. St Julian's Church in Norwich, destroyed by bombing in 1942, was restored to become a permanent place of prayer, and Julian Groups meet in many parts of the world to meditate on her *Revelations*. She is commemorated in the Church of England's Calendar of Holy Days on 8 May.

It is difficult to conceive of a mystic more different from Julian of Norwich or any other reclusive religious woman than Margery Kempe (*c.* 1373–after 1438). Born in Lynn, not far from Norwich, she was the daughter of a prominent public figure who was five times mayor of the town and a member of the regional parliament. Aged about 20 she married John Kempe and had a difficult first pregnancy with life-threatening complications at the time of the delivery. She sent for a priest to hear her confession of a 'secret sin', but he censured her and left before she could articulate her guilt. This induced the fear of eternal damnation and a vision of many devils around her, causing violent hysteria. Deemed to be a threat to her own safety and that of others, she was confined to a storeroom for six months. Mental stability returned after a vision in which Jesus sat beside her and asked, 'Daughter, why hast thou forsaken me, and I forsake never thee?', to which she confessed she had intended to become God's servant but 'could not leave pride and pompous array'.

That Margery had a deeply hysterical personality can hardly be open to doubt. For most of her life she was given to tears, which was not at all uncommon in women mystics, but in her case these were loud and ear-piercing and sometimes accompanied by shrieks and groans that disturbed the devotions of others in her company at the time. This has led to the fairly common view that she was a mentally unbalanced woman who is not to be treated seriously. Yet she nurtured 14 children and engaged in at least two business enterprises – a brewery and a granary – which flourished for a time until hit by declines in the local economy.

Margery was a devout yet feisty woman with an earthy sense of humour and considerable family responsibilities. After the failure of the granary, however, she decided to 'enter the way of everlasting life'. An overwhelming conviction of the love of God reinforced her calling to holiness of life and led to an agreement with her husband that they should both commit themselves to chastity. This was formalized in 1413 in the presence of the Bishop of Lincoln, but before long her husband found that he could only cope with its demands if they lived apart.

Margery thereupon embarked on a series of pilgrimages (exacting experiences at that time) which took her over a period of several years to the Holy Land, Rome, Santiago de Compostela, Norway and, finally, Danzig. In or about 1412 she visited Julian in her cell at Norwich to be counselled on her visionary experiences and was advised that these could be regarded as orthodox if they led to a higher quality of life.

Others were less certain as to her orthodoxy since she exhibited certain sympathies with the Lollards – followers of John Wycliffe – who constituted one of the earliest Reformation movements. She was arraigned before the Bishop of Lincoln, then before the Archbishop of Canterbury, Thomas Arundel, who was a persecutor of the Lollards and decreed that under no circumstances should women be allowed to preach. The fact that she also dressed in white, a symbol of virginity, also aroused some suspicion and hostility, though she explained that this was part of her campaign to gain acknowledgement of the fact that the way of holiness could be embraced by those who lived outside the cloister.

In 1431, her husband was badly injured after falling downstairs, so she returned to nurse him until his death not long afterwards. She was, it seems, unable to read or to write and dictated to two priests successively *The Book of Margery Kempe.* This was autobiographical, consisting of accounts of her pilgrimages and certain other aspects of her life, including some of the visions. Aware always of close communion with God, she also had a deep compassion for the sins of the world. The book is thought to be the first autobiography in English, and the only surviving manuscript was in private hands until acquired by the British Library in 1980. A modern English version was published in 1936 and a Penguin edition in 1985.

The first signs of what would become a major reformation of the English Church appeared as early as the second half of the fourteenth century with the preaching of John Wycliffe (1310–84). His followers, often known as Lollards, were not very numerous, but their influence became considerable. Wycliffe stood for the equality of clergy and laity and therefore the right of the latter to read and interpret the scriptures for themselves, and to receive both the consecrated bread and wine at Holy Communion. All of which, taken together, represented a strong assault on what had become the Church's traditional faith and order. Wycliffe was also believed by his followers to have declared that Christ left 'apostolic power to every good, true Christian man and woman living virtuously'.

Consequently women played an important part in the preaching and leadership of the Lollard movement – so much so that in the course of its severe repression Margaret Baxter in Norfolk, Agnes Grebhill in Kent, Joan Washingby in Coventry and at least nine others, together with many more men, were burned at the stake in southern and central England.

When the Reformation proper achieved dominance in the sixteenth century its emphasis on the centrality of the Bible in Christian witness did nothing to improve the lot of women. But it placed on the throne of England a woman, Queen Elizabeth I, who overcame any bias against feminine rule by firmly espousing Protestantism and promoting anti-popery. She thus became the most influential force in English religious history, changing the nation's culture. This did not involve the acceptance of women as leaders in any other departments of Church or State, but the teaching of Saint Paul and its reinforcement by the Church across the centuries proved to be no impediment to her receiving the title 'Supreme Governor of the Church of England', with the power to appoint bishops, cathedral deans and some other dignitaries. This title passed to all her successors, including Queen Anne, Queen Victoria and the present Queen Elizabeth II.

Far from increasing the opportunities open to women, the dissolution of the monasteries and abbeys at the time of the Reformation actually deprived women of those spheres where they could exercise distinctive, albeit limited, forms of Christian witness. During the next three centuries the only available outlets for ministries of any kind were provided by the Quakers (the Religious Society of Friends). The founder of the movement, George Fox (1624–91) had the burning conviction that every man and woman has direct access to God, who guides them by an 'inner light'. There was therefore no need for formal acts of corporate worship or for a set-aside ministry of any kind. This immediately opened the door to any woman who might feel guided by the 'inner light' (ignited by the Holy Spirit) to preach and lead.

Many did – chief among them in the early days Margaret Fell (1614–1702). Married while in her teens to an old man who, being a distinguished judge, was often away, she was sometimes called on by George Fox in the course of his missionary travels. This led to her involvement in his work and, when her husband died in 1658, the family estate, Swarthmore Hall, became the centre of Quaker activities. She came to be regarded as the co-founder of the movement.

The persecution experienced by the Quakers during the Common-wealth intensified considerably with the Restoration of the monarchy in 1660, and until the Toleration Act of 1669 they received no mercy. Margaret Fell was in prison during the last five of these years and took the opportunity to write a defiant pamphlet, *Women's Speaking: Justified, Proved and Allowed by the Scriptures*. Time has neither outdated nor invalidated her claim. On her release from prison she resumed her missionary activities and in 1699 married George Fox. By this time, however, neither of them had much longer to live and it seems they spent little time together. The nineteenth century saw Quakers involved in extensive social work and the heroic ministry as a prison reformer of Elizabeth Fry (1780–1845).

3

The Slow Awakening

Although Hannah More died in 1797, her pioneering work in the education of poor children, as well as her involvement in the campaign for the abolition of slavery, has often led to her being described as 'the first Victorian'. The decades following her death witnessed an extraordinary expansion of social and philanthropic activity which did something to mitigate the acute suffering created by the rapid transition of Britain from an agrarian to an industrial society. Hannah More also prepared the way for women to spearhead this expansion of social work and exercise a ministry of care and compassion beyond their own homes.

Edward Munroe, in his *Pastoral Work* (1850), saw this involvement as providing women of leisure and means with 'objects on which to bestow strong sympathies and yearnings which otherwise have no special channel for exhaustion'. Moreover, it would provide a serious purpose in life for women who were aware that 'they are responsible beings approaching an eternity in which they will have to render an account of hours given for higher uses, but spent perhaps on vain trifles'.

By the end of the century a contributor to a volume of essays, *Woman's Mission* (1893), edited by a prominent social reformer, Baroness Burdett-Coutts, estimated that half a million women were occupied more or less continuously or semi-professionally in philanthropic work of one kind or another. An edition of the *Church of England Year Book*, published in the same year, reported that 47,112 district visitors (mostly women) were at work in the 80 per cent of parishes making returns. By 1916–17 this had increased to 76,249, and it can be supposed that the overwhelming majority of these were motivated by something more than 'relief from idleness or from occupations of a trivial character'.

The truth is that, as Brian Heeney pointed out in his classic *The Women's Movement in the Church of England 1850–1930* (1988), when women were at last given the opportunity to exercise some form of useful social work, they seized this eagerly and demonstrated that they could bring to it the skill, compassion and zeal required in Christian ministry. That most, perhaps all, were from the upper and middle classes was only to be expected, since the others were preoccupied with the survival of themselves and their families. The men who were ministering as bishops and priests were, for different reasons, drawn from the same, more privileged classes. There were, however, a few women drawn from near the bottom of the social ladder. These were the so-called Bible Women recruited by Ellen Ranyard from 1857 onwards into the Bible and Domestic Female Mission. Modestly paid, and the first professional social workers, these were employed to distribute Bibles and offer advice on domestic matters to wives and mothers in the very poorest parts of London. About 250 were soon in action and 80 of these were trained as nurses. The Ranyard Mission expanded considerably during the early decades of the twentieth century, when it was supported mainly by the Church of England. Ranyard Nurses continued the work until taken over by the district nursing services in 1965.

Another move in this direction came in 1882, when the Revd Wilson Carlile founded the Church Army. This was born of the conviction that only working-class evangelists stood any chance of converting to the Christian faith the alienated urban masses. For the first five years of its existence he recruited only laymen as Captains, but then women were drawn in as Sisters to exercise significant ministries as nurse-evangelists. These have continued, though in a modified form, to the present day.

The revival of the Religious Orders in the Church of England started with women's communities, most notably Priscilla Lydia Sellon's Community of the Holy Trinity, founded at Devonport in 1848. These were initially committed to social work, including nursing and teaching, in slum areas. A little later Deaconess communities, imported from Germany and inspired in England by Elizabeth Ferard, provided similar opportunities for women who did not feel called to embrace the particular disciplines of the Religious Life. Both required an unusual degree of commitment and dedication.

More opportunities eventually came to women with the remarkable expansion of the overseas missionary enterprise into the still largely unknown and invariably hazardous territories of Africa, Asia and the Pacific. The Church Missionary Society sent two women, one accompanying her brother, to Sierra Leone in 1819, but these proved to be exceptions to a policy that regarded conditions overseas to be unsuitable for women. The Bishop of Calcutta also believed that they would be almost certain to marry within a month of their arrival. The Society for the Propagation of the Gospel felt bold enough to run this risk by sending a single woman missionary to Madagascar in 1874 but not again until the next century.

There was no real breakthrough until it was recognized that the millions of Indian women, condemned to spend the whole of their lives in purdah because they were deemed unsuitable for marriage to educated men, could only be reached by women missionaries. This led to the establishing in 1880 of a Church of England Zenana Missionary Society, with 32 women missionaries assigned to stations in India. It also became evident that in Muslim societies only women could minister to women.

These practical factors, combined with a change of attitude by the Church Missionary Society, led to the recruitment of women on a fairly large scale, and by the end of the century there were nearly 300 of them on the books of CMS. Other missionary agencies of all the churches also recognized that neither theology nor tradition stood in the way of women preaching, teaching, leading worship and healing the sick, often heroically, in distant lands. In the end the number of women missionaries, including the wives of missionary bishops and priests, became the majority. Without them the shape and speed of the Christian world mission in the nineteenth century would have been different.

Less inspiring, but still significant, the 1860s witnessed the first stirrings of lay involvement in the Church of England's government. Up to this point lay parliamentarians were deemed to be the mouthpiece of the laity and could exercise considerable power. The bishops now began to encourage the formation of church councils to assist the parish clergy, not least in the raising of money, and although these got off to a slow start they had by the end of the century spread widely. It was not until 1919, however, that women were allowed to play an influential part in the modest revival of lay responsibility.

In 1866, the Bishop of Ely was bold enough to set up a diocesan conference to which laymen as well as the clergy were summoned. This was a purely advisory body and harmless enough to encourage nearly every other bishop to establish similar conferences during the 1870s. They met whenever the bishop felt moved to address them, and in some places laypeople were invited to join the clergy at Rural Deanery meetings. There was no question of women attending either bodies.

Next, in 1886 and 1892, came the inauguration of Lay Houses to meet alongside the exclusively clerical Convocations of Canterbury and York. The membership of these new Houses, drawn from the leisured and professional classes, was by no means undistinguished but, again, its function was only consultative and women were excluded. Soon after this the Church Reform League published a pamphlet calling for sweeping changes in several areas of the Church's life, including the setting up of a formal system of self-government within the framework of the historic Establishment. The bishops of the Convocation of Canterbury responded in 1897 with a number of proposals for modest reform. These acknowledged the need for councils but with the proviso, 'Elected councillors shall be male communicants of the Church of England of full age'.

An attempt by some bishops to get the word 'male' deleted was defeated by only two votes, but it then turned out that there were already a number of women churchwardens (these being elected to an office that was civil, as well as ecclesiastical) who qualified for ex-officio membership of their parish church councils. A year later 1,100 churchwomen signed a petition to the bishops protesting at their exclusion, and their anger was only inflamed when the Convocation's Lower House of Clergy endorsed the bishops' decision by 39 votes to 18. In the debate the Archdeacon of Exeter expressed his belief that women were not made by God to engage in public discussion even in parish church councils. Another archdeacon was of the opinion that 'the most truly feminine women would refuse to seek office' and that others who were elected would make the councils 'weak instruments in local public affairs'. It is hardly surprising that the rise of Church feminism is generally reckoned to have started at the time of this debate.

When in 1903 a Representative Church Council consisting of bishops, priests and laity was formed, women were not only excluded from membership of this powerless body but also prohibited from voting for the lay delegates. Another 11 years would pass before any of them were allowed to vote for and serve on parish church councils, loud protests having secured a concession that women whose property-owning rights entitled them to vote in municipal elections might be trusted to behave responsibly in church affairs.

Meanwhile, a 5,000-strong Church League for Women's Suffrage, which had been formed initially as part of a national campaign to win parliamentary voting rights for women, was turning its attention to their disabilities in church government. In a petition to the representative Church Council in 1915 the League stated its case with crystal clarity:

1 The exclusion of women from the Ruri-decanal and Diocesan Conferences and from the Representative Church Council is an infraction of that spiritual equality of the sexes which is a fundamental principle of the Christian faith.
2 It forbids the direct expression in these assemblies of women's views, upon all of which women claim the right to be heard, and upon some of which they can almost claim a monopoly of first-hand knowledge.
3 The authority of the decisions of such assemblies is thereby weakened.
4 A stumbling-block is thereby placed in the path of many women who regard their exclusion, deliberately decreed, as an infringement of their spiritual status.
5 All women are thereby deprived of the stimulus that comes from a sense of equal opportunity and responsibility for both sexes alike.

By this time, however, the Church's leadership was preoccupied by preparations for a National Mission of Repentance and Hope designed to set something constructive alongside the fearful devastation being wrought in the trenches of France and Belgium. The influential council responsible for its organization included Maude Royden, the most ardent and courageous of the church feminists, who naturally urged consideration of the best use of women speakers in the Mission. The decision about this was left to the diocesan bishops, who decided against their use, with the exception of the Bishop of London, Arthur Foley Winnington-Ingram, who was soon prevailed upon to withdraw his permissions.

The Mission's impact was minimal. Not so the Life and Liberty Movement spearheaded by William Temple, the outstanding churchman of his time. This had the enthusiastic support of the services chaplains and many others who saw the need for substantial church reform once the war had ended, and believed the freedom of the Church to order its own affairs without overbearing parliamentary control was essential to this process. The earlier, tentative moves towards this required a different approach, and in the end statutory authority. In 1919, the existing

Representative Church Council prepared the way by authorizing women to vote for and sit on all the Church's councils, and when the new National Assembly of the Church of England met for the first time in 1920, there were 46 women among the 357 lay representatives.

Progress of this sort and on this scale was not sufficient, however, to meet the demands of the more militant church feminists. At the end of the war the Church League for Women's Suffrage changed its name to the League of the Church Militant. Its campaign for wide-ranging reform included, in 1920, a report on the Ministry of Women which emphasized 'the primary importance of effecting equalization of the ministries of the Anglican Church'. This was in marked contrast to an Archbishop of Canterbury's report on the same subject, published in the same year, which went so absurdly far as to assert, 'The restriction of the ministry of the priesthood to men originated in a generation which was guided by special gifts of the Holy Spirit.' Without going quite as far as that, the Lambeth Conference, also meeting in 1920, came out firmly against the ordination of women to the priesthood.

At the same time, however, the bishops seemed ready to acknowledge for the first time, albeit in negative terms, the existence of the Order of Deaconesses, warning this to be 'the one and only Order of Ministry which has the stamp of Apostolic approval'. Any rejoicing on the part of the deaconesses was immediately inhibited by the proviso that, while they might, under conditions laid down by their bishops, speak and pray in a consecrated building, they could not do so at any of the Church's official services. No apostolic authority was cited to justify this restriction, but lest the intentions of the Lambeth bishops be open to doubt the Lower House of the Convocation of Canterbury passed by a large majority in 1922 a resolution specifically prohibiting deaconesses from speaking and praying in church other than to congregations of women and children.

At the next Lambeth Conference, held in 1930, the attitude to deaconesses hardened and attempts to give them authority to share in some of the functions of male deacons were firmly rejected. Indeed, a committee dealing with this subject stated unequivocally that the deaconess was not a deacon at all but was 'outside the historic Orders of the ministry . . . supplementing and complementing them'. Thereafter their status in the Church was never clear and any hope that they might become a large element in the Church's ministry soon expired.

The prospect of women entering the priesthood was obviously even less bright, but the flag was kept flying by the courageous Maude Royden who, frustrated by her own church's attitude to women, exercised a notable preaching and pastoral ministry at the Congregational Church's City Temple in London. When this ended in 1920, she entered into a joint venture with Percy Dearmer which involved the setting up of a para-church, the Guildhouse, in which she preached to crowded congregations throughout the 1920s and into the early years of the 1930s.

The League for the Church Militant reminded the rest of the Church of its existence in 1926 with a declaration, 'The cause for which we stand uniquely by reason of our churchmanship is that of the open-ness to women of the ministry of Word and Sacraments', and the negative attitude of the 1930 Lambeth Conference led to the formation that year of an Anglican Group for the Ordination of Women. The membership of this was never large but included some highly gifted women who would eventually play an important part in the campaign that led to the realization of their aims. Throughout the 1930s they were very much 'a voice crying in the wilderness', and even that voice was drowned by the outbreak of war in 1939. The Royal Air Force, however, employed a few women as chaplains' assistants.

The exigencies of war also led the Bishop of Hong Kong, Ronald Hall, to take the momentous step in 1944 of ordaining Deaconess Florence Li Tim-Oi to the priesthood. When peace returned in the following year, his action was condemned by the Archbishop of Canterbury, Geoffrey Fisher, and also by the 1948 Lambeth Conference. By this time Florence Li Tim-Oi had ceased to minister as a priest (she never formally relinquished her Orders), but nonetheless her ordination had caused a chink of light to penetrate the Anglican bastion, and this became a sign of hope for many.

4

On the Move – At Last

The 1958 Lambeth Conference was content to commend the wider employment of trained women church workers, but a decade later, when there was much talk about a radical reform of the Church's life in the Western world, the bishops were emboldened to acknowledge that the theological factors relating to the ordination of women to the priesthood were inconclusive. This disavowal of what their predecessors had proclaimed with the utmost dogmatic certainty meant that doors were opening that could never again be closed.

Indeed, a mere three years later, in 1971, the Anglican Consultative Council – a recently created body authorized to consider issues and make decisions between Lambeth Conferences – advised the Bishop of Hong Kong, now Gilbert Baker, that if he went ahead with a proposal to ordain two women priests, his action would be acceptable to the Council. The Bishop seized the moment and ordained them almost immediately. Two years earlier the Church of England had, less adventurously, allowed women to become Servers (a move fiercely denounced by the Guild of the Servants of the Sanctuary) and also Readers, thus disregarding the warning of a leading lay member of the Church Assembly, given in the 1940s, that this would be 'a slippery slope to the priesthood'.

Across the Atlantic, the American Church's House of Bishops voted in 1972 for the ordination of women, not only to the priesthood but also to the episcopate. This was rejected by its House of Deputies 12 months later, but in 1974 11 women were, in the presence of 2,000 people in Philadelphia, irregularly ordained by three retired bishops. The pace of change was now accelerating quickly. In November 1976 women were ordained in Canada, in January of the following year they were (this time officially) in America, and at the end of that year in New Zealand. The 1978 Lambeth Conference confirmed that Anglican provinces were free to make their own decisions in the matter.

The Church of England was, however, still a long way from exploiting this freedom, though its General Synod had made in 1975 the highly significant decision that there were no fundamental theological objections to the ordination of women to the priesthood. In spite of this it steadfastly refused to remove the legal barriers to the carrying out of such ordinations. A proposal in 1978 by Bishop Hugh Montefiore of Birmingham that legislation be prepared to enable women to become both priests and bishops was carried in the Houses of Bishops and Laity, but rejected by a large majority in the House of Clergy. The silence that followed the announcement of the negative vote was immediately broken by the cry of Dr Una Kroll, of the Christian Parity Group, from the public gallery, 'We asked for bread, but you gave us a stone' – a dramatic gesture which the media transmitted across the world.

Permission for women ordained abroad to exercise their priesthood when visiting England was also refused, and the combination of these negative responses proved to be the last straw even for the moderate campaigners. In July 1979 a Movement for the Ordination of Women (MOW) was launched. This had influential support, the first Moderator being the Bishop of Manchester, Stanley Booth-Clibborn, and the highly competent administrative leadership of Margaret Webster, the wife of the Dean of St Paul's.

A sustained and brilliantly organized campaign began with the formation of branches in virtually every diocese. Membership eventually rose to over five thousand, with many more offering support. Meetings, conferences, leaflets, books, demonstrations at cathedral ordinations and, in defiance of the General Synod, celebrations of the Eucharist at which women priests from overseas presided, all generated massive publicity, informed education and helped to sustain pressure. Yet it took another 13 years to achieve the desired change, and there was much frustration along the way as the General Synod refused to move forward.

The theological issue having been settled, though only up to a point since a substantial number of opponents still clung to the conservative line, the debate raged over two points which had first been raised far back in the 1890s. An unbroken tradition, dating it was alleged from the choice by Jesus of an all-male apostolate, and the dire threat to ecumenical relations with the Roman Catholic and Orthodox Churches – these were still advanced as the main reason for opposition. There was the further claim that the Church was in danger of submitting to secular women's liberation ideas.

By 1984, however, the time seemed ripe for another attempt to move things forward, and in November of that year the Bishop of Southwark, Ronald Bowlby (translated from Newcastle in 1980), proposed to the General Synod that its Standing Committee should bring forward legislation to permit the ordination of women to the priesthood in the provinces of Canterbury and York. He spoke of the experience of women in the priesthood and of the theological issues – 'I want to argue that the only way to safeguard the doctrine of God in its fullness is to ordain women as well as men.' It was a powerful speech, but did not convince the Archbishop of Canterbury, Robert Runcie, that there was any urgency about the implementation of such a doctrine and he counselled a policy of 'gradualism'. Deaconess Diana McClatchey was less patient:

> If you want a church that retains the atmosphere of an exclusive men's club on ladies' night, you will have little sympathy with Christian feminism or this motion . . . Do not be surprised, however, if in ten years' time you find even fewer young women in the parish church and even more in the feminist house groups.

This paved the way for the passing of the motion by a substantial majority, but it was for no more than the 'bringing forward of legislation'.

Robert Runcie was uncomfortably placed at the centre of a heightening controversy throughout the 1980s. His predecessor, the devout evangelical Donald Coggan, had been strongly in favour of women priests, though his influence was never great. Runcie, the moderate liberal-Catholic, was far less certain. During his time as Bishop of St Albans he had been co-chairman of a joint Anglican/Orthodox Theological Commission which brought warmth and a measure of understanding to relations between the leaders of the churches. The earliest signs of the Anglican Church moving in the direction of women priests was sufficient to bring closure to the talks, which distressed Runcie greatly. Later, contact was resumed at a lower hierarchical level, but things were never the same again.

In 1986, however, Runcie happily presided over a debate in the General Synod when, by a large majority, legislation was passed allowing women to be ordained to the diaconate on the same terms as men. Among the supporters of this was the Bishop of London, Graham Leonard, the leader of the opposition to women priests. He believed, or perhaps hoped, that women would settle for the diaconate, but there was never any possibility of this, and the effect of the change was to accustom congregations to the leadership of women in worship – an experience that influenced positively many waverers.

Runcie was a bold Archbishop in many ways, particularly in secular political matters, but in church affairs he had a well-deserved reputation for sitting on the fence. This was a position that suited his own temperament, since he was genuinely uncertain about some things. But he had a fervent desire to keep together in one Church of England those whose different beliefs were powerfully held, and in this he was successful, though his dealings with the women leaders of MOW were not always sensitive. After his retirement, when women were finally ordained, he expressed his pleasure and wished that he had taken a stronger supportive position when in office. He had at least been there when in 1984 the General Synod agreed that the necessary legislation be prepared.

George Carey, who succeeded to the Primacy in 1990, rose unexpectedly from an evangelical base and in the opinion of many made the worst of what had long been recognized as an impossible task. But his unwavering support for the ordination of women may well have been of critical importance when the time for decision came on 11 November 1992. Although the General Synod vote in favour was substantial – 75 per cent in the House of Bishops, 70.4 per cent in the House of Clergy and 67.3 per cent in the House of Laity – it was wafer thin in relation to the two-thirds majorities required in each of the Houses. Without Carey's leadership, the result could have been different.

The Moderator of MOW during the final years of the campaign was Catherine Milford, a deacon who at the time was Adult Education Adviser for Winchester diocese. At the final gathering of the Movement held in Coventry Cathedral shortly before the crucial vote, she felt confident enough to say, 'There is a groundswell of understanding of the far-reaching implications of the change that cannot now be stopped.' She had good reason to know, since she had spent much of the previous 12 months in close touch with the dioceses encouraging synodical voters to support change. Earlier she had introduced into Central Council meetings a period of worship after the first half of the business had been concluded. This helped to strengthen considerably the bonds between members. It seemed specially appropriate that she should be among those ordained in 1994, and she went on to become Team Rector of a group of rural Norfolk parishes and an Honorary Canon of Norwich Cathedral.

11th November has, since 1918, been observed as a Day of Remembrance of the millions the who sacrificed their lives in the cause of justice and peace, but it did not in 1992 mark the end of hostilities in the Church of England. Members of MOW and very many others naturally celebrated the historic decision and its future promise, but most of the bishops returned to their dioceses deeply worried men: how were they to deal pastorally with those, mainly among the clergy, who were feeling devastated? What should have been a widely observed joyful celebration was in the event sacrificed to fear and bitterness.

This was not confined to the immediate aftermath of the decision. The much-respected Archbishop of York, John Habgood, disappointingly promoted further General Synod legislation designed to placate and keep on board the minority who were hostile to women priests. This was enshrined in what became a notorious Act of Synod, designed to 'protect' those who wanted nothing to do, not only with the new women priests, but also with their own diocesan bishops who had ordained them. An accompanying document, *Bonds of Peace*, introduced the novel concept of 'two integrities'.

In flagrant denial of traditional Catholic order, itinerant bishops (soon to be known as 'flying bishops') were provided to minister to and, as it turned out, encourage the dissidents. The effect was to create, in effect, a church within a church – one that by refusing to recognize the validity of its parent church's ministries and by placing itself out of communion with this church could only be regarded as schismatic and a denial of the unity it was purported to maintain.

Strenuous opposition to this was mounted by a Group for Rescinding the Act of Synod (GRAS) and Women and the Church (WATCH) which was also concerned to ensure that, with the passage of the years, women priests were not excluded from consideration when their merits equipped them for senior office in the Church, such as canons, archdeacons and deans. Neither organization has been able to attract the support, or develop the campaigning energy, that marked the heady days of MOW, though after some pressure a certain number of women have been given senior appointments. The need for this to include the opening of the episcopate to women has been the prime concern, and for 13 years WATCH had the outstanding leadership of Christina Rees, a writer and General Synod member.

Little progress has been possible, however, in overcoming the effects of the Act of Synod, and a serious impediment to this was created by the formation in 1992 of Forward in Faith. With a membership consisting almost exclusively of disaffected Anglo-Catholics, it has campaigned vigorously to ensure that the schismatic arrangements are maintained and never diluted. Moreover, it has strongly opposed the move towards the consecration of women bishops and sought to extend the provisions of the Act of Synod should such consecrations take place. A network of conservative evangelical clergy and laity, formed in 1993 with the name Reform, seeks to uphold what it believes to be biblical standards of doctrine and morality. This includes, for some, opposition to the leadership of women in any role in the Church on the grounds that it is contrary to the teaching of Saint Paul.

Three years before the General Synod approved the ordination of women to the priesthood, Barbara Harris had become a Suffragan Bishop in the American diocese of Massachusetts. In 1990 Penelope Jameson was appointed Bishop of Dunedin, in New Zealand. Other consecrations of women followed in Canada, Cuba and Australia, and in 2006 Katharine Jefferts Schori, who had been Bishop of Nevada since 2001, was elected Presiding Bishop of the Episcopal Church in the USA, becoming the first and so far the only Anglican Primate.

In July 2000 Judith Rose, long experienced as a parish worker, deaconess, deacon and priest, and now Archdeacon of Tonbridge, got the General Synod to ask its House of Bishops to initiate further study on the episcopate in preparation for a debate on women in episcopal orders. It was not easy to discern what theology that allowed women to become priests might inhibit them from becoming bishops, but it was deemed expedient to consider this possibility if only to clear the ground for action. The bishops duly produced an interim report in 2002 and a final report two years later.

This was favourable and, after it had been discussed by the General Synod in 2005, it was agreed to start the process of removing any legal obstacles to the consecration of women. But the Synod was hesitant about taking a firm step in the direction of women bishops and asked the Bishop of Guildford, Christopher Hill, to produce a further clarifying report on certain matters. When this appeared, it did not satisfy everyone, including several bishops, so further clarification was commissioned. Five months later, however, in July 2006, the General Synod resolved:

That this Synod welcomes and affirms the view of the majority of the House of Bishops that admitting women to the episcopate of the Church of England is consonant with the faith of the Church as the Church of England has received it and would be a proper development in proclaiming afresh in this generation the grace and truth of Christ.

The Synod went on to endorse a resolution of the 1998 Lambeth Conference that those who dissent, as well as those who assent to women priests and bishops, are loyal Anglicans.

There was no indication, however, of what arrangements for dissenters might be consonant with unbroken fellowship within the Anglican Communion. This left open the door to the continuation and intensification of the disagreement over 'flying bishops', which had bedevilled the decision to ordain women priests. It was a door that Forward in Faith eagerly entered. Led by the then Suffragan Bishop of Fulham, John Broadhurst, and supported by some of the past and present 'flying bishops', it attracted a good deal of media attention by the violence of its language and the frequency of its threat to lead large numbers of Anglicans into the Roman obedience. There was even talk of requiring the creation of a third, dissenting, Province to function alongside those of Canterbury and York.

More restrained were those who sought, unconvincingly, to argue with subtlety that bishops are a different case from priests and that their apostolic leadership is not open to the same considerations as those advanced in support of women priests. It was also stated that the consecration of women bishops would sound the death knell to any kind of Anglican/Roman Catholic ecumenical progress.

What provision might or might not be made for dissenters remained, however, the chief bone of contention, and for many who fervently wished to see an end to the subversive 'flying bishops' it was a matter for considerable surprise that the Archbishop of Canterbury, Rowan Williams, was not on their side.

Others remembered that he had, when much younger, been opposed to women priests. At the time of his appointment as Bishop of Monmouth in 1992, the Church in Wales had been sharply divided over this issue and refused to move forward. But in 1993 Williams seconded in the Church's Governing Body (the equivalent of the General Synod) a second attempt at change which this time secured a narrow majority. His speech had been impressive and probably influential but it concluded strangely, 'We must be prepared to be taught by each other in the debate and, if the final result is not what we prayed and hoped for, to ask what God is saying to us in that.' Those who had long campaigned for the recognition of women's ministry were in no doubt that God's response to another Governing Body refusal would be, 'You have made a serious mistake.'

Williams' equivocal attitude, expressed again when the issue of women bishops reached the Church of England's agenda, appears to have been influenced by three factors. The first of these was his deeply rooted Catholic spirituality and attachment to tradition, neither of which permitted the easy embracing of so radical a reform. The second was his understanding of episcopacy as a focus of the Church's unity, as emphasized by the Orthodox Church. The third was his long-standing concern for the underdog, normally relating to social victims but in this case the minority whose convictions had not won the day.

In July 2008 the General Synod reaffirmed by substantial majorities in each of its three Houses the intention to consecrate women bishops. At the same time it rejected a proposal that unfortunately titled 'Super Bishops' should be appointed to cater for the minority, continuing in an unspecified way the role of the 'flying bishops'. The Archbishops of Canterbury and York were each dismayed by this rejection and the Bishop of Winchester, Michael Scott-Joynt, went so far as to describe it as 'profoundly short-sighted and mean-spirited'. Forward in Faith's supporters threatened to seek the supervision of conservative bishops in overseas provinces – a step already taken by some in the USA after losing their battle against the acceptance into the ordained ministry of homosexuals.

Much work on legislative matters was now needed in England before a final decision could be made, and this was entrusted to a revision committee chaired by the Bishop of Manchester, Nigel McCulloch. No fewer that 114 submissions were received from General Synod members and 183 from other interested parties. The long-suffering Bishop was in the end driven to postpone his retirement in order to see the legislation through to final acceptance.

The Committee's final report recommended that, although special arrangements, including the provision of bishops of whom they approved, should certainly be made for the dissenting minority, these should be under the authority of the diocesan bishop, acting in accordance with a statutory code of practice. This was fiercely opposed by Forward in Faith, partly because of lack of trust of the bishops but chiefly because the ultimate authority of the diocesan bishops would mean an end to the freedom to exist as a separate entity within the Church of England. Nothing short of legal backing for schism would satisfy them. Without necessarily sharing these views, a good many bishops and others supported the dissenters because they saw this as the only way of preventing them from migrating to Rome.

Among their supporters were the Archbishops of Canterbury and York who, a few days before the critical General Synod meeting at York in July 2010, tabled an amendment designed to give legal status to the special arrangements. This seemed extraordinarily unwise at the time and proved to have been when the General Synod's decision was announced. After a highly charged debate in which it was evident that the archbishops had laid their authority on the line in a doubtful cause, the Synod narrowly rejected the amendment – the House of Laity alone, but decisively, refusing to take a step backwards.

Meanwhile the Pope, responding to a request from the Bishop of Fulham and the 'flying bishops' had, without informing the Archbishop of Canterbury, announced the formation of an Ordinariate to enable those Anglicans who wished to become Roman Catholics to do so, while retaining some of their former, unspecified traditions. By mid-2011 these bishops and about fifty active and retired priests, together with about a thousand laypeople, had accepted this invitation – many fewer than originally forecast. To the astonishment and dismay of women priests and their supporters, the Archbishop of Canterbury replaced the 'flying bishops' with two others.

Following the General Synod's decision that women could become bishops, the matter was remitted to the diocesan synods for their decisions, but without the liberty to discuss the special arrangements for the minority. Provided the majority of diocesan synods give their approval, the proposal will return to the General Synod, probably in 2012. Final approval there will then have to be sought from Parliament, which is unlikely to raise problems, and submitted for Royal Assent. The year 2014 appears to be the earliest realistic date when women could become bishops.

5

The Religious Life Restored:
Priscilla Lydia Sellon

Although Priscilla Lydia Sellon's Community of the Most Holy Trinity (often known as the Devonport Sisters) was not, strictly speaking, the first Religious Order to be established in England since the Reformation, it was the first substantial development in this direction.

In 1845, Edward Bouverie Pusey, who became *de facto* leader of the Oxford Movement after the secession of John Henry Newman to Rome, established in a villa in London's Regent's Park a small Sisterhood of the Holy Cross. This was associated with Christ Church, Albany Street, one of the outposts of the revived Catholicism, and had the support of Lord John Manners (a future Duke of Rutland) and a number of other influential laymen. Its objectives were observance of a Religious Rule by women who were dedicated to visiting the sick and the poor in their homes, hospitals, workhouses and prison, finding clothing and instructing destitute children, and assisting at the burial of the dead.

After two years it had outgrown its villa and moved to two houses near Christ Church, but it always lacked strong leadership and survived through union with Miss Sellon's community in Devonport, which was founded in 1848, again with the assistance of Dr Pusey. In spite of long periods of Protestant persecution the united communities flourished and became a landmark in the history of Anglicanism.

Lydia was born in 1821, the daughter of a naval commander who had left the service because of ill-health and became a landowner in Monmouthshire. Following the death of her mother when she was only three, he remarried and had 14 more children, creating a large and happy (albeit strongly disciplined) family life. Later the family's name was changed from Smith to Sellon in response to a substantial inheritance from an unmarried aunt of that name.

Lydia developed a strong character which combined acute intellect, considerable charm and a determination to get things done. In 1847 she visited the infant community in Regent's Park and was greatly impressed. She was also inspired with the vision of a much larger community with wider aims and influence. Before she could pursue this, however, she had one of the bouts of ill-health – breakdowns of some sort – that occurred periodically throughout her life. On this occasion a few weeks in Madeira were prescribed, but shortly before embarking on the ship she read in *The Guardian*, a church newspaper, a letter dated 1 January 1848 from the Bishop of Exeter, Henry Phillpotts.

Phillpotts, who was at Exeter from 1830 to 1869, was in many ways a nightmarish figure. It was he who led Sydney Smith to declare that he felt bound to believe in the Apostolic Succession because only so could he explain the descent of the Bishop of Exeter from Judas Iscariot. He was a throwback to the eighteenth century and played a large part in ensuring that for much of the nineteenth century bishops would be deeply unpopular. He ruled his diocese largely by fear rather than by love, yet he was strikingly ahead of his time in the matter of church reform, and this was reflected in his letter to *The Guardian*.

The subject was 'an appeal on behalf of the spiritual destitution of Devonport'. He pointed out that the town, which had developed rapidly with the growth of the naval base, was probably the most densely populated in England, with some 26,000 people congregated within less than one-fifth part of a square mile. The town had no parish church or chapel – the nearest being at Stoke Damarel, some distance away. He proposed therefore to create four districts, build at least four large churches, and establish a large number of schools. Furthermore, three districts in the adjoining town of Plymouth, while not as poor as those in Devonport, were still deprived and no less in spiritual need. But Phillpotts had insufficient money to carry out his plans, so 'presumed to make this unwonted application to the Christian charity of England'.

On reading this, Lydia, as would often prove to be the case in the future, suddenly recovered her physical and emotional strength. The voyage to Madeira was abandoned, and she went to see Phillpotts, explaining to him that, while she could offer no money, she was now offering her services for the Church's mission in Devonport, Plymouth and adjoining Stonehouse. The bishop immediately accepted her offer, recognizing a kindred spirit (some said 'a sister autocrat'), and she went to Devonport to see for herself the problems and form some idea of what contribution she might make to their solution.

She then returned to London to describe what she had discerned with a number of friends, and also with Dr Pusey who advised her to concentrate her efforts on the most destitute district in the Three Towns and put her in touch with the Revd Martin Kilpatrick, who had been appointed to the newly constituted district of St James's, Morice Town. He readily accepted her assistance and suggested that she rent a room in George Street – one of the worst in Devonport.

This was in April, and she adopted the clothes and lifestyle of the more respectable of her neighbours, soon winning their friendship and trust. Her first approach was to the young people of the neighbourhood, who, she noted, inhabited 'every haunt of vice and misery, whose evils were not even veiled'. There was no school and only one place of worship – a room over a beer-shop. She estimated there to be about 9,500 'wild and neglected children', most of them under the age of 14, all of them unbaptized, 'swarming the streets and living like savages'.

None of these had responded to the priest's attempt to establish a school, but about 100 enrolled in the classes she formed and every evening 40 or 50 came to learn reading and writing. A schoolmaster was recruited to lend a hand, but it was tough work, with frequent fights among the scholars. Not surprisingly, she had another breakdown in the summer. This led her once again to consult Dr Pusey who recommended the foundation of a Sisterhood to provide companionship and stability. Her father offered his support and, besides augmenting the small fortune she had inherited from her mother and the inheritance she would have received on his death, he negotiated the purchase of a Dissenting mission chapel, with seating for about 700 people. The minister himself decided to become an Anglican, along with a large number of his congregation.

Having recovered her health, Lydia set before Bishop Phillpotts her plans for a Sisterhood. He readily agreed, and at Dr Pusey's suggestion she paid a second visit to the London community. It was his hope that she might join this community and extend its work to Devonport, but she thought the strictness of its Rule too severe and decided to form her own. A friend, Catherine Chambers, and a member of the London community, Anne Terrot, decided to join her.

The next move was to announce the opening of a 'Home for the

Orphan Daughters of British Sailors and Soldiers', and an appeal for funds brought contributions from the Queen Dowager, other titled people, members of parliament, bishops, navy and army officers, as well as many smaller gifts. Suitable accommodation having been obtained, the home was opened on 16 October 1848, when Lydia Sellon and Catherine Chambers knelt before Bishop Phillpotts to receive his blessing and to inaugurate 'The Church of England Sisterhood of Mercy of Devonport and Plymouth'. Anne Terrot, already professed as a nun, arrived from London a few weeks later, and a Rule, consisting at this stage of a few paragraphs, was adopted to regulate their worship and way of life. Provision was made for any Sister to withdraw if she felt moved to do so. The objectives of the Sisterhood were stated to be

[t]he education of the female children of sailors and soldiers who shall have lost either parent; the visiting of the sick and needy; the superintendence of schools, infant or adult, industrial or educational; the visiting of female immigrants on vessels landing at the port of Plymouth; and any other purpose, such as the care of hospitals and infirmaries, the temporary shelter and training of distressed women of good character, which God shall open to them.

The habit, which would later be modified, consisted of a black woollen dress with long flowing sleeves; a woollen girdle to which was attached a small ebony cross; and a white cap, with long black strings, worn over closely cropped hair. Out of doors, a cloak was worn over the habit, and over the cap a large black bonnet and a black crepe veil. The founder's vision was wide, and for any woman to initiate such a project was unprecedented – many believed it to be scandalous and full of danger; others were relieved to know that it would be subject to the direction of local priests and the authority of a bishop. She was known initially as the Lady Superior and later as Mother Lydia.

Dr Pusey visited the Sisterhood at the end of the year and reported that 'the works of mercy opened in Devonport embrace the whole range of which our Blessed Lord speaks relatively to the Day of Judgement', and he concluded. 'One can only say, "This is the Lord's doing, and it is marvellous in our eyes".' A few more women joined their ranks, and within a matter of months the vocations of all were tested to the utmost by a serious outbreak of cholera.

41

The origin of this was traced to a ship, *The American Eagle*, anchored in Plymouth harbour, but by this time it was rampant through the over-populated insanitary Three Towns. Mother Lydia, who was herself ill again, immediately offered her own and the Sisters' services in the local hospitals and sent for reinforcements from the London community. Over the next five months they worked tirelessly and heroically in caring for the sick and the dying. A temporary wooden building with 60 beds, provided by the Court of Guardians, had an altar placed at one end of it so that dying victims might receive Communion, and at this the clergy said prayers every evening with the patients and the nurses. One of the Sisters, Amelia, died of the disease but the rest escaped, even though Mother Lydia often had to leave her own sick-bed to share in this ministry. Afterwards the national as well as the local press praised their courage and devotion.

In 1850, the foundation stone was laid of St Dunstan's, Plymouth – so named because Dunstan initiated the restoration of monastic life in England in the tenth century. The famous Victorian architect, William Butterfield, designed, without fee, a substantial building to provide a permanent convent for the Sisterhood, though it was, for financial reasons, possible to complete at this stage only a parish church, which served as a chapel and sufficient accommodation for the community at the time. This consisted of five professed Religious, five novices and several ladies 'in residence' who wore the novices' habit and shared in most of the activities. The ceremony was a notable event, attended by over 1,000 mainly poor people, together with about 50 clergy, including a few bishops. At a dinner held afterwards in a field, 11 hundredweight of roast beef were consumed and 'a vast amount of good-sized and pleasant looking plum puddings'.

The community's rapidly developing work now led Dr Pusey to believe that the activity needed to be sustained by concentrated, uninterrupted prayer. By 1852 three Orders or 'Rules' had been inaugurated: the Sisters of Mercy of the Holy Communion, who were engaged in social and educational work; the Sisters of the Sacred Heart were 'those who from sickness or other causes were unable to undertake laborious work, but who wished to have a quiet life engaged in reading and prayer, and such occupations as needlework and writing'; the Sisters of Charity of the Holy Ghost were what today would be called a Third Order, consisting of devout women 'married or unmarried who lived in the world, not in a community, but who wished to belong to a Religious Society and to assist in its work in various ways'.

In 1854 the community received a request for eight Sisters to accompany Florence Nightingale on her mission to provide nursing for the wounded and sick soldiers fighting in the Crimea. Mother Lydia, who was not well enough to go herself, and in any case did not wish to provide a rival authority, recruited five from the Devonport community and three from the London. These joined ten Roman Catholic nuns, 11 professional nurses and some other ladies to form a team that embarked, to cheering crowds, at Folkestone on 23 October. After travelling by train to Marseilles they had an appalling voyage in a vermin-ridden, insanitary ship that became enveloped in a violent storm and finally landed them at Scutari, opposite Constantinople, on 4 November.

As at the time of the cholera outbreak in the Three Towns, the Sisters worked heroically, with few resources – this time among soldiers, more of whom died of fever than of their battle wounds. As leader and inspirer of the nursing team, Florence Nightingale naturally received most of the credit, but the contribution of the Sisters during their two years of service was hardly less meritorious.

The return of the Sisters in 1856 coincided more or less with Mother Lydia's taking control of the London Sisterhood. The two communities were formally united, and she was designated Abbess. Not everyone was happy with this development, and the London Sisters were resentful at what seemed to them the somewhat arbitrary transfer of some of their number to St Dunstan's, where the discipline seemed to them to be slack. But the London convent had always lacked effective leadership, and union appeared to be the only way of solving this problem. Mother Emma, the supervisor, who had served at Scutari, was given responsibility for a small mission house opened in Bethnal Green.

During the absence of the Sisters, Lydia had taken the opportunity to learn the art of printing. This was to enable her to teach the older girls in the orphanage a craft that would enable them to avoid the much lower-paid domestic or shop-girl occupations and the temptation to augment their incomes with 'the more remunerative wages of sin'. Pusey, who approved, had conveniently bought some years earlier a printing press from a Bristol clergyman and had this transferred to Bradford-on-Avon. There the Sisters had just been given, by another clergyman, the use of a magnificent Tudor and Queen Anne mansion which proved to be ideal for the Sisters of the Sacred Heart to exercise their contemplative vocation. The existence of a printing press among them did nothing for the training of the Devonport girls but it enabled the production of beautifully bound editions of Pusey's sermons and some other works that won high praise from connoisseurs.

A year later, in 1861, Mother Lydia had a stroke. She was still only 40 and, although she made a partial recovery, her health, which had never been good, restricted her activities even further. Thereafter she gave most of her instructions while reclining on a *chaise longue*.

The number of Sisters and the cash resources also suffered a decline. Nevertheless she found sufficient energy and enthusiasm to enter with Pusey into a project that involved the purchase of 40 acres of heathland and pine woods near Ascot and the erection on this of a permanent convent for the contemplative Sisters who moved there from Bradford-on-Avon. The refreshing air of the pine woods also made it an ideal site for a convalescent home for sick people, and members of the community's other two orders, including Mother Lydia, also went there for rest and refreshment. It was paid for by Pusey with the large part of a legacy left to him by his mother, Lady Lucy.

This was by no means the end of the community's expansion. In 1864 Pusey asked them to start a home for indigent mill-girls in a newly constituted parish in Leeds. Mother Lydia was glad to respond, but when Pusey discovered that the high-church priest, the notable Father Stanton, whom he proposed to appoint to the parish, was only willing to accept the project if the Sisters were to work under his direction, he withdrew his offer to Stanton and for some reason the mill-girl project never materialized. Pusey now believed that the Sisters had a pioneering role and that the clergy should become involved only if mill-girls required their particular help.

Mother Lydia then acquired a house in the cathedral close at Norwich with a view to establishing a branch of the community there, but this proved to be impracticable and she turned over the house to an embryonic Community of Benedictine Oblates – the first step in the renewal of the Benedictine life for women in the Church of England.

In the same year, 1864, the Bishop of Honolulu asked Mother Lydia if her community would take charge of a school on the Sandwich Islands for local girls who 'might be trained in the ideals of Christian womanhood'. Three Sisters, including two who had been at Scutari, were selected and these sailed from Southampton on 17 September. A farewell service was conducted by John Keble in his village church at nearby Hursley, and Mother Lydia, having prayed with the Sisters on the ship, saw each of them separately and gave each her blessing.

The voyage took about ten weeks, and the Sisters were given an enthusiastic welcome on their arrival in Honolulu not only by the bishop and other members of the Anglican mission but also by the king and the queen. Thereafter Queen Emma took a particular interest in their work, providing strong support and, during a visit to England the following March, went to see Mother Lydia to ask for more Sisters to establish a girls' school in Honolulu. Three were chosen.

Meanwhile the others had established themselves at a girls' school on the Island of Lahaina where they opened with 25 boarders and 40 day-girls. The Rule of the Religious Life was observed in the context of a mission station that was attracting large and enthusiastic congregations. At various times two of the Sisters were detached to nurse the victims of 'Chinese leprosy', and a free dispensary was opened for the poor.

Back in England, an outbreak of cholera in the East End of London took Mother Lydia to supervise the nursing of its victims in an improvised hospital in a disused warehouse in Spitalfields. Sisters from some other Orders joined in the work and when, after three months, the hospital closed, it was reported that 400 cases, most of them severe and virulent, had been treated and of those 'only' 130 had died. Medical researchers said that the most valuable insights into the nature of cholera, so far obtained, had come through the accurate observations and careful management of the Sisters. Many of the survivors were sent for convalescent treatment to the priory at Ascot.

Mother Lydia, still battling against her own ill health, was also in need of a period of recuperation once the cholera had been taken in hand, and after two months at Ascot she set off for Honolulu with the promised reinforcement of Sisters. At the end of the ten-week voyage, they were met by a prince who would later become King of Hawaii and by his mother Queen Emma, the bishop and the rest of the clergy.

Work soon began on the erection of a Priory and a permanent school in the grounds of the future cathedral – $7,000 was provided from the community's funds – and on Ascension Day 1867 the Bishop dedicated the new foundation of St Andrew's Priory. A few days later Mother Lydia embarked on a ship to San Francisco on the first stage of her journey back to England. Crowds of ordinary people assembled to bid her farewell. Some pleaded with her to stay and she was showered with gifts – pigs, chickens, sugar canes, mangoes, eggs and native craftwork – such as were normally given only to royalty and high chiefs.

She was by this time exhausted by her exertions on the islands, but the voyage brought refreshment, and by the time she reached England in August 1867 she was ready to deal with the various problems that had arisen during her long absence. These were mainly related to the fact that the community's activities had been extended some way beyond its capacity to meet them. A number of Sisters had grown old, some had died, a few had become Roman Catholics, and the foundation of other Religious Orders had led to a decline in the number of postulants and novices joining the pioneering foundation.

In England, Lydia's ministry was subjected to what amounted to long periods of persecution, sometimes of a vicious character. This came largely from a Protestant fear that the Oxford Movement, of which the Religious communities were an integral part, was an attempt to return England to Roman Catholicism. Shortly after the community started at Devonport the Vicar of St Andrew's, Plymouth, and a local solicitor launched a vitriolic attack which attracted a good deal of publicity. This not only caused the Queen Dowager and some other notables to withdraw their support but drove Bishop Phillpotts to initiate a formal enquiry to ensure that no laws of Church and State were being infringed by the Sisters. Held in public and in the presence of a large audience, the complaints were articulated by the editor of the Devonport *Daily Telegraph*. After Mother Lydia had entered a powerful defence, the Bishop delivered his judgement that no laws were being broken and that the Sisters were doing a wonderful work for which he had nothing but admiration. He admitted, however, that he wished that a cross and flowers had not been placed on the altar in their oratory, yet 'ladies are ladies and if the irregularities were strange, they were by no means so strange as the works of mercy the Sisters had performed'.

The Roman Catholic Bishop of Plymouth evidently did not believe them to be in any danger of moving in his direction, for during a later epidemic he warned his own flock: 'If you prefer a few attentions to your poor perishing bodies to your soul's eternal happiness, receive them, but if not reject them.' Neither he nor his church provided alternative care.

The Revd Herbert Seymour, addressing a fashionable audience in Bath, described Mother Lydia as 'a petty despot', 'unladylike', 'capricious' and 'like a crafty old owl preying on poor little mice'. He concluded that 'the pillory was the only appropriate punishment for her'. Tracts were published, some making use of material supplied by rejected postulates, and a local newspaper accused her, libellously, of improper use of funds. A national newspaper reported a 'rumour' that she and Dr Pusey were soon to be married.

So the persecution went on, sometimes for years on end, and Bishop Phillpotts felt driven to withdraw his public support of the Sisters, while privately continuing his encouragement. Periods of peace were broken by further attacks, but Mother Lydia rarely attempted to repel them and, although her health was undoubtedly affected, she never wavered in her commitment to the way of Christian life to which she had so obviously been called.

Thus the remaining years of Mother Lydia's life were devoted largely to retrenchment and reorganization, though important work was undertaken in Shoreditch when 4,000 cases of smallpox were reported in 1871. The Sisters were responsible for the nursing in the parish hospital and the homes of victims, and once again convalescent patients were sent to the Ascot Priory where tents were erected in the grounds and extra kitchens set up.

Mother Lydia's own death came on 20 November 1876, when she and another Sister were staying with Dr Pusey at Osborne House in West Malvern. She was 56 and had been a professed Religious for 29 years.

A fulsome obituary in *The Times* described her as 'the founder of Sisterhoods in the Church of England' and, after paying tribute to the social work she had initiated and which her community had carried out, concluded that 'the good effected under Providence would remain as a record of what might be done by a woman's properly directed energy, devotion and good judgement', and would be a lasting tribute to her name and to the value of the institutions she founded. *The Morning Post* was no less generous and went so far as suggesting that the Religious communities would not have returned to the Church of England 'had it not been for the fact that Miss Sellon acted as a pioneer in the work of their foundation and braved the outbursts of public opinion with which they were first met'. The church paper *The Guardian* and the *Church Times* also paid tribute to her life and work, and some 18 months later an archdeacon, presenting a resolution on Sisterhoods and

Deaconesses to the Lower House of the Convocation of Canterbury, took the opportunity to remind its members that 'the value of Sisterhoods was brought before the eyes of the nation by the Crimean War in such a way that the name of Miss Sellon will long be remembered with that of Miss Nightingale as having taught the people of England the value of women's work'.

6

'The Lady with the Lamp' and Medical Reform: Florence Nightingale

In a now frequently quoted letter to Dean Stanley of Westminster Abbey, Florence Nightingale explained, somewhat bitterly:

> I would have given her [the Church] my head, my hand, my heart. She would not have them. She did not know what to do with them. She told me to go back and crochet in my mother's drawing room. 'You may go to the Sunday School if you like' she said. But she gave me no training even for that. She gave me neither work to do for her nor education to do it.

While regretting that the Victorian Church could not use her gifts, it is, to say the least, doubtful if it could ever have provided her with the opportunities that enabled her to become a legend (or perhaps a myth) in her own lifetime and an iconic figure in English history. This image is related, however, to the two years in her long life when she was heroically engaged in nursing soldiers engaged in the Crimean War (1854–6), and in many ways it obscures her other massive achievements. It also hides the true nature of a highly complex personality.

After *The Times* had drawn attention to the unbelievably appalling conditions being endured by the wounded and disease-afflicted soldiers, and Florence had responded to the call for women to alleviate their suffering, the newspaper sent a journalist to report on the effect of her arrival in the Crimea. In just two sentences a picture was painted that stirred a nation and soon went around the world:

> She is a 'ministering angel' without any exaggeration in these hospitals and as her slender form glides gently along each corridor, every poor

fellow's face softens with gratitude at the sight of her. When all the medical officers have retired for the night and silence and darkness have settled down upon these miles of prostrate sick, she may be observed alone, with a little lamp in her hand, making her solitary rounds.

Hence 'The lady with the lamp' – a heroine, portrayed by a drawing in the *Illustrated London News* and distributed even more widely than *The Times*. Over 150 years later, at an annual service for nurses held in Westminster Abbey, a small lamp of a similar type is carried to the altar. Many of the nurses have been trained just across the Thames at the Nightingale School for Nursing and Midwifery.

Yet Florence Nightingale's greatest work was not in this brief period of personal nursing, but in her many years as a major reformer of medical care. When she, the daughter of a wealthy, upper-middle-class family, first set foot in a hospital, nursing was regarded as a menial task suited only to uneducated women who could find no better employment. The transformation of this to the concept of nursing as a high vocation demanding both skill and dedication owed everything to Florence Nightingale.

More than this, she carried out in the face of hostile opposition a root and branch reform of the Army's medical services, serviced a Royal Commission on sanitary conditions in the hospitals of the Indian Army, was consulted by foreign governments, was responsible for the building of new hospitals, and initiated a specialist nursing service for the more than 200 squalid workhouses in England. Two handbooks on nursing and hospitals remained classic, influential guides for well over a century, and not everyone is convinced that their supercession by a more modern approach has been entirely beneficial.

Such massive achievements, with their untold benefits to human life, were hardly likely to be accomplished by a slender, saintly figure gliding along the corridors of society with nothing more than a little lamp to guide her. Florence Nightingale was a tender nurse, but she was also a woman possessed by what she believed to be a calling from God – a calling that brooked no obstacles to its fulfilment. She was visionary, determined, plain-spoken, endowed with unusual leadership and administrative skills, and usually more than a match for the men who tried to stand in her way. That this frequently made her an uncomfortable colleague or companion is not surprising, but the tough unyielding side of her character has sometimes been grossly exaggerated by a number of her more than fifty biographers. Sustained by a deep, albeit unorthodox Christian faith, she often felt herself to have been a complete failure. This was true only of her strenuous attempts to avoid celebrity status.

Florence (Flo to her family and close friends, but to no one else) was born in Florence in 1820 during one of her parents' not infrequent continental tours. They were very wealthy, thanks to a major legacy from a fairly distant relative which had required the adoption of his name – Nightingale. There was a large estate in Derbyshire, with a fine house, Lea Hurst, and another, Embley Park, on the borders of the New Forest in Hampshire. They were country gentry, rather than aristocratic, but extremely well connected, particularly among the Whigs, with whom they were aligned.

Their religious connections were Unitarian, and Florence's maternal grandfather, William Smith, was a notable social reformer and, in spite of his Unitarianism, a member of the Evangelical Clapham Sect. He had worked closely with William Wilberforce and Thomas Clarkson in the campaign for the abolition of the slave trade.

At Lea Hurst in the summer, and Embley Park in the winter, Florence was taught by her father and a series of governesses under an exacting regime that made her proficient in Latin, Greek, German and Italian, as well as competent in history and philosophy. Her chief delight, though, was in the English language, and her early compulsion to write led posthumously to an edition of her selected writings that will, when completed, extend to 16 volumes.

Otherwise, her life was increasingly that of high society – parties, balls, country pursuits and, in the season, stays in London. She was presented at Court in the second year of Queen Victoria's reign. There was the expectation that she would in due course make a good marriage but in this, as in so many other ways, her parents were to be disappointed. Several suitors were turned down, the most serious of these being Richard Milnes, who later became the first Baron Houghton. They had quite a lot in common, and he persisted for a number of years, but Florence eventually concluded that marriage to him would condemn her to lifelong confinement to a form of family life from which she was desperate to escape.

Her parents confessed to friends that the duckling they thought they were rearing had turned out to be a swan. Lytton Strachey, in a famous essay on her in his *Eminent Victorians*, suggested that 'an eagle' would have been a better description. Much later in her life Florence explained: 'the first idea I can recollect when I was a child was to nurse the sick'. At 17, she 'felt called by God to some great unspecified cause'. She was attending church at East Wellow, near Romsey – her parish church – and it was perhaps at this point she realized that the Church of England would not provide her with a cause.

But she was also visiting the homes of cottagers on her father's estates and spending an unusual amount of time with those who were sick. In 1842 she heard about Kaiserswerth, on the Rhine, where Protestant deaconesses were being trained in nursing as well as in teaching, and from then onwards she was constantly day-dreaming about involvement in nursing. This took a practical turn in 1845, when, having felt a clear call in this direction, she spent three months at Salisbury Infirmary learning to be a nurse. Her idea then was to establish in East Wellow some sort of Protestant sisterhood that would care for the sick in the surrounding area. This did not materialize, and her parents were totally opposed to her becoming a nurse. It was out of the question that a woman of Florence's social background and education should 'descend to this level'.

A period of depression in 1847 led to her spending the winter, with her maid and family friends, in Rome. This proved to be important on several counts. Contact with the powerhouse of the Roman Catholic Church included an audience with the recently elected Pope Pius IX and a first encounter with Cardinal Manning, the former Anglican Archdeacon. The ceremonies in St Peter's impressed her greatly and she made a study of the Church's doctrine, but in the end decided that its demands were oppressive rather than liberating.

Of special significance, however, was a chance meeting with a nun at the Convent Trinità dei Monti at the top of Spanish Steps. This led to her undertaking a ten-day retreat at the Convent and a further conversation with the nun which renewed her conviction that she was called by God to surrender her will 'to all that is upon the earth'. This was a turning point in her life. Hardly less important was her meeting with Sidney Herbert, a scion of the Earl of Pembroke, who with his wife was also staying in Rome. A close lifelong friendship developed, and his position in the government as Secretary of State for War at the time of the Crimean War and subsequently was a critical factor in most of Florence's achievements.

Further spells of depression followed her return to Embley Park and these were not alleviated by the breaking of her relationship with Richard Milnes. So, once again, in 1849, she went with the same family friends on a long tour, this time to Greece and Egypt. After visiting the ancient sites, some time was spent in a hospital in Alexandria where two sisters of St Vincent de Paul were treating poor Arabs from the surrounding villages. This impressed her, but as the time for the return journey approached she was overcome by the recurrence of deep emotional problems that would, in various forms, disturb her mind and influence her actions for the rest of her long life. These were partly religious, partly the result of intense frustration caused by the constraints of family life, and almost certainly the symptoms of a bi-polar personality. A diary entry while in Egypt contained a lament: 'My history is a history of woe, mistake and blinding vanity of seeking great things for myself.' This was followed, the next day, with 'God, I place myself in thy hands ... if it be thy will that I go on suffering, let it be so.'

Returning home through Germany, however, she took the opportunity to spend a fortnight at Kaiserswerth. This impressed her greatly, not least the Christian commitment of the deaconesses which, she came to see, appeared to be the secret of effective nursing. At the request of Pastor Fliedner, the founder of the institution, she wrote a booklet about it to make the work better known in England. This was published anonymously and provided an opportunity for her to present the issue foremost in her mind – 'What were God's intentions with regard to unmarried women and widows? How did he mean to employ them, to satisfy them?' The answer, she suggested, lay in the office of deaconess.

Her depression nonetheless reoccurred, and soon after returning home she wrote in her diary, 'I have no desire now but to die. There is not a night when I do not lie down in my bed wishing that I may bear it no more. Unconsciousness is all that I desire.' With the risk of suicide so evident, Florence's parents agreed that she could go back to Kaiserswerth for three months to train as a nurse, and before she went she met, almost by chance it seems, Elizabeth Blackwell, who had overcome formidable opposition in order to become the first woman to qualify as a doctor – receiving her training, along with 150 men, at a medical school in New York. This inspired Florence to persevere in her vocation.

The Kaiserswerth experience did her a great deal of good, but it was not until April 1853 that she, now aged 33, was allowed by her parents to go to Paris for training in a hospital run by nuns, then to become superintendent of a small hospital for invalid gentlewomen in London's Harley Street. In the same year, however, the Russian army invaded Turkey, and Britain and France went to Turkey's aid. Thus began what became known as the Crimean War in which the chief enemy for the British and the French was not so much Russian arms as raging cholera, typhus and malaria, against which the soldiers had no protection. Within a few weeks of their arrival in Turkey, 8,000 British troops had become seriously ill, many of them terminally.

Reports of this having reached England, a letter to *The Times* compared the lack of medical care in the British Army with the much more adequate provision in the French, and asked, 'Are there no able women among us willing to go out to treat our soldiers as the French are being treated?' Florence immediately offered her services to the War Office in a letter that crossed with a request from her friend Sidney Herbert that she should respond to this challenge.

A week later she was on her way, leading a party of 28 women, six of them nuns from Lydia Sellon's Devonport community, ten from two Roman Catholic convents, the rest from a variety of backgrounds. The journey to Constantinople, which included the experience of a violent Mediterranean storm, took a fortnight, and when they arrived at Scutari, a suburb of the Turkish capital, they were greeted by a scene of barely describable horror. A huge military barracks had been turned into what purported to be a hospital. The rooms adjoining the main corridor, 450 yards long, were packed with men brought from the front, still in their uniforms, often stiff with mud and blood. There was no running water, no sanitation, no blankets and only inadequate food. The few army doctors and the handful of untrained women nurses could not cope and, after more and more patients had poured into the barracks and an adjoining hospital, it was estimated that over 2,300 of them were occupying a total of four miles of beds. Yet only one in ten died of wounds, the rest of disease. The death rate was 42 per cent.

Florence immediately initiated a total reorganization. Some of those who had accompanied her from England turned out to be unsuitable for the task and had to be sent home, but a second party of 36 led by Mary Stanley, the sister of Dean Stanley, brought valuable reinforcements. By the end of the war well over 200 women of varying calibre had offered their services. The proposed reforms inevitably led to conflict with the military authorities, most notably General John Hall, the chief army medical officer, who reported to the War Office, 'Miss Nightingale shows an ambitious struggling after power, inimical to the true interests of the medical department.'

Florence, who had, however, been given plenary authority, with the title Superintendent of Female Nurses in the Hospitals of the East, knew how to use it and simply appealed over his head to the War Office where she had Sidney Herbert's full support. When at the end of the war Hall was appointed KCB, she said, 'This must mean Knight of the Crimean Burial-grounds.' She used her influence with Herbert and her contacts at *The Times* to publicize what she was attempting, and this attracted gifts of money which, added to gifts from friends and some of her own money, enabled her to buy large quantities of medical supplies and nourishing food.

Of the greatest importance were the sanitary reforms, and the death rate in the hospital was reduced dramatically. Besides the administrative work, she was engaged most of the time in her first love, that of nursing. She worked 20 hours of every day, and although she drove her nurses hard, she insisted on their ceasing at 8 p.m. Hence the image of 'the lady with the lamp', derived from her night-time tending of the suffering soldiers. Her gentle sensitivity with them was in marked contrast to her tough-mindedness with anyone who stood in the way of her plans for their care. She became greatly loved, news of her work spread rapidly throughout the Army and, during a short visit on horseback to the front at Balaclava, she was cheered by large gatherings of soldiers and presented with flowers by many of those whose lives had been saved by her skill and care. During this visit she contracted a fever and was herself at death's door for 12 days.

When peace came in 1856, she went to Balaclava and remained there for four months until the hospitals there were closed. A heroine's welcome awaited her in England, but on arrival she refused to make any public appearances or to write a book about her Crimean experiences. 'I only did what God called me to do', she explained, but she agreed, with some reluctance, to the launching of an appeal for money to mark the nation's gratitude. This was conditional upon her having complete control of its use, which was to support a campaign to improve the quality of nursing in all military hospitals.

Queen Victoria had followed her work in Scutari with the greatest admiration and sent her a brooch, designed by the Prince Consort and bearing the inscription 'Blessed are the merciful'. She now invited her to Balmoral to hear more about her work at first hand, so Florence took the opportunity to lobby for the Prince Consort's support of her campaign. The Queen had apparently gathered from the reports that she was a bit of a 'dragon' and awaited her arrival at the castle with some apprehension, but in the event she was pleasantly surprised and told Florence, 'You have no self-importance or humbug, no wonder the soldiers love you.'

Her proposals for reform, presented in 1859 after meticulous gathering of statistical and other evidence, were quickly implemented and led to the founding of an Army Medical College at Chatham and the first military hospital at Woolwich. In the same year she published *Notes on Hospitals* and *Notes on Nursing*, both of which became classic textbooks on their subject, remaining in print until well into the next century.

Meanwhile, the public appeal was enjoying tremendous success. Money poured in from every quarter, including from many parish churches, and totalled over £44,000 – about £2 million in today's values. This was used to found in 1860 a Nightingale School of Nursing at St Thomas's Hospital which was closed in 1991 but then resurrected by King's College, London to train 1,200 nurses and midwives. After prescribing the basis of the training to be offered, however, she lost interest in the project and became no more than a figurehead in its development under a capable matron.

It was also the case that her health was now in decline – a mixture of physical and emotional problems. It has been suggested that she contracted brucellosis, sometimes known as Crimean fever, which can have long-lasting symptoms, and she became virtually a recluse, emerging from her house in South Street, Mayfair, only rarely. But this did not mean inactivity. On the contrary: from her couch in an upper room she directed several more enterprises, some of the greatest importance. In this she was assisted by Dr John Sutherland, an authority on sanitation, who became a close friend and visited her every day to help with her correspondence and diary. Her Aunt Mai, whom she had known since childhood and who was also a close friend, dealt with the many visitors, protecting her from all but the heads of state and of governments who wished to consult her. Most of the communication between Florence and these assistants was in the form of notes, and besides several domestic servants and a personal maid, there was a messenger who took her letters to various parts of the capital. There were usually one or two cats in attendance.

She was consulted by the military authorities involved in the American Civil War and the Franco-Russian War, and a major project was a Royal Commission to inquire into the sanitary state of the Army in India where there was an unacceptably high death rate from disease among British soldiers. Although she was unable to travel to the subcontinent herself, she amassed and analysed a vast amount of material, ensured that the most qualified people were appointed to the Commission and wrote a 92-page summary of the findings of its report which appeared in 1863. This was given the title *How People May Live and Not Die in India.*

Nearer home, she discerned the need for a major reform of the War Office, where Sidney Herbert was still in office but where many of the reforms of the medical department she had initiated were in danger of being frustrated by incompetence and often deliberate obstruction. She saw clearly what was needed and pressed Herbert to see that her proposals were carried out. But he was now far too ill to do much about it and this aroused little sympathy from Florence who saw her plans being thwarted. She was, however, devastated by his death, and not only because this meant the end of War Office reform. Their friendship had been close for many years and she described herself as his 'true widow'.

A more modest project, and one that was wholly successful, was the provision of proper medical facilities for the inmates of the more than 200 workhouses which had been established as a consequence of the 1834 Poor Law Amendment Act. Again, it was a letter to *The Times* that drew public attention to a scandalously cruel situation, but Florence had herself visited workhouses in London and had no doubt that specially trained nurses to serve in them was the right solution. It was Scutari all over again and there was no one better to deal with it, even now from a distance.

In 1860, not long after her withdrawal from public life, Florence produced *Suggestions for Thought to Searchers after Truth among the Artisans of England* – a three-volume work which was published privately and circulated to only a few friends. One of the volumes, *Cassandra*, had started as a novel but was turned into a report on the enslavement of young women by the oppressive demands of upper- and middle-class family life. It was in fact a *cri de cœur* and the ferocity of its language and style owed everything to the intense pain that she had herself experienced at Lea House and Embley Park. It was an early plea for women's liberation.

The other volumes contained a rich mixture of material – extensive quotations from the Spanish mystics, John Bunyan and other spiritual writers, together with many of her own thoughts about religion and life's meaning and purpose, but lacking a framework necessary for cohesion. Benjamin Jowett, the legendary Master of Balliol College, Oxford, who is believed by some to have proposed marriage to her, saw the material before its publication and suggested that it consisted of the basic elements for a book, rather than a finished volume. John Stuart Mill, the philosopher, agreed.

Nonetheless the two volumes of 'Thoughts' and 'Practical Deduction' provide important insights into her beliefs. These are not easy to categorize. She was brought up in a Unitarian household, but was baptized in the Church of England, went with her parents to the Anglican church at East Wellow when they were at Embley Park, and to the Methodist Chapel when they were at Lea Hurst. Her Unitarian background was reflected in her commitment to Christian action rather than doctrinal orthodoxy, though unlike her parents she believed in the Trinity and the Incarnation. Until she was 37, she attended the Church of England with reasonable frequency, but then lost patience with the disputes that occupied so much of its leadership at the expense of social action. At various times she turned to the Roman Catholic Church for insight, and for a few years corresponded with Mother Mary Clare Moore, of the Bermondsey Sisters, who had been with her at Scutari and now introduced her to the Catholic mystical tradition. Conversations and correspondence with Cardinal Manning were constructive but led to the conclusion by both of them that she would never become a Roman Catholic. She had in fact much more in common with her friend Benjamin Jowett, sharing his controversial liberal views on such matters as biblical criticism, the miracles and the impossibility of eternal damnation.

Underlying all this, however, was a deep awareness of her relationship with the God who had called her to a particular task and who continued at various times in her life to point to the direction in which she should move. She never doubted that 'with God all things are possible'.

In his award-winning and now definitive biography of Florence Nightingale (2008), which is indispensable to the serious study of her life and work, Mark Bostridge suggests, surely correctly, that her attitude to feminism was ambivalent. For the first half of her life it barely existed as a concept, and her own success in escaping from the tyranny of middle-class family life occupied more than thirty years. When accomplished and retailed in *Cassandra*, she was recognized as a pioneer in the field. On the other hand she was, for much of her life, opposed to women becoming doctors. This was partly because she believed they would be better employed as nurses, but also because those who had become doctors were behaving like their male colleagues and had therefore brought no improvement to the profession. A certain amount of grudging support was given to the Women's Suffrage Movement, but on the whole she believed that women would achieve more by exerting influence on men of power, as she had done, rather than themselves seeking power. She nonetheless advocated equal pay and property rights for women, and Mark Bostridge is certain that had she been alive today she would have supported the ordination of women.

By the end of the century Florence's health had deteriorated considerably, and, although she lived for another ten years, the quality of her existence was poor. She became almost blind, her memory deserted her, and towards the end she seemed hardly aware of her surroundings. In 1907 she became the first woman to be appointed to the Order of Merit, and in the following year she was given the Freedom of the City of London, but both honours had to be received on her behalf.

She died in 1910, and, having given instructions that there was to be no great public funeral in Westminster Abbey, was buried, in the presence of local people, in the family plot in the churchyard at East Wellow, where the stone over her grave is inscribed 'F. N. Born 12 May 1820. Died 13th August 1910'. Later there was a Memorial Service in St Paul's Cathedral, and a statue was erected in Waterloo Place, not far from Trafalgar Square: she is commemorated in the Church of England's Calendar of Holy Days on 13 August.

7

Rediscovering the Deaconess:
Elizabeth Ferard and Isabella Gilmore

The ministry of deaconess was of considerable importance during the early Christian centuries, but although it survived in some parts of the Church until the eleventh century, it largely went into desuetude some 500 years earlier. Its revival in the early part of the nineteenth century was due to the initiative of Pastor Theodor Fliedner of Kaiserswerth, in the Rhineland. He recognized the need for an organization of women who would devote themselves to the care of the sick and to the education of neglected children.

He had in mind something akin to the work undertaken by some Roman Catholic women's religious orders, but without the taking of solemn vows or other distinctive elements of the Religious Life. They would, however, have a defined role – that of a deaconess – be recruited from the unmarried and the widows, and undertake to serve for at least five years. In 1836 he appointed two women to work in his own parish and, as interest in this development grew, undertook to train others who would go out in pairs to other parishes – one to nurse and the other to teach.

By the end of the century Kaiserswerth had grown to a considerable size and became a colony of charitable institutions, including a hospital and dispensary, a home for 60 infirm ladies, an asylum for mild psychiatric cases, an orphanage for the children of middle-class parents, and a 'Rescue Home for Released Female Prisoners and Magdalens'. There were also smaller daughter houses in Alexandria, Berlin, Constantinople, Jerusalem, Rome, Smyrna and other cities.

The organization was administered from Kaiserswerth, which now had several thousand deaconesses on its books, all of whom had been through its training programme, and most of whom were engaged in specialist nursing and teaching, rather than parish, ministries. Florence Nightingale received the early part of her training at Kaiserswerth without, of course, ever becoming a deaconess, and she wrote a pamphlet which made its work known in England.

The Bishop of London, Archibald Campbell Tait, who later became Archbishop of Canterbury, went to Kaiserswerth to see for himself in 1858. He was introducing several new projects designed to enable the church in London to minister more effectively to the multitude of mainly poor people who were quite outside its influence, and was sufficiently impressed by what he saw to initiate a discussion in the Convocation of Canterbury about the possibility of reviving the deaconess order in the Church of England.

Another visitor to Kaiserswerth at about the same time was Elizabeth Ferard. Descended from an old Huguenot family, she was born in London in 1825 and had for some years been looking for an opportunity to serve God in full-time work in the Church of England. This was not possible while she was caring for her ailing mother, but after her mother died in 1858 she went to Kaiserswerth, where she stayed for about three months. In spite of difficulties with the local German dialect, she worked in an orphanage and also learned nursing skills.

She also became aware of the extent to which the revival of the deaconess order had spread to other parts of Europe and wrote:

> I again heard of the continual spreading of the deaconess work in every direction except in England, and more than ever wished we could have something of the kind in England where the materials for it are so abundant, could we but found a Deaconess House on the right principles without falling on the stumbling block of Romanism.

She did not feel, however, that Kaiserswerth provided a model for the Church of England, neither did the answer lie with the recently founded religious community of All Hallows at Ditchingham, in Norfolk, which was committed to nursing and the care of children. The Mildmay Deaconess House, established in London's East End in 1860 by a Church of England clergyman, the Revd William Pennefather, was deemed to be too Protestant in its ethos and subsequently developed more within the Methodist Church.

Encouraged by Bishop Tait, she therefore discussed her ideas with the

Revd Thomas Pelham Dale, to whom she was related by marriage. He had wanted to establish a women's society to work among the poor but one that was more flexible than a rigidly structured religious order. They were in full agreement over this, and after she had undergone some training and got two kindred spirits, Ellen Meredith and Anna Wilcox, to join her, she founded in 1861 the Community of St Andrew in a house near King's Cross Station, which was named the North London Deaconess House. This was with the enthusiastic approval of the bishop who in July 1862 ordained Elizabeth as a deaconess – the first ever in the Church of England.

The Deaconess House was located in a notorious slum district, and she and her Sisters found a great deal of work in the parish of Somers Town, to which they were attached. They also taught in local schools for girls and infants, and Elizabeth took charge of the nursery at the Great Northern Hospital. The Community was not bound by religious vows, and it was not until the twentieth century that these were introduced and it became a religious order. Nonetheless it was regulated by strict rules concerning conduct, dress and worship. Morning and Evening Prayer were offered daily, and time was set aside for private prayer and Bible study. Recruits, who came from the ranks of the more highly educated, were enrolled first as a Provisional Sister, then spent two years as candidates before ordination and admission to the community.

The issue of authority led before long to a disagreement between Elizabeth and Thomas Dale. She was, according to his daughter and biographer, 'a manager of decision and power, and not inclined to brook interference in the Head Sister's prejudice in favour of autocratic rule which grew stronger. Her conviction that strict authority was necessary and that if the work was to prosper this must be in the hands of the Sister Superior become firmer.' Disappointed by this development, Dale resigned as chaplain in 1868.

In spite of this parting of company, however, the work flourished and other dioceses began to send women to the community for training as deaconesses. But not all dioceses and women wanted their ministries to be exercised in the context of communities that, although not strictly speaking religious orders, nonetheless exhibited many of the marks of such orders. This led to the emergence of different models.

The clearance of Somers Town slums to make way for the development of the St Pancras Station railway yards led to the removal in 1873 of the community to a much larger house in Tavistock Square, which became the London Deaconess Institution. Soon after this Elizabeth's health began to fail and she resigned from the leadership. The next ten years were devoted to running a convalescent home for children she had founded at Redhill, in Surrey. She died on Easter Day in 1883.

In a book *The Ministry of Deaconesses* (1899) Celia Robinson, the sister of John Armitage Robinson, the great scholar Dean, and herself a deaconess, described Elizabeth Ferard as

> a strict disciplinarian, with an indomitable will and a strong love of justice. She was generous and affectionate, but intensely reserved with a shy manner that gave her an appearance of haughtiness. She had not that gift of ready sympathy which would have enabled her to win many helpers for the cause, but those who knew her well loved and respected her deeply.

She is commemorated in the Church of England's Calendar of Holy Days on 18 July – the date of her ordination.

The Bishop of Rochester, Anthony Thorold, had also been to Kaiserswerth and came away impressed. He was aware of the work of Elizabeth Ferard in London and that Deaconess Houses had also been established in Ely, Canterbury, Chester, Salisbury, Winchester and Durham. At that time a large part of south-east London was in the Rochester diocese, and Thorold was keen to have deaconesses working in the squalid slums where the Church was making little impact.

His first choice for this pioneering enterprise was a Miss Martin, but she died very suddenly before any real progress could be made. He wrote to the matron of Guy's Hospital, Victoria Jones, to see if she could recommend a woman with initiative and gifts of leadership who might take on the task. Although she had only recently become matron of the hospital, Victoria had formed a very high opinion of one of the ward sisters, Isabella Gilmore, and suggested her to the Bishop. He was equally impressed and went to enormous pains to overcome her initial reluctance to accept his invitation. Eventually she did and became the most influential figure in the growth of the deaconess ministry beyond the semi-religious order model adopted by Elizabeth Ferard.

*   *   *

Isabella Gilmore was born in 1842 at Woodfall Hall on the edge of Epping Forest. Her father was a City businessman who had made a fortune from copper mining in Devon, but he died when Isabella was only five, leaving eight other children, including William Morris, who became a famous architect and designer. She was then brought up by governesses before attending a private school in Brighton, followed by a finishing school in Bristol until she was 17.

Twelve months later she married Arthur Gilmore, a naval officer, ten years her senior. He was often away at sea, but had fairly long leaves, and sometimes she was able to accompany him on summer cruises. In 1882, however, by which time he had risen to the rank of Commander, he died of tubercular meningitis, whereupon she returned to her mother's home, now in the Hertfordshire village of Much Hadham.

Having considered what to do with the rest of her life, Isabella decided to take up nursing at Guy's Hospital. Nursing was still in a primitive state and staffed by rough, ill-disciplined and often drunken women of limited skill and less compassion. Conditions were, however, changing at Guy's. Margaret Brast, who was matron when Isabella joined the staff, was a reformer. She was recruiting well-educated, upper- or middle-class women of good social background who were designated lady pupils. These were to become well-trained, responsible, ward sisters or matrons of other hospitals. Isabella also established good relationships, sometimes long-lasting friendships, with the consultants, and it was during her time at Guy's that antiseptic surgery was introduced.

Although it was not her intention to stay long at the hospital, she signed a three-year contract as sister of a medical ward, but soon afterwards her brother Rendall, an Army officer, died leaving five daughters and three sons who had been deserted by their mother. Isabella immediately undertook complete responsibility for their upbringing, though her sister Emma provided them with a home until she had completed her contract.

It was then that Bishop Thorold made his approach, having first let her see a booklet he had written about his plans for tackling the problems of increasingly industrialized south London:

While we cannot stir ourselves too much, too rapidly, to give the working class the things they have a right to claim and so seldom receive – air, water and house room – let us not slacken effort in recognising and supplying their moral and spiritual needs ... We want three things, after the one indispensable and essential gift of all, the fullness of the Spirit of God. They are – men, alms and devotion. Men, yes, and women too, prophets if you like to call them, who shall come to us to live and preach and represent Christ.

When she went to see him, he asked, 'What are your plans when you leave the hospital?' She responded, 'Look after my brother's children and also work among the poor.' 'Then', said the Bishop, 'why can't you do for us what you are going to do for yourself?' Isabella recognized the importance of what he had in mind; it was simply that she was not convinced that it was for her. Visits to several deaconess houses did nothing to convince her otherwise. 'I was not impressed by anything I saw, and I disliked much; in fact the whole thing did not commend itself to me in any way.'

Nonetheless, Thorold, who was a bishop of deep spirituality and great pastoral sensitivity, was not ready to let her go and over a quite long period wrote letters and arranged meetings to see if she might change her mind. Still uncertain, she went one Sunday morning to her local church, where there chanced to be a visiting preacher who chose as his text, 'Go, work for me today in my vineyard.' That did it. The sermon that followed went unheard by her, she remained on her knees until it was finished – 'It was just as if God's voice had called me, and the intense rest and joy were beyond all words.' That evening she wrote to the Bishop: 'I humbly accept your offer.'

Responsibility for the children, who now called her 'Mother', remained, but many discussions with the Bishop followed in which together they planned the establishing of a Deaconess Institution with a governing Council and herself at its head. Initially it was intended to start in a house amid the slums of Bermondsey, but the cost was more than the Council could afford, so another was chosen in Park Hill, near Clapham Common, which was a more salubrious area in which to live but still easily accessible to the slums.

Isabella's brother, William Morris, undertook responsibility for the furnishing and decoration of the chapel in his now characteristic style, though he did not favour what she was undertaking, and on 16 April 1887 the house was officially opened. After Evensong the Bishop ordained her:

I admit thee to the office of Deaconess in the name of the Father, and of the Son, and of the Holy Ghost. Amen.

God the Father, God the Son, God the Holy Ghost, bless, preserve and sanctify you; and so fill you with all spiritual benediction and grace, with all faith, wisdom and humility, that you may serve here before Him to the glory of His Great Name, and to the benefit of his Church and people; and make you faithful unto death, and give you the crown of everlasting life. Amen.

He then handed her a cross, saying:

Receive and wear this badge, a symbol of thy profession as a Deaconess. Be not ashamed to confess the faith of Christ crucified; bear ever in thy heart the remembrance of His love who died on the cross for thee. Amen.

She was clad in the uniform which she and the Bishop had agreed to be fitting for the office and the ministry. It consisted of a blue merino dress with velvet cuffs, a deep white collar and a lawn cap of the sort she had worn as a Guy's sister. Out of doors there was the covering of a long black cloak and a plain cottage bonnet, tied with a bow under the chin, and a long gauze veil. Quality was always to be of the best because she believed this would indicate to slum dwellers that deaconesses' work was of the highest importance. With great sorrow she parted with her engagement and wedding rings which were incorporated into a chalice, still in use.

It had been intended that three other women probationers would be in residence at the time of the opening, but recruiting in the early stages of the institution proved difficult. A number came to test their suitability for the work of a deaconess, but most departed after a quite short time, unable to cope with the strict discipline and austere way of life. By the autumn of 1889, however, a strong group had been formed and embraced a routine which began at 7.30 a.m. with a half-hour period of meditation in the chapel. Prayers were said again at 9.00 a.m. and more prayers at 1.30 p.m. for those who were not out working in the parishes. Evensong was sung at 5.30 p.m. and the day ended with family prayers at 9.45 p.m. A fairly large number of Associates, who were closely attached to the institution, attended a monthly Friday morning service.

At first it was not easy to find parishes that wanted to make use of their ministries, but eventually they found more than enough work to do in two Battersea parishes. These were predominantly working class, employed in riverside mills and factories, some on the railway. Both had gifted, zealous clergy and church life was vigorous, but the response from the poor was negligible.

Isabella and the other deaconesses undertook much welfare work, and her brother William once told her, 'I preach socialism, you practise it.' But like many of those who engaged in heroic work among the poorest of the poor in the Victorian era, she was a long way from socialism in her convictions. While she deplored the gulf between rich and poor and was saddened by the indifference of most of the rich to the plight of the poor, it was never in her mind that the social and economic order might be changed to create a more just and equal society.

In fact, she preferred her recruits to come from the middle and upper classes, as had her matron at Guy's, and in one of her reports on the Deaconess Institution she said,

I want strong women in body, soul and spirit – ladies if possible. A woman cannot be too much of a lady for this work. There is nothing that requires more tact than getting among the people and they are the first to find out what you really are, even if they do call you 'the mission woman' or 'trade woman'.

She went on to emphasize, however, that the ladies were of no use if they were afraid of hard work, unwilling to learn and content to 'sit and think about doing good, but not doing it'. In her 1888 report she recorded that in one district of the main parish 349 families had been visited and 4,753 visits paid. In one district of the other parish 245 families had been visited and 16,625 visits paid; 732 families were now being visited, another district having been taken into their care.

Probationers were given intensive training before being allowed onto the streets. Isabella emphasized that, although there were rules to be observed, these must never be allowed to stand in the way of meeting human need. There was to be no hint of patronage in the practical duties of nursing and poor relief. If rebuke was ever necessary, 'it must be done gently, and by loving, humble, patient ways'. Antagonism against the Church was 'never to be met in a contentious spirit, but with gentleness and a real understanding and sympathy for people'.

The clergy were encouraged to hold special services for the many children who had never been near a church, and Isabella, being appalled by the number who had not been baptized, arranged for special baptism services to be held in the church hall on dark weekday evenings, when families could attend without being ashamed of their clothes. Sometimes 100 or more children would be presented. Within her own Institution, suitably qualified clergy were brought in to strengthen the theological education of those under training. An increase in the number of these, as well as of those ordained, eventually made the Park Hill house much too small for the purpose, and in November 1891 Isabella took her Institution to a much larger property on the north side of Clapham Common. This, already named 'The Sisters', was not only spacious but also nearer to the outdoor work. Three large rooms were combined to make an impressive chapel, and a small house nearby was purchased for use as a 'Preventive Home'. Six girls from bad homes were cared for by a matron and trained for a new and better life in domestic service.

Early in 1906, after 20 years as Head of her Institution, Isabella retired to Reigate, and when she had recovered from a serious operation, embarked on visits to many of the deaconesses she had trained. Among these were the Head Deaconesses of Exeter, Manchester, Newcastle, Winchester and New York, as well as others in China, Japan, New Zealand, Australia, Canada and South Africa. She retired from public life in 1921 and died at Parkstone in Dorset on 15 March 1923. She is commemorated in the Church of England's Calendar of Holy Days on 16 April – the date of her ordination. Gilmore House, named in her honour, continued to train deaconesses for more than another fifty years.

By the time of her death the deaconess order was firmly established in the Church of England. It had been recognized by the Lambeth Conference in 1897, but it was not formally restored by the Convocation of Canterbury until 1923 and York in 1925. Even after then, however, there was much futile debate as to whether deaconesses were in Holy Orders, but this was resolved in 1987 when most were admitted to the diaconate. Those who chose not to take this step continued to minister as deaconesses, but the days of the Order are now numbered – and for the best of reasons.

8

Clearing the Urban Slums:
Octavia Hill and Henrietta Barnett

Improvement of the housing conditions of the urban poor and the provision of open spaces in which people of all classes might find relief from the pressures of Victorian urbanization were the twin objectives of Octavia Hill. In both spheres there was ample scope for reform, especially in housing. It is not now easy even to imagine the inhumanity of the nineteenth-century slums in which a family of ten was often crowded into a single room, alongside similar families, with grim courtyards lacking adequate water supply, sanitation and other basic needs.

But Octavia Hill became aware of the suffering this caused, and the measure of her achievement is demonstrated by the fact that, having started with an experiment involving three houses, she was by the time of her retirement supervising 6,000 London houses and flats, most of them with two or three bedrooms. Many had gardens or other open space nearby.

More than this, she trained a new style of housing manager who undertook similar housing renewal in London and in other towns and cities. Henrietta and Samuel Barnett were inspired and instructed by her, as was Emma Cons who started as one of her rent collectors and went on to manage other large housing projects as well as to found Morley College for the education of working-class men and women, and what became the Old Vic Theatre to give them a chance to experience Shakespeare.

Octavia's broad, humane vision, which found expression in her book *Homes of the London Poor* (1875) owed much to her socially conscious family upbringing, but also to the early influence of the Christian Socialists, especially that of Frederick Denison Maurice, a controversial theologian and social reformer. He prepared her for baptism and confirmation, and she became a friend as well as a disciple. Charles Kingsley also impressed her deeply.

She was born in Wisbech in 1838 – the eighth daughter and ninth child of James Hill, a corn merchant, local banker and social utopian. Her mother, his third wife, was a writer and an educationist committed to the ideas and methods of Pestalozzi, which she applied to the upbringing of her own family. Her maternal grandfather, Dr Southwood Smith, worked in the London Hospital in the East End where he became an authority on sanitation and fever epidemics and told her how the health of the poor was adversely affected by their squalid housing conditions. He also campaigned against the employment of child labour in coal mines.

When Octavia was only two her father went bankrupt for the second time and consequently suffered a breakdown which removed him from his family. Her mother took the five remaining children to live in Finchley, then a village just north of London, where their grandfather, who lived in nearby Highgate, became a surrogate father.

Her mother became manager and book-keeper of the Ladies' Guild, a central London co-operative crafts workshop founded by the Christian Socialists to teach poor schoolgirls to make toys. Octavia joined in and as a result met F. D. Maurice. She also met John Ruskin, who supervised her artistic development and encouraged her to learn by copying the paintings of great masters. He too became a lifelong friend and an abiding influence.

After her baptism and confirmation, and when she was still only 17, F. D. Maurice asked her to become secretary of the women's classes held at the Working Men's College, of which he was the principal, in Red Lion Square, also in central London. This also involved standing in as a teacher when members of its staff were absent.

She left this to join her mother and sisters in a new project – a school in the house in Nottingham Place in central London to which they had moved from Finchley. This was intended originally for the children of a few friends, but its numbers soon grew and Octavia also started a weekly gathering in the kitchen to teach poor women to make clothes. This soon brought her to an awareness of the appalling housing conditions in which they all lived.

She went to discuss this problem with John Ruskin and asked him if he would finance the purchase of three run-down houses in south London to enable her to do something about it. He had recently received a large inheritance from his father, which she may or may not have known about, so he readily agreed to advance the money on a business footing, with a return of five per cent.

Thus, in 1864, began Octavia's great experiment in the housing of the poor. One of her sisters, Miranda, to whom she was specially close and who always provided strong support, took over responsibility for the expanding school, leaving her free to improve the houses and instal the tenants. These were visited weekly for the collection of the modest rents and to discover any family needs. There was a weekly tenants' meeting and occasional outings to the countryside, all of which proved to be so successful that she expanded the scheme as other houses were put up for sale. Other landlords, impressed by her management skills and results, put their properties in her hands for improvement and rent collection. Gradually her responsibilities spread to other parts of London, and her reputation led the Ecclesiastical (later Church) Commissioners in 1884 to take her onto their staff to deal with a number of their major housing problems.

They owned large areas of land, mainly in south London, which had been leased earlier in the century to developers who had created some of the capital's worst slums. As the leases on these fell in, serious decisions about their future were needed and Octavia was brought in to advise and administer. The tenements were pulled down and replaced by decent houses and flats, and she persuaded the Commissioners to deal with their housing on a large scale rather than piecemeal. This enabled estates of cottages, subsequently known as Octavia Hill estates, to be built in Walworth, Southwark and Deptford, with plenty of space and community facilities. Tenants due for rehousing were consulted about their needs, and the large team of rent-collectors, reinforced by socially conscious middle-class volunteers, were trained to deal with welfare problems

A letter to fellow workers in 1887 indicated what was involved in the creation of a public garden in Southwark, part of a new estate:

It was, when handed over to me, a desolate place. There had been a paper factory on one half of it, which had been burnt down. Four or five feet of unburnt paper lay in irregular heaps, blackened by fire, saturated by rain and smelling most unpleasantly. It had lain there for five years and much rubbish had been thrown in. A warehouse some storeys high fronted the street on the other half of the ground, with no forecourt or area to remove its dull height further from the rooms in the modest dwellings which faced it. Our first work was to set bonfires alight, gradually to burn the mess of paper. This took about six weeks to do, though the fires were kept alight day and night. The ashes were good for the soil in the garden, and we were saved the whole cost of carting the paper away. Our next task was to pull down the warehouse and let a little sun in on our garden, and additional light, air and sight of the sky to numerous tenants.

Then came the erection of a covered playground for the children; it was the whole length of a huge warehouse which bounds the garden on one side. It is roofed with timber from the warehouse we pulled down and the roof is supported by massive pillars. The space is paved with red bricks set diagonally, so as to make a pretty pattern. At one end of this arcade is a drinking fountain.

The scheme also involved the building of a community hall, which was used for a great deal of social and cultural activity. The interior walls had murals portraying peacetime acts of heroism. Financial support from friends and many others who admired her work helped to finance non-housing projects.

Octavia's concern for deprived young people led her to close involvement with the Volunteer Cadet Corps which had been formed in 1879 when there was still the threat of a French invasion. The military element in its programme was fairly minimal and it was more of a well-structured boys' club, with a strong emphasis on discipline and physical fitness. It was, however, anticipated that some of its members would eventually join the Army or the Navy, which a good many did.

She saw the VCC as an ideal means of training for the boys on her estates – better than the Church Lads' Brigade or the Boys' Brigade because it appealed to 'the more manly kind of lad'. But her involvement with what many saw as a neo-military organization caused some eyebrows to be raised, including those of her mother who was worried lest her daughter might be condoning war. To her she argued that, while a defensive war could be right, she greatly doubted if one would be needed. What is more, a volunteer element in the Army would be less likely than a wholly professional body to hurry the country into war. Most importantly, the training offered 'will be to our Southwark lads the very best possible education'. By 1912 over 8,000 boys had passed through the VCC's First London Battalion and Octavia protested strongly when the War Office reduced the maximum age limit to 17.

Her concern for the creation of open spaces in former inner-city slum areas led her into membership of the recently formed Commons Preservation Society. This took her into the company of Canon H. D. Rawnsley and Sir Robert Hunter and to the co-founding with them of the National Trust. This was for her a realization of an earlier dream and analysis expressed in a book *Our Common Land* (1878) and she travelled extensively in Britain to secure places of beauty for the benefit of all. Nearer home, her persistence saved from development the important Parliament Hill Fields in north London which remain a source of pleasure and refreshment for many.

Octavia had, however, no serious political concerns. Indeed, she opposed the campaign for women's suffrage on the grounds that women were temperamentally unsuited to making decisions about budgets, defence and international affairs. They might, she conceded, get involved in local government where matters related to housing and other aspects of social welfare were decided.

When a Royal Commission on Housing was appointed in 1884 its chairman, Sir Charles Dilke, invited her to join, but this was vetoed by the Home Secretary on the grounds of her gender. The issue went to the Cabinet where the Prime Minister, W. E. Gladstone, said that, while he supported her appointment in principle, he 'could not in person', which presumably had something to do with her being a woman.

A fine portrait of her by John Singer Sargent, presented to her in 1898 by her friends, now hangs in the National Portrait Gallery. She bore a striking resemblance to her mother, with dark eyes and a warm smile, which seems to confirm the common view that her undoubted despotism was always exercised benevolently. Certainly she had a strong personality, a determination to get things done and a consequent impatience with bureaucracy and inefficiency.

Her Christian faith ran deep and was expressed in practical action, rather than the doctrinal controversies of her time. She was in touch with successive bishops of London and so influenced Frederick Temple, before his translation to Canterbury, that he seriously considered the possibility of moving from his palatial London house to a more modest dwelling in Clerkenwell so as to be near the poor. This was not feasible, but he told a meeting held at the even more palatial Fulham Palace that Miss Octavia convinced him and the other Ecclesiastical Commissioners that they were wrong and she was right about certain points of their housing policy. He added, 'When she had talked to us for half-an-hour we were quite refuted.

I never had such a beating in my life. Consequently I feel a great respect for her.'

Although blessed with extraordinary energy, she tended to work until she dropped, with the result that her life was punctuated by breakdowns which often required long periods for recuperation. One of the earliest of these was also related to a broken engagement, and she remained unmarried for the rest of her life. She lived with her sister, Miranda, and also for 30 years with a Miss Yorke, who accompanied her on holidays and cared for her when her health began to fail. This was in 1912, and she died on 13 August of that year. Burial in Westminster Abbey was suggested but she had requested a grave in the churchyard at Crockham Hill, a Kent beauty spot for which she had a special affection. She is commemorated in the Church of England's Calendar of Holy Days on 13 August.

The memory of Octavia's great work did not, however, inhibit the Church Commissioners from selling the south London estates to private landlords during the first decade of the present century, thus reducing substantially the supply of social housing in the area. In spite of protests and demonstrations, the last of these sales, involving 1,630 houses and a £266 million deal, took place in the spring of 2011. A group of local clergy held a service of repentance, including the depositing of ash, outside the Commissioners' offices on the Tuesday of Holy Week and said that the sales would destroy their communities. The Commissioners said they would 'further the mission of the Church'.

*   *   *

At a birthday party for Octavia Hill held in the parish of St Mary, Bryanston Square, in London's West End, Henrietta Rowland, whose second name also chanced to be Octavia, met Samuel Barnett, the curate. She was 21 and the daughter of wealthy parents who lived in Champion Hall, Kent. Hunting, gardening and other outdoor pursuits, as well as parties, had until recently occupied most of her life, but now she was working with Octavia Hill in the slums of St Mary's parish.

Samuel Barnett's background was different. Born in Bristol in 1844, he was the son of the first manufacturer of iron bedsteads. Until he was 16, he was educated at home but then went to Wadham College, Oxford, to prepare for Holy Orders – much to the displeasure of his father. On coming down from Oxford he taught at Winchester College for a couple of years in order to earn sufficient money to finance a visit to America. There he found the memory of the Civil War still fresh, and the experience led him to say later, 'Born and bred in an atmosphere of Toryism, what I saw and heard knocked all the Toryism out of me.'

He then worked as a lay helper at St Mary's before becoming its curate in 1867. The parish had some fine houses, occupied by the rich, but it was working in its appalling slums, in company with Octavia Hill, that had a profound effect on the rest of Samuel's life – as did his meeting with Henrietta Rowland to whom he wrote in 1872 proposing marriage. She felt flattered but was not immediately attracted by the offer. Marriage to an impecunious parson required some consideration. But in June 1872 she accepted. 'I realized that his gift of love was too holy to refuse', she explained.

Shortly before they were married, Barnett was offered a country living near Oxford, but this was not the direction in which either he or Henrietta felt drawn. So Octavia Hill used her influence to get him offered instead St Jude's, Whitechapel, in the East End of London. In his letter the Bishop of London told him that there was no hurry for a reply, since it was 'the worst parish in my diocese, inhabited mainly by a criminal population, and one which has, I fear, been much corrupted by doles'.

The Barnetts were not deterred and stayed for 21 years, plus another 13 years when he was Warden of Toynbee Hall, the East End settlement he had founded. The Bishop's description of the parish was not exaggerated. The 6,270 parishioners were housed in only 675 dwellings, many of them lodging houses in which each room, furnished with a sack of hay, a table and a chair, was let to one or more families for eightpence a night.

Packed together in squalid courtyards and alleys, with unmade roads, some of the buildings were three storeys high, with pits in their cellars for sanitation purposes. In some alleys each inhabitant had only four square yards of space. Lower buildings were usually made of wood and soon became dilapidated. Broken windows everywhere were repaired with paper or rags. Standpipes provided water, but the people were dirty and bedraggled. Most buildings were infested with vermin. One-fifth of the inhabitants were without adequate food or clothing and, with fever and other afflictions never far away, the annual death rate was 40 per thousand.

The vicarage needed a good deal of renovation before it was fit for habitation; small and dark, it had an underground kitchen and no bathroom. St Jude's church had been built of cheap common brick in the Gothic revival style with a substantial tower – all now discoloured by grime and showing signs of decay. Inside, it was equally unattractive, its huge galleries blocking the windows and making it very dark. On his first Sunday Barnett had a congregation of six old women who had come in the expectation of receiving a dole when the worship ended.

This was the challenge facing the Barnetts. They were to have no children and she devoted her considerable intelligence and energy to sharing in the revival of the church and improving the lot of the poor in the East End and beyond. In many ways she was the more able of the two – bold, assertive and with considerable organizing ability. He was a sensitive man of quiet speech, somewhat diffident and careless of dress, not physically strong, and sometimes depressed. He used to say that he was but the mouthpiece of his wife and had the courage of her opinions. Or, sometimes, that all the important strategic decisions were made at his wife's tea table. These were exaggerations and an expression of his humility, for he was a great parish priest and a notable social reformer, but it is fair to say that he would have been unable to achieve so much and to maintain his work for so long in such grim social conditions without her sustaining presence. It was a remarkable partnership based on mutual love and a shared vision.

On their arrival in Whitechapel, Samuel declared that his aim was 'that everyone may know God as Father', and added, 'Nothing short of the best is good enough for his parish.' The interior of the church was transformed, with the assistance of G. F. Watts and William Morris – leading artists of the time – and was open every day. Samuel was well aware that three Prayer Book services on Sundays did not meet the needs of the people, but did not feel able to break the law in any significant way. So Henrietta, who never liked the traditional services, organized on Sunday evenings at 8.30 what she called a 'Worship Hour'. Normally conducted by the curate, this consisted of a mixture of hymns, readings, anthems, solos and prayers on a particular theme, but with no sermon. It attracted large congregations. 'Chuckers-in' went about the streets and alleys urging people to give it a try and assuring them that there were dark corners where they could sit if they felt ashamed of their clothes. Besides this, the attendance at the end of the first year at the traditional Sunday morning Eucharist had risen to 30, with 150 at Evensong.

Beyond the church their work was extraordinary. A parish library was started with 638 books – Scott, George Eliot, Dickens, Trollope and the like – with volunteer librarians on hand to offer advice. Within five years the number of books had risen to a thousand, and from this small beginning grew the Whitechapel Public Library – masterminded by the Barnetts – which was opened in 1892 and soon had over six thousand borrowers. The church schools, ill-designed and more or less derelict, were refurbished and re-opened, with flowers in the classrooms, coloured illustrations of Aesop's fables on the walls, and soap, towels and mirrors in the cloakrooms. Regular meetings of parents and managers were held, but an experiment in co-education had to be abandoned when the girls rebelled.

These and other innovations brought many conflicts with the education authorities and led them to form in 1884 the Education Reform League to 'enlist the co-operation of the working classes in the effort to infuse more life into the dry bones of State-aided Elementary Education'. Several of its aims were a very long way ahead of their time and included education to be compulsory and free to the age of 15 or 16, with continuation college, again compulsory to 18 or 19; free breakfasts, staggered summer holidays, school journeys, university education for primary school teachers and equal opportunities for all children to attain their highest capability.

Visiting the homes of parishioners was always a high priority, and they often went incognito in order to meet families on their own terms. At one point Henrietta proposed that they should move out of the vicarage and identify themselves more closely with the poor by living in a slum house, but Samuel disagreed as he needed more, not less, domestic space in which to develop his work. Hospitality was a central feature of their shared ministry and this led to another project which achieved spectacular success. It started when they displayed interesting and beautiful objects acquired during an extended visit to Egypt and explained these at their Sunday afternoon tea parties. Encouraged by the response, they borrowed more items from friends and museums and displayed them in the church schools. Such was the popularity of these exhibitions that they convened a committee which raised sufficient money to build a Whitechapel Art Gallery – now among the most important in London.

Arrangements were made for ailing children to go on a country holiday, and within seven years this initiative had become the national Children's Country Holiday Fund, which over the ensuing years benefited some hundreds of thousands of children. Henrietta also served on a national departmental committee to enquire into the condition of Poor Law children, and this led to the formation of a State-Children's Association, of which she became the secretary. Another concern was the plight of girls whose parents were for the most part beggars or criminals. These were recruited for service in West End homes where they received friendship and training. The needs of boys were different and they were found some means of employment locally or prepared to go to sea. Others lived in a house, which became a self-governing hotel and from which they went out every morning to work as shoe-blacks on the London streets. Soon after he became Prime Minister in 1908, H. H. Asquith described Henrietta as 'the custodian of the State's children'.

Housing was always a major concern for the Barnetts, and they worked closely with Octavia Hill in the formation of the East End Dwellings Company. This built houses for unskilled labourers, day workers at the docks and the many men and women who lived by casual employment – none of whom was eligible for assistance by the main housing charities. A House of Commons committee on housing spent a day in Whitechapel to inspect this project, and new legislation led to more speedy demolition of slums and the erection of replacement housing.

Toynbee Hall was founded in February 1884 to enable Oxford and Cambridge graduates and undergraduates to live for a time with a permanent community of curates and professional men who were engaged in social work in the East End. This grew rapidly to become a major centre of social and educational work which still flourishes. Samuel was its first warden.

It was hardly surprising that when in 1893 the Master of Balliol College stayed with the Barnetts he found Samuel looking very tired. This led to his appointment as a Canon Residentiary of Bristol Cathedral, it being understood that he and Henrietta would spend three months of the year in Bristol and return to London for nine months to continue his work as Warden of Toynbee Hall. This arrangement worked well for the next 13 years. Plenty of reform was needed at the cathedral and there were many slums in the city, so they were not idle, but Bristol provided much-needed refreshment and a degree of relaxation impossible to find in Whitechapel.

Samuel declined the offer of two cathedral deaneries but in 1906 accepted a canonry of Westminster, at the same time resigning the Wardenship of Toynbee Hall. By this time his health was declining, though between them there was still vision and energy enough for the making of many proposals for the much needed reform of the Abbey's life. None of these was accepted and there were more than raised eyebrows when Samuel included Henrietta's name on the front-door plate of their house in the Little Cloister. The introduction of a telephone was said by their neighbours to be 'intrusive.' The Abbey's daily round of formal worship did not meet Henrietta's spiritual needs, but she still had huge social work responsibilities, and Samuel's failing health, which extended over several years, demanded her attention until his death in 1913. She still had another 23 years to live and during this time wrote a massive two-volume biography of her husband, which was actually an account of their shared ministry. Besides much more innovative social work she continued what was said to be 'one of the most remarkable achievements of human urban planning'. This was the creation of Hampstead Garden Suburb in north London. On learning that the London Tube railway was to be extended to Hampstead, she envisaged land on the edge of the Heath being ruined by ugly urban development. A Hampstead Heath Extension Council was formed and money was raised to purchase 80 acres of land for a social experiment that would enable people of all classes to live in a beautiful environment. Sir Raymond Unwin, a mining engineer turned planner, was engaged to produce a scheme, and Sir Edwin Lutyens, a famous architect, to design the public buildings.

Henrietta prescribed cottages and houses at no more than eight to an acre suitable for people of all incomes and for the handicapped – no walls, only hedges or trellises, wide roads lined with trees, the public gardens and woods to be open to all, no intrusive noise such as church bells. A central open space was to have on its edges an Anglican church and a Free church, along with a community hall. The Anglican church, dedicated to St Jude, was given a fine tower and spire, paid for by Henrietta's friends as an eightieth birthday present. It was her hope that many of Whitechapel's poor would take the opportunity to start a new life in the new community, but few of them, apart from a small group of Jews, chose to move. Today its singular attractiveness has ironically made it one of the most expensive places in London in which to live.

As part of this development Henrietta wished to provide an opportunity for girls from poor families to have the same educational opportunities as the more privileged, hence the founding in 1911 of the Henrietta Barnett School. This is now considered to be the best state, voluntary aided grammar school in the country. Absence of fees attracts 1,000 applicants every year, and of these 93 are given places after passing two competitive examinations and an interview.

At the age of 72 Henrietta took up painting and was soon good enough to have her work exhibited in the Royal Academy. Besides her work in England she propagated the Settlement idea in the United States and became Honorary President of the 480-strong America Federation of Settlements. She was made a Dame in 1924 and, following her death in Hampstead in 1936, her name was added to Samuel's fine memorial in Westminster Abbey. They are commemorated together in the Church of England's Calendar of Holy Days on 17 June.

9

Mothers of the World Unite:
Mary Sumner

One of the most remarkable developments in the life of the Church of England and the worldwide Anglican Communion during the nineteenth and twentieth centuries was the growth and influence of the Mothers' Union. For the first nine years of its embryonic life it consisted of no more than a meeting of mothers under the tutelage of the wife of the Rector of the rural Hampshire parish of Old Alresford. It now has four million members distributed throughout the Anglican Communion.

The original objects of the organization were, and remain, the upholding of marriage, the enhancement of stable family life, and the spiritual development of mothers to enable them more effectively to play their key role in the home. Arising from this, members of the Mothers' Union soon became immersed in the life of their local churches and, apart from the nascent women's Religious Orders, were the first women to be entrusted with even a modicum of responsibility. Eventually they became in many parishes the mainstay of the Church – their devotion, zeal and commitment often far exceeding that of the men in their congregations.

Founded by Mary Sumner, a Victorian of deep evangelical faith, wide vision and enormous organizing skill, the Mothers' Union stood firmly behind the belief that marriage is God-given, lifelong and therefore incapable of termination by divorce. Membership was therefore never open to the divorced, whatever the circumstances of their lives. This position, exclusive rather than inclusive, was not significantly different from that of the Anglican Church as a whole and created no serious problems until the 1950s and 1960s. Then immense social changes in Britain and the rest of the Western world, involving the relationship between men and women, left the Mothers' Union stranded with an uncompromisingly conservative stance which seemed at first to be a vital bulwark against the disintegration of Christian family life, but soon became a severe handicap to its attempts to meet the needs of many women.

Thus the membership in the provinces of Canterbury and York fell from a peak of half a million in 1939 to about 100,000 at the present time. Changes in the Mothers' Union constitution made eventually in 1974 and again in 2007 have freed its members and branches to make a distinctive Christian witness in a world that would be unrecognizable to Mary Sumner.

Whether or not it will be able to do so for very much longer is now an open question. In a scholarly, perceptive and illuminating *History of the Mothers' Union: Women, Anglicanism and Globalization, 1876–2008*, Dr Cordelia Moyse concludes, sadly, that the prospects of revitalizing the largest mission organization in the Church are seriously hampered by the Church's continuing refusal to take the laity seriously. Added to this are what she calls 'the genteel misogyny' the clergy seem to lavish on the MU, and also the tendency of many clergy to project onto the organization, their frustrations with the mundane reality of parish life. She points out that 'while clergy relations with the MU in Africa are not always harmonious, in African dioceses there is a greater sense of partnership in the mission of the Church'.

It would have been unreasonable to expect that an organization which had for so long focused its witness on motherhood and the nurturing of the family as virtually the sole female vocation would be in the forefront of the feminist movement and the campaign for the ordination of women to the priesthood. In fact, for most of its history it was strongly opposed to both. But the recent reforms have changed this, and about 150 Mothers' Union members are now in the priesthood.

Mary Sumner was born in 1828 into a distinguished and prosperous Lancastrian family that could trace its roots back to the twelfth century. Her father, Thomas Haywood, was a Manchester banker who also had literary interests but, although she was born at Swinton Park in Lancashire, the family of three children soon moved to Hope End near Malvern. This was a substantial country house with spacious reception rooms, 22 bedrooms, peacocks on the lawn and 500 rolling acres.

Theirs was an idyllic childhood, educated at home in an evangelical atmosphere with daily prayers and Bible reading, and with ample time for pony riding and parties. There were annual travels abroad in the family coach, and stays in Tours, Dresden and Rome to perfect her language skills and complete her musical education. At one time she aspired to be an opera singer, but at a New Year's Eve ball in Rome in 1845 she met George Sumner, a son of the Bishop of Winchester, Charles Sumner, who had recently come down from Oxford and was now staying in Rome while on the Grand Tour. It was apparently love at first sight for both of them, and 18 months later they were married.

Thus Mary entered a notable ecclesiastical family. Charles Sumner, who was at Winchester from 1828 to 1868, was one of the nineteenth century's moderate reforming bishops. Appointed just before major reforms considerably reduced episcopal stipends, he enjoyed an annual income of about £1.4 million in today's money. He was an uncompromising evangelical, who owed all his appointments (he had previously been a Canon of Windsor, Dean of St Paul's and Bishop of Llandaff) to the favour of King George IV. His elder brother, John Bird Sumner, also an evangelical, was Bishop of Chester, then, from 1848, Archbishop of Canterbury. The Sumners intermarried with the Wilberforce family, which included William the Emancipator, and Samuel, the greatest of the Victorian reforming bishops, who succeeded Charles Sumner at Winchester, having previously been Dean of Westminster and Bishop of Oxford.

Young George was brought up at Farnham Castle in Surrey – one of his father's three episcopal residences, where visitors ranged from Queen Victoria to a multitude of poor people seeking the Bishop's alms. On his return from the Grand Tour he was ordained to a curacy at Crawley, near Winchester, combining this with that of chaplain to his father at Farnham. Meanwhile, in 1848 he and Mary had been married from her home at Hope End. This was a grand occasion at which 600 tenants, employees and their families were entertained at what became a long-remembered fête. Three years later George was appointed by his father Rector of Old Alresford, a few miles from Winchester, where he and Mary remained for the next 34 years.

A few years before their arrival it was recorded that the parish had a population of 578, of whom 202 were children and 59 over the age of 60. Of the 152 communicants, the women heavily outnumbered the men. There were a few large houses, the occupants of which strongly supported the church, and 107 spartan cottages housing what was still essentially a peasant workforce. The lot of the women, as described by Mary Sumner in 1850, was far harder than that of the men and now seems barely human:

Woman's toil in the fields was almost necessary to the maintenance of the family. She was consequently roughened and hardened . . . More commonly wives had to go through their work like dumb driven cattle. Up betimes to snatch a poor breakfast, then leave the eldest child to guard those too small for school while she was picking stones, weeding with stiff fingers on frosty mornings, cutting turnips . . . Haytime and harvest were like holiday times, hard as was the work. Generally one day was reserved for washing and cleaning, or when work was lacking going to the wood and coming home laden with sticks . . . The family food was almost entirely bread, with potatoes for those who had gardens or allotments, a scrap of bacon for Sunday, and tea of the thinnest always ready. The mother fared worst of all, for she fed her husband and children before she herself ate. She had no time for cooking recommended meals, little time for anything and if she kept her cottage and family clean and whole she was a heroine in exertion. It is no wonder that she aged prematurely, and that it was often difficult to guess whether she was thirty or fifty years old.

Life in the huge Rectory, Old Alresford Place, was different. Besides the large reception rooms, study and kitchen, there were 15 bedrooms, extensive servants' quarters and stables. The 40 oil lamps took a maid a whole morning to trim. At £580 a year the living was very comfortable rather than affluent, though doubtless it was augmented by family subventions. In fact George and Mary, with their three children, lived fairly simply, faithful to the evangelical tradition, with daily family prayers and Bible readings, learning the Prayer Book collects and the Catechism. Mary had a daily cold bath, would not use the telephone or, when they came in, a motor car. Mary was nonetheless a lively, amusing personality who enjoyed parties. Unlike many of his predecessors, George was a diligent parish priest – assiduous in visiting the homes of the people, organizing meetings for married men, young men, a Girls' Friendly Society and, later, a library and reading room. He preached twice on Sunday, gave lectures in Lent and taught in the school.

Although the Rectory became the centre of parish life, Mary devoted her early years at Old Alresford primarily to the upbringing of her children, believing this to be essential to their moral and spiritual development. After the birth of their first child, when they were still at Crawley, Mary, only 20, combined her joy with a marked seriousness:

I shall never forget the awed sense of responsibility as I took her in my arms. It struck me how much I needed special training for so great a work and how little I knew. I felt that mothers had one of the greatest and most important professions in the world and yet there was none had so poor a training for its supreme duties.

Here was the beginning of the idea that led to the creation of the Mothers' Union.

A large domestic staff able to meet some of her children's needs as well as her own eventually left her free to undertake quite a lot of parish work. A niece said that she doubted whether her aunt had ever put on her own stockings. She was organist and choir mistress, visited the cottages and lent a hand with the Sunday School, but she became increasingly aware of how ill-equipped the mothers, both in the big houses and the cottages, were for nurturing their children's moral and spiritual upbringing. Something more than the existing Mothers' Meeting was needed, since this was attended only by cottage mothers.

The ladies from the big houses and some from the cottages were therefore summoned to a meeting at the Rectory one summer afternoon in 1876. Although normally a confident speaker, Mary lost her nerve on this occasion, and George had to be brought from his study to present her ideas and explain a simple card. This was headed 'Remember that your children are given up, body and soul, to Jesus Christ in Holy Baptism, and that your duty is to train them for his service.' The practical points that followed included

[n]ever allow coarse jests, bad angry words, or low talk in your house. Speak gently. Do not allow your girls to go about the streets at night and keep them from unsafe companions and from any dangerous amusements. Kneel down and pray morning and evening, and teach your children to pray.

Appended was a prayer to be said daily. At the end of the meeting those attending were invited to take a card and sign it as a sign of their commitment and also have their names entered on a register. 'Enrolling Member' remains the title of branch leaders to the present day.

The cards were taken and signed enthusiastically, and for the next nine years the Old Alresford group met monthly at the Rectory where Mary, and sometimes George, spoke to them about the Christian faith and its implications for family life. Not forgetting the responsibility of fathers for the lives of their families, a similar group for men was held on Sunday evenings and these were also addressed by Mary who urged them to share in the upbringing of their children and to give their wives birthday presents as a sign of their love for them. The men were apparently greatly influenced by her.

Apart from a similar meeting for women at Lichfield, started by a friend of Mary, this remained a local enterprise until 1885. Then, as part of a Church Congress held in Portsmouth (at that time in Winchester diocese) a meeting was arranged for working-class mothers. In a packed hall, Bishop Harold Browne, who had succeeded George's father in the bishopric, took the chair and called on Ernest Wilberforce, a Canon of Winchester who was about to become the first Bishop of Newcastle upon Tyne, to address the gathering. At the sight of his audience, he recognized that his prepared address was quite unsuitable for the occasion. So, in a moment of panic, or possibly inspiration, he called on Mary Sumner to take his place.

Totally unprepared and unaccustomed to addressing large meetings, she naturally protested, but eventually gave in and delivered an impassioned speech. This began by declaring there to be 'a very terrible want of morality and high tone in the homes and among the people of this country' and went on to ask, rhetorically, 'What can be done to raise the national character?' She had no doubt as to the correct answer:

It is the mothers who can in great measure work the reformation of the country. Those who rock the cradle rock the world, because the mother has charge of the child for the first months and years of its life; and those years are all important to the future of each child, and may I tell you one reason why the tone of character in England is not as high as it should be? It is the neglect of the mothers. Forgive me for speaking plainly, but I feel that if only they knew their power, they would use it – and if they knew their duty they would arise and do it . . . My sisters, God will ask us as mothers, at the last great day 'What have you done with that child – those children I gave you to train for Me?'

The sight and sound of a woman addressing a large church meeting was a unique experience for all present and the power of Mary's impromptu speech made a great impression.

Within a matter of days, Bishop Browne had decided to convene the Mothers' Union, for which Mary had asked at the meeting, as a diocesan organization. Responding immediately, she went about the diocese in her coach to help with the formation of branches. In 1887 she spoke at 69 meetings, usually accompanied by George, who had recently become Archdeacon of Winchester and a Canon Residentiary of the cathedral, with the privilege of occupying the best house in the Close. A year later the Mothers' Union was established in 18 dioceses and the first quarterly journal was published, achieving a circulation of 13,000 by 1890. Growth now became phenomenal. In 1900 there were 170,000 members and by 1909 this had increased to over 316,000 in 6,000 branches, some of these in Dublin, New Zealand, Hong Kong, India and Madagascar.

Fortunately, Mary was not only a woman of vision but also a highly competent organizer. She realized that some sort of structure was needed if the movement was to retain a degree of coherence. The parish branches were by 1892 linked to others in their local deaneries and these in turn with diocesan councils, of which the bishop's wife was invariably President, as indeed the parish priest's wife was Enrolling Member of the branches.

In 1892, Mary summoned delegates from 21 dioceses to a meeting in Church House, Westminster, with a view to setting up a national organization. Initially, however, this invitation was frustrated by the Archbishop of Canterbury and the Bishop of London whose objections remain unknown, though they may have been related to the fact that the wives of both were involved in an embryonic Women's League. Nonetheless, an annual conference found favour.

Four years later another special meeting was called, this time of the Diocesan Presidents, who attended with the support of their episcopal husbands, and this time no objections were raised. Mary became the first National President of a Central Council, and the constitution stated the objectives of the Mothers' Union:

1 To uphold the sanctity of marriage.
2 To nurture in mothers of all classes a sense of their great responsibility as mothers in the training of their boys and girls (the future fathers and mothers of England).

3 To organize in every place a band of mothers who will unite in prayer, and seek by their own example to lead their families in purity and holiness of life.

This third objective was encapsulated in a slogan which Mary had accepted at the time of her own marriage – 'Be yourself what you wish your children to be.' A modest annual subscription was now required, and a badge consisting of an intertwined 'MU' became a common sight in both rural and urban districts. Queen Victoria, to whom Mary was devoted, was enlisted as Royal Patron in 1897, and thereafter queens entered into a continuous succession.

Several factors contributed to the Mothers' Union's extraordinary growth. In the early stages Mary was able to exploit her connections with the wives of influential bishops in order to extend the movement beyond Winchester diocese. It was also the case that many parishes already had what were called Mothers' Meetings – valuable in themselves as a focus for the clergy's pastoral work among women, but lacking in the dynamic high purposes that were introduced at Old Alresford. These meetings were easily converted into MU branches. No less significant was a social change during the latter years of the nineteenth century in which there emerged, in the context of a broad desire to improve the nation's quality of life, a multitude of voluntary organizations under dedicated and skilled leadership. That said, the development of the Mothers' Union took place during an era when women still lacked many basic human rights, had few opportunities and hardly any place in the life of the Church, apart from attendance at services.

Few of these, however, were concerned with the radical social and economic changes that some saw as necessary to real improvement, and Mary Sumner was certainly not among them. Moreover she discerned early in her movement's life that her original intention of uniting peeress and peasant in local meetings would not work. The barrier of class was far too high to be easily broken down. The occupants of the big houses and the cottages did not mix.

Again, the challenges to the two categories presented by Mary did not always coincide. The original membership card with its injunction not to permit daughters to frequent public houses or roam the streets had to be supplemented with another that urged mothers not to delegate all their responsibilities to a nurse. The quarterly journal with its homely advice about investing in strong shoes and warm woollen clothes was hardly needed in the affluent surrounds of a house approached by a long, tree-lined drive.

A separate category of 'subscribing member' was soon formed. Its members were not expected to attend branch meetings, but rather to drawing-room gatherings at which papers were read and discussed. At a Church Congress in Hull in 1890 Mary reported that, of the 9,000 members in Winchester diocese, no fewer than 1,300 were 'high rank women'. Clergy wives and other ladies involved in the leadership at every level were categorized as 'associates' and the distinctions remained until 1912. Meanwhile a special publication, *Mothers in Council*, for educated leaders had appeared in 1891 under the editorship of the best-selling novelist Charlotte Yonge, who lived most conveniently at Otterbourne, just a stone's throw from Winchester. Although herself unmarried and now aged 67, she had no difficulty in becoming deeply involved in the work of the Mothers' Union, and, besides her editorship of *Members in Council*, which extended over several years, her name added lustre to what was becoming a popular movement.

In 1909, Mary handed over the Central Presidency to the Dowager Countess of Chichester, but retained that of the Winchester diocesan branch for another seven years, thus completing 30 years in office since its foundation. By this time she was 87, and, until her death five years later, continued to comment on developments in the movement's life. On her ninetieth birthday she received a letter and a signed photograph from Queen Mary, and, although she had requested the simplest of funerals, when the time for this came in 1921, several diocesan bishops were in the packed Winchester Cathedral. She is now commemorated in the Church of England's Calendar of Holy Days on 9 August – the date of her death.

The Mothers' Union began, and has remained, firmly rooted in the life of the Anglican Church. The fact that its founder's husband was a son of the Bishop of Winchester and a nephew of the Archbishop of Canterbury and himself destined to become an Archdeacon, then a Bishop, was sufficient to ensure that it would not remain on the fringe. So did the early support of several senior diocesan bishops. The extraordinary growth of a movement that became an institution was characterized by its appeal to women and the support of the clergy of all the Church's traditions. Launched at a time of often bitter strife between 'High' and 'Low' elements of Anglicanism, it managed to sail through the seas of controversy and provide a bond of unity among Christian women. This often under-estimated contribution to the Church's life has been sustained to the present day.

From the earliest days at Old Alresford members have been admitted at a special service based on that provided in the Book of Common Prayer for The Baptism of those of Riper Years. Initially these services were held wherever the Mothers' Union meeting was held – in the Rectory, or the church hall, or sometimes in the homes of members. After some years, however, they began to be held in church, though this was opposed by some bishops who feared that it might encourage members to believe that they could have an active part in the Church's worship. Before long, members from the branches in a rural deanery were permitted to gather in one or other of their churches for a combined service, or even in a cathedral for a diocesan event.

These were, and still are, usually held on or near the Feast of the Annunciation to the Blessed Virgin Mary, otherwise known as Lady Day. As early as 1897 Mary Sumner declared this to be an annual day of prayer, intercession and thanksgiving, and its observance thereafter not only provided another focus of unity but also a model of Christian motherhood. At the same time it led, uncontroversially, to the recovery of devotion to the Mother of Jesus in the Church of England during a period when a still dominant Protestantism regarded such a devotion as a clear symptom of popish leanings. Representations of the Madonna and Child now appeared on the branch banners, embroidered by members or bought from professionals, and were carried in procession on great occasions, and between times were, irrespective of their quality, allowed to adorn parish churches and cathedrals.

The Marian devotion was rendered uncontroversial largely by the fact that it focused on Mary the human mother rather than the bearer of the Divine Son of God, to whom other miracles could be attributed and to whom prayer might be addressed. In the not so long run, however, the image of the humble, servile Mary proved to be an inhibiting factor in the quest for women to be accorded their right place in the Church's life at every level. It promoted a deeply conservative attitude in which members not only willingly accepted a subservient role but actually opposed proposals that women should move into leadership positions. This took a long time to change, but perhaps not much longer than it did among most of the Church's female members.

Meanwhile there was a movement from a merely passive role in which members met mostly to receive instruction in religious or domestic matters to one of active participation in certain aspects of parish life. Catering for church events became a primary responsibility, along with cleaning the building, visiting sick members, delivering the parish magazine and the products of the Harvest Festival to the aged and sick, or sharing in some way in the parish mission. Most of this was humdrum, but they were tasks that needed to be done, that men were never going to do, and that created a strong sense of community. Before long, members of the Mothers' Union had become the backbone of very many congregations. Their support of the Church was constant, they brought in new members, led a disciplined life of prayer, and were often present at mid-week as well as Sunday celebrations of Holy Communion. Without the Mothers' Union the life of the Church of England in the twentieth century would have been different – and weaker.

And not only in England. Just three years after the inauguration of the Mothers' Union in Winchester diocese there was a branch in New Zealand and another in Canada. In 1904 Mary Sumner reported to the Central Council that the movement had a foothold in nearly every British colony. As early as 1896 she had recognized the potential for growth in an Empire created not only by acquisitive greed but also by a civilizing mission that aimed to bring light and Christian values to places where, in the words of a favourite missionary hymn, 'the heathen in his blindness bows down to wood and stone'.

Thousands of dedicated men and their wives gave themselves to this great task, and the Mothers' Union provided the wives with a valued link with home as well as mutual support in a strange and sometimes hostile environment. The same was true for the wives of soldiers serving overseas. During her early propagating tours of Winchester diocese Mary quickly became aware of the potential in garrison towns such as Aldershot and Winchester itself. An Army Division was immediately formed and within three years had over a thousand members who, naturally, maintained their enthusiasm when accompanying their husbands overseas. Chaplains welcomed this opportunity to extend their ministries.

Missionaries also recognized the usefulness of the Mothers' Union, not so much for evangelical purposes but for the introduction of Christian values into the family life of the indigenous people. During the first decade of the twentieth century the Society for the Propagation of the

Gospel formed many non-European Mothers' Union branches in India. Through various agencies and in some variety of forms the movement spread throughout the Anglican Communion. In 1921 a Wave of Prayer was introduced to encourage members in Britain to pray daily for branches and dioceses in specified places overseas. This has continued to the present time and over the years has helped parishes to a better awareness of their place in a world Church. The first worldwide conference held in 1930 brought together 38 diocesan presidents from overseas.

In 1940 there were about 80,000 overseas members and, after an inevitable wartime slowdown, growth continued steadily until the 1980s when a massive expansion of the Anglican Church in what came to be known as the Global South (mainly Africa) brought with it a no less massive increase in Mothers' Union membership.

Such dramatic developments could hardly have been experienced without the arising of some problems. The change from Empire to a Commonwealth of independent nations required a high degree of authority to be granted to national Mothers' Unions. This was already taking place and had to be accelerated. More fundamental was the problem of applying Christian values of the Victorian family to the very different, sometime polygamous, cultures of the developing world. Again, some flexibility in the interpretation of the rules overseas had always been allowed, and this continued, but not sufficiently quickly to satisfy the demands of the national Councils in highly Westernized Canada and Australia where the inflexible rule about marriage and divorce conflicted sharply with radical changes in the patterns of family life.

By the 1960s the pressure of this was being experienced equally in the United Kingdom. On the outbreak of war in 1939 membership in the United Kingdom had reached what turned out to be a peak of half a million. With many men away on active service, members found even more to do in their parishes, and strong support of family life became more challenging. A mini-revival of church life in the 1950s helped to sustain the size of membership, but anxiety about its age-profile led to the formation of Young Wives' Groups from which it was hoped a younger generation of women would graduate to the senior body. In 1952 there were 3,000 of these groups, each with 20–30 members.

At the same time a younger generation of clergy engaged in pioneering ministry in new towns and housing estates was displaying a marked reluctance to include the Mothers' Union in its tools of mission. The 'Swinging Sixties' confirmed their decisions as a major social change came suddenly, created by new forms of contraception, co-habitation, marriage breakdown, easier divorce, youth rebellion and a new emphasis on the priority of relationship over rules. Although members of the Mothers' Union could not escape the consequences of this, their organization, like the Church itself, could only stand by its long-held, uncompromising commitment to lifelong marriage. And when the Church began to respond to the new situation with changed attitudes and pastoral policies, the Mothers' Union was too deeply entrenched in its traditional position to be able to move.

The failure of the Central Council to lead in new directions led to much disagreement and unhappiness in the branches and some loss of support from parish clergy who found the existence of a branch a hindrance to their pastoral work among the divorced and unmarried. Membership went into rapid decline, and many branches were closed. Overwhelming pressure from below and from overseas led to the setting up in 1969 of a commission chaired by the then Bishop of Willesden, the deeply conservative Graham Leonard, who would 20 years later lead the opposition to the ordination of women to the priesthood before leaving to become a Roman Catholic.

The commission collected a massive amount of evidence from members and deliberated for just over three years before delivering a divided report under the misleading title *New Dimensions*. In the end the Central Council, taking full account of overseas as well as national membership opinion, produced in 1974 a new Constitution which radically altered its approach to marriage and family life in Britain and granted to the many and varied overseas units absolute authority and therefore complete freedom to order their affairs to meet local needs.

Five new objects for members in the United Kingdom continued to stress the sanctity of marriage, the importance of nurturing children in the faith and life of the Church, but also 'To help those whose family life has met with adversity', thus opening its doors to the divorced. The increased momentum of social change during the remaining years of the twentieth century led to further constitutional changes in 2007 when the appeal to Christ's teaching on the nature of marriage was replaced by 'To promote and support married life', and the nurturing of children in the faith and life of the Church gave way to 'To encourage parents in their role to develop the faith of their children'.

Mary Sumner would have been shocked by this and also saddened by the decline in membership in England, but she would not have allowed anyone to believe, unchallenged, that the upholding of family life is now an outdated objective – or that 100,000 women could not still do something about it.

10

Church Songs and Stories: C. F. (Fanny) Alexander, Frances R. Havergal, Catherine Winkworth and Charlotte M. Yonge

No woman has had a greater influence on the hymnody of the Anglican Church, and most other churches for that matter, than Fanny Alexander. It is impossible to imagine the celebration of Christmas, whether in the chapel of King's College, Cambridge, or in a rural parish church, without the singing of 'Once in Royal David's City'. Equally, Holy Week and Easter would seem incomplete without 'There is a green hill' and, although 'All things bright and beautiful' does not receive quite the same attention, it remains one of the few hymns widely known and loved in Britain's increasingly secular society.

Eric Routley, the foremost twentieth-century authority on hymnody, described the author of them as 'the greatest of women hymn-writers in English'. Others have described her as 'the queen of children's hymn-writers', and these three hymns first appeared in 1848 in her collection *Hymns for Little Children*, which had a preface by John Keble and was designed to explain the Church Catechism, including the Apostles' Creed, the Ten Commandments and the Lord's Prayer. The book was an immediate success and the profits from 100 impressions went to support a school for deaf and dumb children.

Not all of the 250 or so hymns she wrote were, however, intended for use by children, and it is a mark of her genius that the best known three have won the affection of people of every age and widely differing circumstances. Of the hymns she wrote for adults a few remain in use. 'He is risen! He is risen!' for Easter and 'Jesus calls us; o'er the tumult' for St Andrew's Day are probably the best known. But none of these can rival in quality or popularity her magnificent versification of *St Patrick's Breastplate*, 'I bind unto myself today the strong name of the Trinity'.

Cecil Frances Alexander was born in Dublin in 1818; her English father had been a major in the Royal Marines who served in the Napoleonic War and under Nelson at the Battle of Copenhagen in 1801. His career was, however, cut short by wounds received in the West Indies, and, after serving as a staff officer in Dublin for a few years, he resigned. Already a landowner himself, he became agent for the Earl of Wicklow's large estate, and until Fanny was 15 the family lived at Ballykeane House in a beautiful part of County Wicklow. These were happy years during which a visit to Scotland provided an opportunity to meet Sir Walter Scott, and her poetic gifts began to develop. She also came under the influence of the Oxford Movement, and, while visiting an uncle, Sir Thomas Reed, in Winchester, she met John Keble, Dr Pusey, Archdeacon Manning and other prominent members of the Movement.

In 1833, the family moved to Milltown House, Strabane, in Co. Tyrone, Major Humphreys having been appointed agent to the Marquis of Abercorn. The house, of Elizabethan style, oak panelled and adorned by valuable tapestries, enjoyed an idyllic setting, and it was during her next 17 years there that Fanny wrote her most famous hymns and published *Hymns for Little Children*. Her next collection, *Moral Songs* (1849) dealt with behaviour and included a hymn which remained in use until about 1939:

> Within the churchyard, side by side
>   Are many long, low graves;
> And some have stones set over them;
>   On some the green grass waves.
>
> Full many a little Christian child,
>   Woman, and man lies there;
> And we pass near them every time
>   When we go in to prayer.
>
> They do not hear when the great bell
>   Is ringing overhead;
> They cannot rise and come to church
>   With us, for they are dead.

She also came under the influence of the Rector of the parish – the

Revd James Smith, an able evangelical priest of Calvinist leanings, whose preaching and ministry made a considerable impact on her. At the same time she admired and learned a good deal from Walter Farquhar Hook, the legendary Vicar of Leeds, and, like him, she embraced for the rest of her life a powerful combination of evangelical and Tractarian insights.

This was reinforced in 1850, when she met and married the Revd William Alexander, six years younger than herself, who had recently been appointed Rector of Termonamongan in Co. Tyrone. He was an outstandingly gifted priest and destined to become Archbishop of Armagh. They had much in common, including an ability to write publishable poetry. His description of Fanny at the time of their marriage may not have been entirely objective but accords in many ways with other assessments of her personality and character:

It is not an exaggeration of affection which says she was a singularly attractive person. Her frame was lithe and active. Her face had no pretension to regular beauty; but it possessed the sensitive susceptibility, the magic quickness of transition, the sacred indignation, the flash of humour, the pathetic sweetness with which genius endows its chosen children.

Termonamongan had a population of only 1,500 but it was, as its new Rector described it, 'a wild one, with the people scattered over bogs and mountains for many miles'. Fanny shared fully in his pastoral ministry, walking many miles, often over rough terrain and in appalling weather, to visit the sick and the poor. A Roman Catholic woman suffering from cancer was visited every day for six weeks in order to have a sore dressed. An elderly, paralysed woman, who had insufficient bedding to keep her warm, was wrapped in Fanny's shawl.

The same quality of ministry was continued, though in different ways, when they moved in 1855 to the parish of Upper Fahan in the beautiful surroundings of Lough Swilly, and again five years later when William was appointed Rector of Strabane on the banks of the River Mourne. It was the most lucrative living in the diocese of Derry.

In 1867 he became Bishop of Derry, and the next 28 years were spent in the Palace in Londonderry, where she became a much loved bishop's wife. In spite of all her pastoral work in the parishes and the birth and upbringing of four children, Fanny had continued to write hymns and, when the pressure was not too great, a lot of poetry – much of this for children. This was considered good at the time, but, unlike her hymns, none has retained its power. And when she took on what were then seen as the essential duties of a bishop's wife, the opportunities for writing more or less disappeared.

Her hymns and poems were always deeply influenced by her environment, particularly the beauty of her surroundings, and it was perhaps her own privileged social status, as well as an acceptance of the established order in Victorian Ireland, that led her to pen the verse in 'All things bright and beautiful':

> The rich man in his castle,
> The poor man at his gate;
> God made them, high or lowly,
> And ordered their estate.

London schools were forbidden to sing these lines in the 1960s, and they have been left out of modern hymn books.

She was however provoked by the passing of Gladstone's Bill, which disestablished the Church of Ireland in 1869, to write an uncharacteristically angry hymn which began:

> Look down, O Lord of heaven, on our desolation!
> Fallen, fallen, fallen is now our country's crown,
> Dimly dawns the New Year on a churchless nation,
> Ammon and Amalek tread our borders down.

She died in 1895, and crowds lined the streets of Londonderry at the time of her funeral. Four months later her husband became Archbishop of Armagh and Primate of All Ireland.

*   *   *

Frances Ridley Havergal, a hymn-writer and the author of more than twenty books as well as innumerable booklets and leaflets, epitomized the mid-Victorian lady of comfortable means and fervent evangelical piety. Her influence was considerable in certain circles, partly through the use of her hymns at a time when hymn-singing was transforming the

Church of England's worship, and partly through the popularity of her writings which sold in huge numbers. She firmly believed that the Christian faith provides an answer to all life's problems.

Her work belonged so firmly to the era in which she lived that, apart from a few hymns, it is quite unusable today, though surprisingly two of her books have in the present century been reprinted in America. A few of her poems, one of which is included in the *Oxford Book of Mystical Verse*, retain their power and 'The Thoughts of God', written while on holiday in the Swiss Alps, speaks of the inadequacy of words for expressing deepest experience.

> And now
> We only bow,
> And gaze above
> In raptured awe and silent love;
> For mortal speech
> Can never reach
> A word of meetly-moulded praise,
> For one glimpse of the blessed rays,
> Ineffable and purely bright
> Outflowing ever from the Unapproachable Light.

'Mountains, real ones, are more to me than any other created thing' she once said, and this poem is obviously designed to suggest the contours of a mountain.

Besides her writing, Frances (or Fanny, as she was known in her earlier years), was deeply immersed in a variety of activities designed to save the souls of the lost. Although she undertook a certain amount of visiting of her clergyman-father's parishioners, she was not drawn to social work, since it was, she believed, their souls rather than their bodies that mattered. In one of his parishes, however, she was instrumental in forming a Flannel Petticoat Society for the clothing of poor children. She collected subscriptions from her friends, and on 5 November every year some 25–30 children attended the Rectory to exchange their rags for a new set of clothes, then stayed on for a slice of cake and hymn-singing.

At various times Frances played an important part in evangelistic campaigns in parishes in other parts of the country. These lasted for a week and involved daily addresses in church, many house meetings, activities for children – all sustained by intensive visiting of homes and general drumming up of support. The outcome was invariably an increase in regular church attendance and often a crop of conversion experiences. Frances was among the speakers, her addresses consisting of hymn-singing interspersed with telling expositions of the meaning of the words. This she called her 'Ministry of Song', and was exercised in many difficult places and surroundings.

Another of her causes was the Irish Society which she first encountered when still quite young. This was during a visit to her sister who had married a rich widower whose business interests required him to live in Ireland, which he did in some style. The Society existed to promote the scriptural education of the Irish-speaking population through the use of their own language. While in itself valuable, this also provided a bulwark against the spread of Roman Catholicism. Throughout the rest of her life she made regular visits to the various centres of the work and raised a great deal of money to finance them.

Frances was born in Astley Rectory, in Worcestershire, in 1836. Her father had been curate of the parish, and when the Rector, who was also the Patron, became ill, he appointed him as his successor. Frances was born late into the family and became its favourite. Although the Havergals were by no means rich, they were comfortably off with an inherited private income. There were 40 acres of glebe, and maids and a governess in the Rectory. There was still money enough to spare to enable the Rector to provide a clock for the church tower and later to finance the building of a north aisle and the installation of a new chancel window.

It was nonetheless an austere household, influenced by a Calvinist evangelicalism, with daily family prayers and much attention to the Bible, in preference to novels or any other reading that might be considered frivolous or a source of temptation. Fanny's early education was handled by her mother and older sister who taught her reading, spelling and a hymn in the morning, and patchwork sewing and a hymn in the afternoon. She also had to memorize a biblical text and repeat this at breakfast the following day. When aged six, she was taken to see a small child lying in a coffin in order to remind her that education was as much for death as it was for life. Later, she was required to learn the Catechism, the Collect, Epistle and Gospel for the week and answer questions about her father's sermon of the previous Sunday.

Yet it was a happy family life whose tranquility was disturbed only when the father was required to vacate the parish in order to make way for the Patron's recently ordained son. They moved to Henwood House, a few miles away, where they stayed for four years, sustained by the private income, the fees of pupils and payments for sermons in other churches. During this time Fanny was very lonely, her siblings having gone away either to marriage or the furtherance of their education. So she began to write poetry, encouraged by her father who was a poet and a better than average composer. When only seven she wrote:

> Sunday is a pleasant day,
> When we to church do go:
> For here we sing and here we pray,
> And hear the sermon too.
>
> On Sunday hear the village bells
> It seems as if they said,
> Go to the church while the pastor tells
> How Christ for man has bled.
>
> And if we love to pray and read
> While we are in our early youth,
> The Lord will help us in our need
> Besides in times of truth.

In 1845, her father was appointed Rector of the city centre church of St Nicholas, Worcester and an Honorary Canon of the cathedral. The Rectory was a much less attractive house than Fanny had been accustomed to, and the death of her mother, after a long illness, in 1848, made a deep impression on her. Two years later she went to a fashionable girls' boarding school in Campden Hill, West London, where she started a broad education which included languages, poetry and dancing as well as fundamentalist Bible teaching, but this closed at the end of her first term.

She then moved to Powick Court, a small private school near Worcester. Once again, however, her education was interrupted, this time by a severe attack of erysipelas. Although she had made good progress in her school work, it wasn't feasible for her to return, and when in the autumn of 1852 her father went to Germany to consult an eye specialist, she went with him and attended a school in Düsseldorf. She quickly became fluent in German, was declared to be a brilliant pupil and after a year was placed first in the school exams.

When her father returned to Worcester at the end of 1853 she remained in Germany and went to live with a Lutheran pastor and his wife at Oberkassel, some 40 miles from Düsseldorf. Now aged 18, she thrived in a somewhat punishing regime which began at 7 a.m., then four more hours of study until the midday meal.

The afternoon was free until about 4 p.m., when she joined the pastor's wife and small daughter for knitting and housework. Then followed an evening session with the pastor, when they took it in turn to read passages from the writings of Goethe and other classics of German literature, interrupted by the pastor's learned and sometimes amusing comments. At the end of 12 months, he reported to her father 'such application, such rare talent, such depth of comprehension, that I can only speak of her progress as extraordinary'.

On her return to Worcester, where she had been confirmed in the cathedral before going to Germany, she threw herself into parish life, spent some time as governess of her sister's four children, took singing lessons and began to write hymns. In 1860, three of these were published in the magazine *Good Words*, and the fee enabled her to buy a silk cassock for her father. Regular publication of her hymns followed, and she began what became an active involvement in the work of the infant Young Women's Christian Association which continued until her death.

A turning point in her life came in 1870, when she started what became an important friendship with the Revd C. P. Snepp, Vicar of Perry Barr, north of Birmingham. He was compiling a hymn book, *Songs of Grace and Glory*, to express his own deeply held Calvinistic beliefs, and invited her to assist him. He was also anxious to include in the book some of the hymns written by her father, who had died in 1870. This proved to be less than straightforward, since her stepmother (he had remarried shortly after becoming widowed) was unwilling to release them for publication. Eventually she relented, but Frances's relationship with her was always difficult.

In many ways Snepp replaced her father in her affections. He was in his late forties when she was 33 and always adopted a protective attitude towards her, while she remained slightly deferential towards him. He addressed her as 'My dear and valued sister' and hoped that she would confide completely in him. But although their relationship became increasingly close, there was nothing about it that disturbed Snepp's wife, with whom she was also on good terms. Besides helping to choose hymns for the new book, she contributed several of her own that were compatible with its aims. When *Hymns Ancient & Modern* appeared, she denounced it as 'the thin end of the wedge of Popery', but when taken to task by Snepp for even examining the book, she explained that she had only glanced at some of the lines in the appendix to its second edition.

Another important influence on Frances's life and work was her discovery of the Alps. She made five visits to the French and Swiss sides in company with a woman friend, and at a time when climbing was a new sport they ascended, with the aid of a guide, Le Grands Mulets in the Mont Blanc range. This involved crossing the dangerous Glacier des Bossons.

Many of her hymns first appeared in leaflet form, and 'Take my life and let it be' was widely circulated as a card, especially at evangelistic campaigns, when converts were invited to sign it as an expression of their commitment. It was translated into French, German, Swedish, Russian and other European languages. Her children's book *Brey* was also translated into several languages, and another, *Little Pillows*, was designed for 12-year-olds and above, providing, as she put it, 'a short, easily recollected text to go to sleep upon for each night of the month, with a page or two of simple practical thoughts about it, such as a little girl might read every night while having her hair brushed'. This was compiled in a fortnight and was sold in millions, as also was *Kept for the Master's Use*.

In 1873 Frances became involved in the Mildmay Institution, which had been founded by the Vicar of St Jude's, Mildmay Park in 1866 and was modelled on German Lutheran deaconess institutions. This undertook a good deal of social work and trained deaconesses, though these did not become members of the Church of England's new deaconess order. Without herself becoming involved in the social work, she joined the Association of Female Workers, an inner group that adopted a common discipline of prayer and mutual support.

Her final years were spent in Cheltenham, and on the eve of another visit to the Irish Society she contracted a severe illness from which she died in Swansea, the port, on 3 June 1879. Soon after her death her sister collected material for *Memorials of Frances Ridley Havergal*, which sold

42,000 copies in two editions. A memorial fund, to be used by the Church Missionary Society for the training of Bible Women in Africa, attracted 12,000 contributions.

* * *

It is to Catherine Winkworth more than to anyone else that the English-speaking world owes the opportunity to sing the great German hymns, including 'Now thank we all our God', 'Praise to the Lord, the Almighty, the king of creation' and 'Christ the Lord is risen again'. She was also an active campaigner for women's rights in the mid-Victorian era.

Born in London in 1827, she was the daughter of a silk merchant who moved with his family to Manchester when she was still young. She remained there for most of the rest of her life and came under Unitarian influence which encouraged her to devote a good deal of time to work among the poor of the slums. Through her father, Catherine met Karl Josias Bunsen, the Prussian ambassador to London. He gave her a copy of a German devotional book that included hymns, and when she displayed interest in these, encouraged her to go to Dresden to learn German.

Martin Luther, the greatest theologian of the Reformation, was also a poet and a musician, and, during a time when hymnody was comparatively undeveloped, recognized that hymns could express Christian identity and also help to spread a message. So he wrote some himself, composed tunes for the work of others, and initiated a remarkable era of German hymnody, to which the music of J. S. Bach made an important contribution.

Catherine began to collect German hymns which with considerable poetic skill she translated into English. Under the general title *Lyra Germanica*, 103 of these were published in 1855 as *Hymns for the Sundays and Chief Festivals of the Christian Year*, and another 121 in 1858 as *The Christian Life*. The first volume ran to 23 editions and the second to 12, and before long German hymnody was influencing, and largely improving, the quality of worship in all the English Churches, most especially those of the reformed tradition. Her books of hymns were followed by *The Chorale Book for England* (1863) and *The Christian Singers of Germany* – a study of hymn-writing from the ninth century.

Besides this she was secretary of the Clifton Association of Higher Education for Women, and played an important part in the foundation of Bristol University. Her involvement in the developing women's rights movement also led her to translate the biographies of two of the founders of the German Sisterhood, whose work among the sick and the poor led to the deaconess order. Her own sister was no less active for women's rights.

Catherine died in 1878, and she is commemorated on 1 July, the day of her death, in the liturgical calendar of the Episcopal Church of the USA and by the Evangelical Lutheran Church of America.

*   *   *

Charlotte Mary Yonge, often described as the 'novelist of the Oxford Movement', wrote over 250 books, many of which were republished several times. She was the best-selling author of the Victorian era. Most of her work was fiction, but there were some history textbooks and a two-volume biography of Bishop John Coleridge Patteson, the first Bishop of Melanesia, whose martyrdom created a deep impression in England.

Her talent was prodigious. She wrote, she said, for young women, but she had millions of other readers worldwide and her work was admired by Dickens, Tennyson, Rossetti and Kingsley. Yet she lacked the spark of genius of Jane Austen and the Brontë sisters that enables books to transcend the times in which they were written. So today her readers are few in number, though there is a Charlotte Yonge Fellowship which holds conferences and publishes a twice-yearly review. Some of her most important novels are available from small publishers and are among those included on the internet.

Certainly they cannot be ignored by serious students of Victorian literature and they are a mine of information about the details of the life of middle-class families, villages and churches throughout much of the nineteenth century. Her own life coincided almost exactly with that of Queen Victoria, and she rarely moved far from the village of Otterbourne, a few miles from Winchester.

Her gifts were those of a highly intelligent and imaginative story-teller, with a sharp eye for detail and an unusual capacity for portraying character and relations between siblings. Her stories often portrayed ideal family life, with loving companionship and much freedom and fun. This was something that had been lacking in her own lonely and strictly ordered upbringing and left her emotionally undeveloped. She was always extremely shy and socially inept. In a sense she never quite grew up and tended to see life through the eyes of a child, which helps to explain the charm of her stories and their attraction for so many readers.

She was childlike, not childish, and had a most serious purpose. A motto often quoted in her novels was *Pro Ecclesia Dei*, and she once explained, 'I have always viewed myself as a sort of instrument for popularizing church views.' By 'church views' she meant those of the Church of England, as expressed by the founders of the Oxford Movement and taught her by John Keble. It was also said of her that 'she made goodness attractive'.

Charlotte was born in 1823, the daughter of an officer who had fought in the Peninsular War but had been obliged to leave the Army in order to manage his mother-in-law's small Hampshire estate. He thus became a county squire, comfortably off but not immensely rich, and he, his wife and the infant Charlotte joined grandmother in Otterbourne House.

As she grew up, she entered the highly disciplined regime, common at the time in families of her sort – rise at 6.30 a.m., two hours of lessons before breakfast, family prayers, two more hours of study, lunch, the afternoon devoted to outdoor pursuits or domestic activities such as sewing or needlework, supper followed by serious reading and conversation. Charlotte received all her education at home, and of a very high quality it was, since both her parents were unusually intelligent and skilled teachers. She in turn was a precocious pupil and at the age of seven taught her first Sunday School class – an occupation that remained very important to her. Her father was a strict taskmaster, but he was to her a loved hero figure and one of the two major influences on her life.

The other was John Keble. The Yonge household was deeply religious, and her father provided money for the building of a new church at Otterbourne. Less happily, he insisted on designing it himself. There was, however, an alternative when, in 1835, John Keble was appointed vicar of the neighbouring parish of Hursley. He was already famous for his widely read poems *The Christian Year* (1827) and for his Oxford Assize Sermon (1833) which is generally regarded as the starting point of the Oxford Movement.

A brilliant scholar, Keble was ready to devote the remainder of his life – he died in 1866 – to the pastoral care of Hursley. Charlotte, who was only 13 when he arrived, took to him at once. He prepared her for confirmation, thus introducing her to the new High Church beliefs and

practices, and remained her mentor until his death. In her biography of
Charlotte, Georgina Battiscombe visualizes the scene in the vicarage when

> Charlotte and John Keble sat together in his favourite corner, with the
> willow pattern china ranged over the chimney-piece, the aspidistra in
> the fireplace, the coloured glass fire-screen standing under the window,
> open to the summer warmth and the hanging basket of ferns swaying
> to the gentle draught. With Prayer Book open before him, and Palmer's
> *Origines Liturgicae* open for reference on the bamboo table at this side,
> Keble went through the Church of England Liturgy, comparing it with
> other and older rites, a method of instruction exactly calculated to
> appeal to Charlotte's historical sense. Tractarian teaching never fell on
> more fruitful soil. So Charlotte fell headlong in love with religion.

She and her parents were often in Hursley rather than Otterbourne
Church on Sundays. There was no sign of the ritualism of the later Oxford
Movement, but the worship was decently ordered and devoutly
conducted, the sermons were thoughtful, sometimes intellectually
demanding, and Holy Communion was celebrated monthly rather than
three times a year. Charlotte often walked over to attend daily Evensong.
Her writings were always submitted to Keble for comment before their
publication.

She first went into print when only 15 with a story, 'Le Chateau de
Melville', written in schoolroom French and interspersed with fairy tales
and fables. Copies were sold in aid of the church school at Otterbourne,
and the royalties from her future books all went to church or other
charities. The first of these, *Abbeychurch*, appeared in 1844, after she had
persuaded her grandmother that publishing was not unladylike if any
profits went to the Church. The book's twin centres were the consecration
of a new church and the attendance of young people at a Mechanics
Institute where they might be exposed to the questioning of religious
faith.

Not all Charlotte's novels were concerned directly with the Church, but
Charity House was the story of how a dull, uncared-for parish was
transformed by the arrival of a new priest, who continued to live the life
of a well-to-do country parson but was influenced by the Oxford
Movement. The peace of the parish was disturbed.

The first of her two most famous two-volume novels, *The Heir of*

Redclyffe (1853), is a tear-jerker that enjoyed enormous popularity. Its hero was not allowed to die of fever while in the Alps until a priest had been found to administer the Church's last rites. *The Daisy Chain* (1856 and republished as a Virago Modern Classic in 1988) was about women's education, involving a bookish, awkward heroine Ethel May, and also containing a great deal reflecting the High Church controversies of the nineteenth century.

Besides her extraordinary output of books, she also edited *The Monthly Packet* for nearly 50 years, starting in 1851. This was intended, as she explained in the first number, 'to help young people from 15–25 to form their own character, not as a guide but as a companion in times of recreation, to make them more steadfast and dutiful daughters of our own beloved Catholic Church of England'. Although she announced in the 1870s 'I have no hesitation in declaring my full belief in the inferiority of women, nor that she brought it upon herself, that is at the time of the Fall', not all of her many readers were willing to be 'dutiful daughters' and some of them went on to spearhead advances in women's education later in the century.

By this time she was also, and surely surprisingly for so dedicated a spinster, editor of *Mothers in Council*, a journal of the fast-growing Mothers' Union. This was at the request of Mary Sumner, the organization's founder, who lived in the Close at Winchester, and still left her with time to become involved in the work of the Girls' Friendly Society. Advancing years hardly reduced her activity, but in March 1901 she was suddenly taken ill with bronchitis which developed into pneumonia and led to a speedy death after receiving the Church's last rites.

This was a national event, with obituaries and tributes in all the main papers, and after a Requiem Mass in Otterbourne Church, she was buried in the churchyard near a memorial cross to John Keble. This she had had erected, and it was inscribed 'To the Master and Inspirer of Charlotte Mary Yonge'. A reredos in her memory was installed in the Lady Chapel of Winchester Cathedral.

11

Rescuing the Prostitutes: Josephine Butler

Josephine Butler was one of the greatest and possibly the most courageous of the nineteenth century's social reformers. Yet, as Jane Jordan points out in her illuminating biography (2001), to which this chapter owes much, she is no longer widely known. Her cause was the rescue of women from the evil of prostitution and with this an affirmation of the right of women to be judged equally under the law.

More than a century after her death, it is difficult to appreciate the extent to which prostitution infested the life of Victorian England. The primary cause of this was the desperate poverty in which a high proportion of the female population was obliged to live. Lacking the basic necessities of life, many were driven by sheer necessity to sell their bodies.

That there was an ample market for what they offered was due largely to the location of military garrisons in almost every part of the country, as well as the existence of ports serving Britain's prosperous maritime trade and attracting a multitude of seafarers who were far from home. Besides these long-standing openings for prostitution, there were in London and other large cities a significant number of upper-class men who, though seemingly happily married and pillars of rectitude in the community (some even occupying the highest places in government) felt the need to seek out prostitutes. A few of the women were of a higher social standing than most, but unimaginably worse than all was the existence of many child prostitutes – girls of nine to twelve years of age – who were in demand by the wealthy perverted. The sale of young children into sex-slavery was common and there was a thriving export trade in young lives from London to Paris and other European capitals.

Not all of this was legal, but officialdom was prepared to turn a blind eye, even to its worst excesses, until the military began to reap the fruit of their exploitation. Syphilis emerged as a more potent cause of disability among soldiers and sailors than any warfare in which they might become engaged. So serious a problem did this become that in the 1860s Parliament passed three Contagious Diseases Acts designed to protect men against the risks they encountered in brothels. These covered a total of 18 towns and owed something to the methods employed by those responsible for state-controlled brothels on the Continent. Later they were extended to include other towns, and there was even a suggestion, fortunately not accepted, that every part of the country should be subject to them.

They required that known prostitutes, and others believed to be prostitutes, should submit every month to an intrusive medical inspection to ensure that they were free of disease. These inspections, carried out by appointed male surgeons equipped with instruments, were often of a brutally sadistic character. Infected women were sent to the harsh regimes of lock hospitals, where they were detained until pronounced free. Those who refused to submit to inspection or go for treatment were committed to prison for six or nine months.

In defence of this monstrous regime it was asserted that, while resort to prostitutes was always regrettable, men were only exercising a natural instinct. It was therefore necessary that women should be available to them and that the women should be free from contagious diseases. What was natural in men was wicked in women.

Josephine Butler's campaign against this manifest evil was focused chiefly on securing the repeal of the final Contagious Diseases Act of 1869. This would deliver prostitutes from medical inspection, with its affront to their dignity, and at the same time remove any semblance of State approval of brothels and other open expressions of vice. She was equally concerned to rescue prostitutes from their plight through the provision of caring homes and alternative occupations.

A deep Christian commitment undergirded by a disciplined spirituality provided the main motivation for what became her life's work. Both in her speeches and writings she denounced the implication that women were less human than men and could therefore be used simply to satisfy male lust. She also pointed out that men were no less responsible than women for the spread of sexual diseases. Furthermore, it was altogether wrong that legislation relating to women's bodies and general welfare should be enacted by a Parliament in which women were not represented.

And of fundamental importance was the elimination of the dire social conditions that enabled prostitution to flourish.

The tackling of so major a social disorder required of Josephine Butler and others who joined her unusual courage and perseverance. In Victorian society it was 'not done' for women, especially of her social class, to speak of sexual issues and of the intimate aspects of the medical inspection of women's bodies. There were also powerful vested interests involved in the maintaining of prostitution, including those who made a great deal of money out of its organization and those of the governing classes who would find its reduction inconvenient.

She was therefore subjected to much personal abuse in the press, ostracism in the circles in which she mixed, and threats and violence at her meetings. When a mob descended on her house in the Close at Winchester, the Dean and Chapter complained, not about the mob but that she, with the support of her husband, Canon George Butler, was engaged in activity that would inevitably disturb their peace. On the other hand, she invariably received strong support from the working classes who perceived that it was the young members of their order who were being cruelly exploited and that wider issues of social justice were involved in the reforms. The repeal of the offensive Act in 1886 marked the triumph of her campaign which had started 17 years earlier, but not the end of her striving for the welfare of women. Her efforts did much to advance the Women's Movement.

Josephine Elizabeth Butler was born in Northumberland in 1828 into the aristocratic Grey family. She was one of ten children, and her father, a substantial landowner, was a prominent public figure and much involved in the campaign for the abolition of slavery. Her mother, a strong-minded woman, was related to Earl Grey, Prime Minister at the time of the passing of the Great Reform Bill in 1832. Reform was in her blood.

She was naturally brought up in the aristocratic manner at Dilston Hall, near Corbridge. Riding, parties and dances were part of the normal routine, and she and her sister Hetty, to whom she was always very close, were educated at home by tutors. They then spent two years at a school in Newcastle. On Sunday mornings they went to Corbridge Parish Church with the rest of the family, but in the evening they were taken by their governess to the Methodist Chapel which was under the influence of a thriving revivalist movement.

A visit in 1847 to Ireland, where one of her brothers was now living, proved to be influential. The potato famine was at its worst and she was deeply affected by the sight of the starving peasants: 'I cannot forget the occasional shrill wail which was sighed out by some poor creature sending her last cry of despair to heaven before falling down in a state of collapse by the wayside.' Another powerful influence was the accounts of the appalling cruelties inflicted on the slaves her brother was campaigning to liberate. And this led to a kind of religious crisis in which she wondered just how God was involved in these desperate situations. The outcome was a deep empathy with the poor and downtrodden, together with a commitment to do everything she could to relieve their plight.

A few years later Josephine travelled to Durham, where her brother Charles was undertaking postgraduate studies, and where she met George Butler who had recently been appointed to teach Classics in the university. His father, who had been headmaster of Harrow, was now Dean of Peterborough. They began to correspond, love poems started to arrive at Dilston Hall, and soon after he returned to Oxford to be a Public Examiner, they were engaged. Marriage in Corbridge Church followed in 1852.

The next 14 years were spent in Oxford, where she soon became pregnant and was appalled by the attitude of many of the dons to women and the double standards on sexuality then prevalent among men. In retrospect it appears that it was during this time that she began to identify the need for the kind of social work that would occupy the remainder of her life.

Meanwhile her health was deteriorating – caused by a mixture of anxiety and depression – but the appointment of George as vice-principal of Cheltenham College enabled them to move to a more agreeable climate and the diverting task of running one of the boys' boarding houses. Disaster struck, however, in the summer of 1864, when their five-year-old daughter, Eva, fell to her death from the banister at the top of the hall stairs. From this Josephine never really recovered, and it was only when not far from her own death that she was able to express her feelings about it in a biography of her husband:

> Never can I lose that memory – the fall, the sudden cry, and then the silence. It was pitiful to see her, helpless in her father's arms, the little drooping head resting on his shoulder, and her beautiful golden hair, all stained with blood, falling over his arm. Would to God that I had

died that death for her. If we had been permitted, I thought, to have one look, one word of farewell, one moment of recognition. We called her by name but there was no answer. She was our only daughter, the light and joy of our lives.

A breakdown soon followed and the winter was spent in Cannes seeking recovery.

In January 1866 George became headmaster of Liverpool College, a boys' school which had been founded a quarter of a century earlier and now had over 800 pupils of various races and religions drawn from Liverpool's rising mercantile class. At this new beginning Josephine felt the need 'to find some pain heavier than my own' and she consulted a Baptist minister who was in close touch with many of the port's social problems. He directed her to the Brownlow Hill workhouse – with 5,000 inmates the largest in the country. Among these were many prostitutes, whom Josephine, on her first visit, found employed in the picking of oakum. She sat among them and, in spite of the vast social gap, immediately established a rapport.

Visiting the workhouse became part of her life. One of the prostitutes, Mary Lomax, was taken into her home, and, with the full collaboration of George, more followed until the house, which also accommodated a number of the schoolboys, was full. All lived together as a family, shared in the evening prayers, and there was great sadness when, after three months, Mary died. No attempt at religious indoctrination was made, but the women often asked Josephine about her faith, and Mary was converted shortly before her death. Love and gentleness were what they were offered, in stark contrast to what they had previously experienced.

Josephine now began to extend her rescue work. Visits to prostitutes in their homes and in the hospitals where they were often incarcerated revealed desperate human need, and among those who were dying she sought to bring faith and hope. 'Woman, thy sins are forgiven thee', were her words to some who were overcome with guilt because of their past lives. But more than this was needed, and a House of Rest, which eventually accommodated 40 women, was opened in 1867, followed by an Industrial Home in which they were trained for a useful occupation or prepared for emigration abroad.

None of which was without a financial cost. Josephine and George contributed as much as they could and members of her family were very generous, but there was no escaping the grind of fund-raising. She used this, however, as a means for spreading her message and concentrated specially on young unmarried men of means, appealing to their consciences as well as reminding them of their responsibilities towards women. She became one of the best-known figures in Liverpool and soon even more widely.

A few weeks after the 1869 Act had passed into law, she addressed a meeting on the subject in Bristol and this led almost immediately to the founding of a National Association for the repeal of all the Acts. Initially membership was confined to men, partly because it was believed, correctly, that they would have most influence, but also there was a certain reticence about discussing the issue in mixed meetings. A Ladies' National Association was therefore formed in the same year with Josephine at its head and chief spokesperson.

Thereafter she travelled tirelessly, often addressing 'men only' meetings, providing most of her audiences with their first ever experience of hearing a woman speaker in public, and all the more astonishing because she dealt with a political subject. At one such meeting her husband thought it necessary to point out that his wife had been drawn by a great moral imperative from the normal privacy and sanctity of the domestic sphere to 'take a lead in directing the energies of their countrymen'. Her speeches were often said to leave audiences spellbound, the horrendous content being delivered in a sweet and gentle voice, yet with passion.

At the end of 1869 a letter organized by the Association and signed by 124 women, including Florence Nightingale, appeared in the national *Daily News* headed 'The Ladies Appeal and Protest'. It set out cogently the objections to the legislation. Subsequently it was turned into a petition to Parliament, with 2,000 women's signatures, causing an MP to report to Josephine:

Your manifesto has shaken us very badly in the House of Commons. We know how to manage any other opposition in the House or in the country, but this is very awkward for us – this revolt of the women. It is quite a new thing; what are we to do with such an opposition as this?

The Association had in fact a sympathetic MP, William Fowler, to express its concerns, and soon after the presentation of the petition he introduced a private member's Bill calling for the Contagious Diseases

Acts to be repealed. The press and the public were excluded from the chamber for his speech, at the end of which the Home Secretary prevented any debate by announcing the appointment of a Royal Commission.

This was not satisfactory to Josephine and the Association who believed that the subject should be debated openly, not in the secrecy of a Royal Commission, and that decisions on such a subject should not be made only by men. It was nonetheless agreed to collaborate with the Commission and £20,000 was raised to finance the collection of evidence to present to it. Although some of the members of the Commission were sympathetic to the cause, many were strongly opposed and these made their views plain when Josephine appeared to present her evidence. It proved to be a considerable ordeal, but she wrote later 'There was One who stood by me. I almost felt as if I heard Christ's voice telling me not to fear.' The Commission was left in no doubt as to her opposition to the double standard applied by the Acts, to an age of consent as low as 12 years old, to the lack of training available to rescued prostitutes, to the trafficking of young girls, and to the grinding poverty underlying the problem.

While the Commission was sitting, another petition, signed this time by 250,000 women, was presented by Josephine to the House of Commons. This was received only with mirth, but not before she had told some members of the Royal Commission who were present on her arrival that she was 'deeply troubled at the sight of so many men with so base and low a moral standard as you seem to have'.

When the Commission reported in July 1871 it was apparent that its members were hopelessly divided, for besides the main report there were five minority documents both for and against the Acts. The main report argued that, while the compulsory examination of women was in principle undesirable, it had nonetheless led to a reduction in the spread of syphilis, and it concluded that 'the temporary suspension of personal freedom in this instance is not to be regarded as an infringement of a clear constitutional principle'. One of the minority reports said that the reduction in syphilis cases was due, not to the Acts but to successful rescue work. Another called for the examination system to be extended for 'general use throughout the country'. Josephine's verdict on the main report was that it was 'a hateful compromise', and that it would set back the cause for Repeal by several more years.

Worse soon followed in the form of a Bill presented by the Home

Secretary, Henry Bruce, which purported to replace the existing Acts with provisions for 'the better Protection of Women'. It proposed that the age of consent should be raised from 12 to 14, and that girls under the age of 16 should be afforded some measure of protection. But women suspected of being prostitutes were to be exposed to new police powers, and the legislation would be extended to cover the whole of the British Isles.

Josephine was vehemently opposed to the new Bill, declaring it to be 'no compromise at all', but some in the Association were ready to support it on the grounds that it was the only available chance to get the 1860s Acts repealed. They also believed that it might be possible to have the punitive provisions removed at the committee stage. This division of view soon encompassed the whole of the Association, leading to the defection of many members, the depletion of funds and a serious weakening of its influence. There were, however, those who believed that the loss of less than fully committed members would strengthen the Association. In the end the Prime Minister, W. E. Gladstone, who was believed to favour repeal, caused the Bruce Bill to be withdrawn and, to Josephine's distress, it was back to square one.

There were several other responsibilities to occupy and give her concern. While on a tour of Switzerland designed to aid the recovery of her health, in 1869, she convened a few small meetings to support the cause of women's higher education in Europe. These meetings led to an encounter in Geneva with a Madam Goegg who asked her to address a drawing-room meeting of Swiss, Italian, French, German and Russian ladies on how best they might oppose the system of government-regulated prostitution then operating on the Continent.

An International Women's Association was immediately formed to campaign against regulation, and thereafter Josephine spent a great deal of time travelling to continental countries to help advance this cause. In Rome, where the problem of prostitution was particularly serious, she found Vatican officials cautious in their expectations that the Pope would pronounce on the subject. Moreover, she had no desire to have an audience with him because of all the flummery involved, but she sent him an Italian translation of one of her pamphlets, *Una Voce de Deseto*, and was delighted to learn that he had been moved by it and intended to make a pronouncement in favour of abolition. She declared him to be 'a true and humble Christian, altho' a Pope'. By this time she had completed a mission of inquiry in all the European capitals and chief cities, and as a result a British, Continental and General Federation was founded in 1875 with herself as its joint secretary.

An urgent matter for the Federation's attention was the widespread child prostitution and the extensive trafficking known as the 'White Slave Trade'. London was a strong source of supply for young girls, since the age of consent in Britain was lower than elsewhere in Europe, and Josephine, ever outspoken, declared the availability of these girls to be stimulating to some men – 'The younger, the more tender and innocent, the more helpless and terrified the victims, the greater their value in the eyes of these accursed beings.' Brussels was a particularly sordid city, and after Josephine and others had submitted damning evidence at a trial forced on the Belgian Government by a Federation campaign, the seven women and five men held responsible for the organization were sent to prison. Thirty-four English girls who had been held against their will in several brothels were released. Her interest and influence spread as far even as India.

George's appointment as a Canon of Winchester in 1882 did not lead to any diminution in her work, and soon after moving there she established a rest and rescue home in a large house just outside the Close. Among the earliest residents was Rebecca Jarrett, who had a particularly sordid history but became a Christian and exercised a remarkable influence for good on other prostitutes. Josephine related her story to W. T. Stead, the editor of the *Pall Mall Gazette* and a well-known London figure who pioneered the modern exposé form of journalism and was conducting a campaign against child prostitution.

Stead met Rebecca and persuaded her to return to London and the underworld of vice in order to provide him with irrefutable evidence of what was taking place. The details of what followed are better not described and they led to a five-day exposé in the *Pall Mall Gazette* under sensational headlines such as 'The Maiden Tribute of Modern Babylon', 'The Forcing of Unwilling Maids', and 'I Order Five Virgins'. This did wonders for the circulation of the paper and led to the holding of mass meetings, some attended by a thousand or more people, calling for an end to the trafficking. Unfortunately, however, some of the evidence had been obtained by the enticement of a pretty 13-year-old named Eliza who was treated horrifically. When the girl's mother, who had actually been paid £1 to make her available, learned of all the publicity surrounding Eliza's experiences, she claimed that she had been abducted.

A trial at the Old Bailey followed, as a result of which Stead was sentenced to three months hard labour and Rebecca to six months imprisonment. On her release Josephine invited her back to Winchester, and it was this visit that led to the mob, inflamed by local brothel keepers, to demonstrate violently in the Close. Eventually she joined the Salvation Army and devoted the rest of her life to its social work.

Although the incident caused Josephine a great deal of distress, the national publicity surrounding it advanced the Repeal cause considerably. During a General Election campaign in November 1885 Josephine published *A Woman's Appeal to the Electorate*, and after 261 MPs in favour of repeal were returned, and the Liberals were back in office, a Bill for repeal was given the Royal Assent on 15 April 1886. Josephine chanced to be in Naples at the time and on receiving the news exclaimed, 'So that abomination is dead and buried. Praise the Lord!' Another ten years would pass before it was finally repealed in India.

Repeal of the Contagious Diseases Acts did not, however, bring and end to prostitution or the many other evils ensuing from it. Josephine continued to campaign therefore for the closing of brothels and, increasingly, for the Women's Suffrage Movement, which she had always regarded as essential to the dignity of women and necessary to the removal of other affronts to the welfare of women. As the end of the century advanced, her own health, which had never been strong, was becoming less and less able to cope with the strains and stresses she had for so long shouldered. She also became increasingly affected by the deaths of many of her relatives and friends.

In March 1890 it was George's turn. He had been ill for some time, and, on medical advice, they spent the winter in Cannes. But this led to no improvement and, while on their return to Winchester, he died in a London hotel bedroom. He had been totally committed to his wife's work and played a significant part in it, yet he always felt the pain of her long absences, as did other members of her family, and she herself accepted the pain of separation as part of the price of the fulfilling of her vocation.

After George's burial she moved to Wimbledon and had another 16 years to live. It was not until 1901 that she announced her 'retirement from public work', and even after that was often called upon to address a meeting or offer advice. It seemed inevitable that when she moved to Cheltenham to be nearer to her son, Charles, the other half of the house chanced to be occupied by a high-class prostitute. This prompted her to investigate the extent of this vice in 'godly Cheltenham' and to close working with the police in reducing its surprisingly large incidence.

When she became very ill in 1906, and cancer had been diagnosed, her sons George and Stanley persuaded her to return to Northumberland to a house on George's estate. There she died on 30 December 1906 and was buried after a service attended only by a few members of her family in the tiny church at Kirknewton. She had asked for her funeral to be 'of the very simplest kind and without any show of deep mourning', but she had also specifically requested to be buried beside her husband in Winchester.

Throughout her life, Josephine was a prolific writer, often in newspaper and magazine articles supporting her campaign, and in a vigorous and sometimes violent language. She also wrote more than twenty books, starting with *The Education and Employment of Women* (1868) and including a biography of *Catherine of Siena* (1878) with whom she always felt a close affinity, *Our Christianity Tested by the Irish Question* (1887) and *Recollections of George Butler* (1892). *Personal Reminiscences of a Great Crusade* (1896) is an important account of her life's work which was, she said, 'a revolt against and an aggressive opposition to a gross political and illegal tyranny'.

An obituary in the *Daily Telegraph* concluded:

She never faltered in her task and it is to her in supreme that the English statute book owes the removal of one of the greatest blots that ever defaced it. Her victory marked one of the greatest stages in the progress of woman to that equality of treatment which is the final test of a nation's civilisation.

There is a memorial window to her in the Lady Chapel of Liverpool Cathedral. A window in St Olave's, Hart Street, in the City of London portrays her, alongside Elizabeth Fry, Florence Nightingale and Edith Cavell, holding a Bible in one hand and in the other a rolled petition to Parliament. She is commemorated in the Church of England's Calendar of Holy Days on 30 May.

12

Marching as to War: Marie Louise Carlile

In 1878, the Revd Wilson Carlile, then one of ten (yes, ten) curates of St Mary Abbots in Kensington, became specially concerned about the failure of the Church to make any significant impact on the large working-class population that inhabited most of the parish. He had himself been born in 1847 into a wealthy family and at the age of 17 set himself to make £20,000 by the time he was 25. This he achieved, but soon afterwards lost most of his money when a trade depression destroyed his City company.

He was deeply traumatized by this but eventually emerged from a period of ill health largely as a result of an evangelical conversion experience. He returned to commercial life for another five years but became increasingly involved in evangelistic campaigns before spending two years at St John's College, Highbury (now St John's College, Nottingham) preparing for ordination.

At St Mary Abbots he began to hold magic-lantern services in the church hall and open-air meetings after 9 p.m., when the local people were on the streets. These attracted large numbers, but also the attention of a so-called Skelton Army of roughs who tried to break up the meetings. Local residents and shopkeepers complained, and in the end the Vicar decreed that the outdoor work must stop.

Carlile was naturally frustrated by this decision, and, with the support of a few influential and moneyed friends, decided to form an independent organization that would, while remaining firmly within the life of the Church of England, concentrate on evangelism wherever and whenever the opportunity arose. This would be a lay movement and he was convinced that only working-class evangelists could ever convert others of the working class. Advertisements in the church press in 1882 sought 'Young men, full of fire and hard work, ready to give up all for the Lord Jesus'. The response was sufficient to enable missions to be held in various parts of the country, and a base was established in a hall in Westminster.

Thus began the Church Army which became, and remains, a significant evangelistic agency not only in the United Kingdom and Ireland, but also in many other parts of the worldwide Anglican Communion. Modelled to some extent on the Salvation Army, founded by William Booth 17 years earlier, it made use of military imagery. The evangelists who had had some training were officers (captains), and given a smart uniform, supporters were soldiers and an early handbill announced 'War declared on sin and Satan under the command of the Revd W. Carlile every night at 8 o'clock. Come if you dare'. Instrumental music and singing were among the weapons.

In 1889, social work began among the poorest and most marginalized in society and was seen as an essential element in the Church Army's mission. During the 1890s there was a rapid expansion, and by the end of the century there were 400 captains and 200 nursing sisters. Their work won the warm approval of the Convocations of Canterbury and York, and by the time Carlile retired from the battle in 1942, aged 95, its significance had won him a place among the distinguished holders of the Order of Merit. In 2000 he was included in the Church of England's Calendar of Holy Days on 26 September.

A key figure in the development was Wilson Carlile's sister, Marie Louise. She was four years younger than he, being the ninth child of a family of 12 (three of whom died in infancy). Theirs was a comfortable middle-class Victorian family life in Clapham Park, then a spaciously attractive south London suburb, and Marie did very well at a local school.

When old enough, she undertook, happily, the duties expected of the daughter of an evangelical family – teaching in the Sunday School of a tough area, helping in a boys' club and an ambulance class, visiting the homes of the poor. Entries in her diary of that time include 'Took a steam kettle to a poor man' and 'gave a dress to a needy woman'. She saw clearly that love of God and love of neighbour were inseparable, though, as with most of her class, saw no need to change the social order.

Her brother's appeal for young men to come forward for evangelistic work drew also a response from a number of women who felt drawn to serve Christ in some substantial way but found no opportunity for this within the life of the Church. Wilson Carlile saw immediately the opportunities this offered and inserted an advertisement in the October

1883 edition of *The Battleaxe* – the movement's journal – for 'Church Army soldiers (sisters only) who are desirous of giving themselves wholly to the work'. Further appeals followed offering 'a small remuneration here, but a great one hereafter'. The earliest recruits came from the middle classes, but this soon changed to conform to the Army's working-class image, though there were always a few of the others involved.

It was not at this stage envisaged that women would become officers but they were given ten weeks of intensive training and soon began to make an impact. The Army's Annual Report for 1887/8 recorded:

A Mission Nurse finds access to every house and a cordial welcome within. She can speak to women, sympathise with them, win their confidence and gain insights into their characters far more appropriately and successfully than anyone of the other sex could do, especially anyone who was above them in education and position, both social and official, which a clergyman is.

At this point Carlile decided to open a training home for Mission Nurses, near his headquarters, now in Edgware Road, and he turned to Marie for help. She was keen to respond, but her father was reluctant to allow her to take on responsibilities that would inevitably involve engagement with women who lived well beyond the boundaries of respectable society. In the end, however, he was persuaded to let her join her brother for a short time, on a temporary basis.

The training home was far from grand, consisting only of a few rooms in 'a smelly old house' over a shop, but it had to serve for the next four years, by which time Marie had been designated Honorary Super-intendent of the Women's Training Home. Neither she nor her brother ever received any remuneration for what turned out to be their lifetime's work. Family resources were sufficient to sustain them, and from the outset of the Church Army's life Wilson Carlile's influential contacts provided substantial sums of money to finance its work. For many years, no one holding senior office was ever paid.

In the spartan surroundings of the Home, recruits were given an intensive training which included Bible study, prayer, ambulance classes, music and conducting open-air meetings in poor areas. This eventually developed to include mornings at a London infirmary to learn about nursing, slum visiting, contact with barmaids in public houses and rescue work – the description given to work among prostitutes. The extent of the problem of prostitution in London and other large cities during the outwardly religious and respectable Victorian era is not now commonly recognized but it became a large element in the work of many Church Army Sisters, some of whom specialized in a task requiring both skill and compassion.

Lectures on the Bible and Prayer Book prepared the trainees for an examination conducted by a Diocesan Inspector appointed by the Bishop of London. In 1889, a year after the move into more spacious accommodation, the Home was visited by the Archbishop of Canterbury, Edward White Benson, who warmly approved of Marie's work, and she also established a friendship with Princess Louise Augusta, a grand-daughter of Queen Victoria, who lived long enough to be present at the Coronation of Queen Elizabeth II. Other titled ladies were drawn in to lend a hand.

Marie, who had turned down an offer of marriage in the year of the Archbishop's visit, was wholly dedicated to her training work and also to the support of her brother with whom she was in constant contact and who frequently turned to her for advice. Although frequently involved in open-air meetings, she never found public speaking easy, but in 1893 gave at a conference in Leeds an important paper on the aims and methods of the Nursing Sisters.

They were to go out with loving hearts and loving hands to work among the sinful, the bad and the suffering – to take a Sister's compassion to even the most depraved, strong in the conviction that the love of God could reach and change the darkest hearts. They were to supply the clergy with Mission Women for work in slums, lodging houses, cottage meetings and mission services and for nursing and rescue work. They were also able to work among caravan people, gypsies and hop and fruit pickers.

Among the recruits were domestic servants, factory workers, governesses, clerks and some hospital nurses who came for training in evangelism. Self-discipline, rather than imposed discipline, governed life in the Home – an innovative approach at the time, but, as Marie explained, the Sisters would be on their own when sent out to care and evangelize. Standards were nonetheless high and only about one-third of those accepted for training were retained at the end of the course. The rest were given financial and other help to resettle, and some went on to make different careers in social work.

Those who completed the course successfully – about 190 by 1893 – were commissioned as Mission Sisters and sent mainly to difficult inner-city parishes, where they were provided with accommodation and were paid a few shillings a week. Although selected for their physical strength and inner resources, many of the Sisters could not cope with the exacting work for more than three or four years. Others left to get married, but there were 250 in service at the end of the century, and Marie declared: 'When we think of the crying needs of the perishing souls around us our little band of women seems very small indeed, but like Gideon's three hundred they will be used to do great things.'

Although most of the Church Army's work continued to be parish based, a pressing need arose for special centres and residential homes for women and girls who needed more intensive care. Young women rescued from prostitution usually needed shelter for a time; girls moving into big cities in search of work, and others who may have lost their jobs in domestic service, had to be saved from the streets; women rescued from violent homes or from crime; unmarried mothers, the elderly and infirm – the need was far greater than the Church Army could ever hope to meet, but many hundreds and eventually many thousands of women came to be grateful for dedicated, caring Sisters. In homes run by men officers for men, the Sisters also had an important role.

The outbreak of war in 1914 brought a massive increase in the scope of the Church Army's work. Soldiers serving in France and also in Britain lacked places for rest and refreshment when not on duty, and Sisters became heavily involved in the canteens and recreation centres provided by the Church Army in company with the Salvation Army and the YMCA. Other opportunities arose in the large munitions factories where women were employed. Family life suffered as a consequence of dislocation, and the widows and orphans of the multitude of casualties needed much care.

Opportunities for evangelism were always seized and open-air and indoor mission services were held in a wide variety of places and circumstances. The deployment of so many officers on work among the armed forces brought freedom to the Sisters to embark on caravan missions without male leadership. Back in 1892 Wilson Carlile had commissioned a fleet of horse-drawn caravans for evangelistic work in rural areas as well as fairgrounds and race-courses. Boldly painted slogans such as 'Caravanning the Good News to Villages', and texts 'Do this in remembrance of me', and 'Be thou faithful unto death' advertised the presence of the missioners. Within the caravan were New Testaments, hymn books, magic-lantern slides and other tools of mission, and the caravan itself provided a focus for the outdoor meetings. By 1914 there were 70 of these operating in every diocese but one in England, and another in Scotland.

From the outset the Sisters formed part of the mission teams but always in a subordinate position and never on their own. The war changed this, at least from 1917 onwards, when a few caravans returned to the countryside with teams of Sisters. The number of caravans employed by the Church Army never again reached its pre-war height, though 50 were in use in 1922, and the last to be laid up was in 1973.

The increased recognition of the importance of women's ministry, stimulated by wartime experience, brought a particular problem to the Church Army. An Inter-Diocesan Council for Women's Work, set up in 1920, decreed that if women wished to have formal Anglican recognition they must have recognized qualifications. Marie Carlile was disturbed by the implication of this:

> The privilege of the Church Army has always been to give an opportunity for church work to women who had only an elementary education, as well as of course to others who have had more chance to study. Some of these very simple women have made such grand workers in their own way. We cannot now close the door on them.

The issue touched upon a fatal weakness of the Church of England which, having become alienated from the overwhelming majority of the working class, has never discerned how to recruit to the ranks of its authorized ministry men and women who will remained anchored in their working-class origins.

In the end, a compromise was reached and it was agreed that the Church Army could continue with its methods, but, although the Sisters had been active in nursing and evangelism since 1887, it was not until 1921 that the first of them were admitted by the Bishop of Willesden to the Office of Mission Sister. An attempt made in 1907 to gain for men official status as lay evangelists failed even though Wilson Carlile assured the bishops in the Canterbury Convocation that any idea that they might one day wish to become priests was 'entirely repugnant to them'.

Marie's crucial work of training the Sisters, which extended to include some responsibility for the training of men cadets, continued until 1913 when it was decided that she should relinquish this in order to become Honorary Secretary of the Women's Work. She was also the only woman member of the Army's executive committee. Although beset by constant health problems which sometimes required quite long periods off duty, she handled what had become immense responsibilities with remarkable dedication and skill.

Her primary task was to retain among the Sisters, now widely scattered throughout Britain, and some overseas, a sense of corporate identity, or, as she always put it, a sense of family. While recognizing that they were an integral part of the local church's life, it was important for them not be absorbed into activities unrelated to the main mission of evangelism and social care. It was also the case that a large proportion were involved in particularly challenging work, the experience of which needed to be shared with others who were also being challenged. With numbers eventually approaching a thousand, it was obviously impossible for Marie to exercise single-handed the necessary pastoral supervision, so a number of senior Mission Sisters were appointed to visit them in their parishes.

Marie herself continued to undertake some of this and received from every Sister a weekly report on her activities, countersigned by the Vicar or another person to whom she was accountable. She had a photograph of every one of them in her room and prayed for each regularly. Twice or three times a year each received a personal letter from her, and regular conferences were held to bring them together. On these occasions, or at other times when she met Sisters, she immediately recognized them by name.

Not surprisingly, they were devoted to her and aware of her deep spiritual depths. This was bound to raise from time to time questions relating to allegiance and jurisdiction, but Marie always emphasized the importance of the wider ministry of women and urged upon the Sisters the need to avoid division. After the 1914–18 war ended she stated her own views on women's ministry with crystal clarity:

The time has come when the whole question of women's service and status in the church should be seriously considered, many of the present limitations removed and permission given for women to speak at non-liturgical services in consecrated buildings under a system of authorised licence such as exists in the case of men. Evangelism has its charisma, not necessarily conveyed by ordination, not limited to the three-fold ministry, and not restricted to one sex. The Church of Him who was born of a woman must find the way to use to the full the powers that God has so generously given to womanhood.

She did not get involved in the women's suffrage movement, but did attend a Service of Thanksgiving in St Martin-in-the-Fields after the voting rights of women had been extended in 1918.

The 1939–45 war made greater demands on the Church Army than anything experienced before. This was due partly to the fact that Britain itself was on the front line for much of the time, and partly because the war spread quickly from Western Europe. During the Blitz canteens and pastors were always on hand both on the bombed sites of the large cities and in London's deep air-raid shelters where brief services were held. When the bedraggled Army returned from Dunkirk, the Church Army was on hand to greet them at the south coast ports and the mainline railway stations.

Two Sisters working in Rouen got away on the last boat from St Malo. Two others who had been working in Nantes were on the ill-fated *Lancastrian* when it was sunk off St Lazaire. They were lucky to escape, having been thrown clear into the sea, from which they were rescued by one of the ship's boats. This was then machine-gunned, and finally they reached England by a French trawler. Two Sisters went to Algiers in April 1943 to work with the Red Cross, before moving to Italy. Another was in Jerusalem, serving in a hostel for seamen on leave and escorting them around the sacred sites. After D-Day the Church Army set up an extensive network of canteens in France, and Peggy Smith, who with her husband Captain H. J. Smith worked near the front, was the first British woman to get into Germany during the war. Once again church services were integrated with the welfare work.

Marie Carlile's last public appearance was in October 1947 at a great rally in London's Albert Hall celebrating the centenary of her brother's birth. A year later, she retired from the leadership of the Church Army's Women's Work, though she continued to be deeply interested in the Sisters' activities and to visit the Training College which was now located in Reading. Shortly before retiring she had entrusted the pastoral care of the Sisters to one of their own number, Sister Benniston, who was also a deaconess, but not before she had written to each of the 500 of them asking for a personal note confirming her choice.

There are now 83 active Sisters, of whom nine are ordained. Since 1996 Sisters who become priests are required to resign their commissions, but there is now a moratorium on this pending certain decisions about a new Church Army structure.

Some Sisters still come from working-class backgrounds with few educational qualifications, but most are middle class and some have degrees. There is no longer a separate women's department, and Sisters are not now restricted to ministering in situations considered most suitable for women. A few are vicars of parishes, others are involved in para-church Christian community work, some occupy diocesan posts, a number have self-supporting ministry roles. All offer something distinctive.

13

A Prophet in a Pulpit: Maude Royden

If a patron saint of women's ordained ministry in the Church of England is ever required, the choice will have to be Maude Royden. A woman of vision and of remarkable gifts of leadership and communication, she had outstanding courage. Denied ordination in the Church of England, she accepted in 1917 an invitation to become pulpit assistant at the City Temple – the foremost Congregational church and at the time one of London's most important preaching centres. This was when services still attracted large congregations, and sermons were frequently reported in the national press.

Her appointment to this post, even in a church that had no beliefs in apostolic succession, priesthood (apart from that of all believers) and other obstacles to feminine ministry, created a sensation. On the Sunday of her first morning and evening sermons (18 March 1917) the police were required to control the crowd seeking admission. Many had to be turned away.

The press had done its best to create indignant interest. The *Daily Express* announced 'Woman Crank's Sermon'. *The Globe*, appealing to a better educated readership, preferred 'A Portia in the Pulpit', while the *Daily Sketch* sank to 'Girl Preacher in Parker's Pulpit' – Dr Parker being the great preacher who had made the City Temple famous. Opposition was not of course confined to the irresponsible press or even to the many in the Church who believed that women had no place in the leadership of public worship. Among Royden's friends and supporters who longed for the day when women would serve equally with men in the Church's ministry, some believed that what they regarded as her precipitate action would hinder, rather than help the cause – a division of opinion that reappeared in the Movement for the Ordination of Women 75 years later.

By the time she entered the City Temple's pulpit, Maude Royden was already well known through her involvement in the Women's Suffrage Movement. She had also been travelling secretary of the Fellowship of Reconciliation, pleading the cause of pacifism during the early stages of the 1914–18 war. Earlier she had, against much opposition, become the first woman lecturer to be employed by Oxford University's Extension Delegacy. Neither did her commitment to reform in church and society diminish in the decades to come.

She was born in 1876, the sixth daughter and the youngest of the eight children of Sir Thomas Royden – a very wealthy shipowner, a highly regarded Lord Mayor of Liverpool and for seven years a Conservative Member of Parliament. Frankby Hall, the family home on the Wirral, was a comfortable establishment with a butler, several maids and other domestic staff, but Maude was born with two dislocated hips which at the time could not be remedied. Much of her childhood was spent in pain. Later this was relieved, but for the rest of her life she was lame.

Her brothers went to Winchester, and she was sent to the Cheltenham Ladies' College, where Miss Beale still reigned over the school she had founded. The Anglican ethos hardly touched her, but she played a full part in the life of the school and was much affected by a visit to its mission in London's Bethnal Green.

At Lady Margaret Hall, Oxford, which still had only 50 students, she read History, but although she passed the same examinations as men undergraduates, she was not allowed to take a degree. Again, she was not affected by the Anglicanism of the Hall, but she learned the art of public speaking at the Oxford Students' Debating Society (an alternative to the Oxford Union to which women were not admitted) and established some lifelong friendships that were to be of great importance to her. No less important was the effect of her fairly frequent attendance at services in the church of the Society of St John the Evangelist – the Cowley Fathers. This brought her under the influence of the Oxford Movement, leading to a struggle with the issue of whether or not she should become a Roman Catholic.

After Oxford she returned home to care for her ill mother and to consider what she might do with her life. Feeling drawn to social work, she read Booth's seminal *In Darkest England*, and, as a result, offered her services to the Victoria Women's Settlement in one of Liverpool's most depressed areas. Initially, she worked just one day a week, then took up residence, but the stress involved proved to be too great. 'Women drink like fiends,' she reported to a friend, 'and so should I if I lived in Lancaster Street.' The warden's lack of administrative skill was also a problem, and after 18 months she resigned.

Maude now returned to the Roman Catholic question and decided to consult the Revd G. W. Hudson Shaw whom she had met briefly in Oxford, where he was a member of the University's Extension Delegacy. This encounter had consequences more far-reaching than her faith decision which she eventually settled in favour of remaining an Anglican.

Shaw, a priest of brilliant mind and radically reforming instinct, combined his lectureship with responsibility for the parish of South Luffenham in Rutland. At the time of his meeting with Maude, his wife was too ill to undertake any parish work (the normal expectation of a vicar's wife), and since for six months of the year he was himself away lecturing on most weekdays, he invited her in 1905 to spend three months in the parish as a kind of unpaid curate, engaged in pastoral and teaching ministry.

She accepted, moved into the Rectory, and began visiting the homes of the villagers. She also ran a Sunday School, a Mothers' Meeting and a sewing class for girls. At the same time, she established what became a close relationship with Effie, Shaw's sick wife. His first wife had died shortly after their marriage, and not long after re-marrying Effie, who was his niece, it turned out that she was mentally unstable. She lived in constant fear, needed much sensitive care, and after the birth of their first and only child, was insane for two years. Shaw himself, perhaps not surprisingly, was subject to bouts of depression.

When the three months were up, Shaw, recognizing Maude's special teaching gifts and wishing to retain contact with her, asked the Extension Delegacy to appoint her to a lectureship. This was resisted. There had never before been a woman lecturer, and it was far from certain that the classes, scattered about the country, would welcome a woman in this role. But Shaw persisted, and eventually it was agreed to employ her on an experimental basis. At first a number of places were unwilling to receive her, but those that did soon discovered her brilliance and before long she was lecturing fairly widely to large meetings on Shakespeare and the Romantic poets.

She continued to make her home in the South Luffenham vicarage and in 1905 recognized that she was in love with Shaw. He felt the same and so there developed an unusual lifelong relationship that was both passionate and chaste and was actually welcomed and supported by Effie who was herself sustained by a love that was mutual. Shaw and Maude realized that marriage was impossible and that Effie was important to their continuing relationship – 'We must always be three. This is our safety', they agreed. When, following Shaw's death 40 years later, Maude came to write about this she entitled her book *A Threefold Cord*.

In the same year that they acknowledged their love, she moved to Oxford, a more convenient base for her many rail journeys. When offered promotion, it came with a warning against acceptance, since the Delegacy officials thought that the higher lecturing fee to which she would become entitled might well price her out of the still prejudiced market. She took this advice and continued to lecture at the lower rate, but also began to be involved in the National Union of Women's Suffrage Societies (NUWSS).

At this time the only women with voting rights were property owners, and these were confined to local government elections. A growing movement to remedy this was divided between the NUWSS which adopted a 'winning the argument' approach under the leadership of Millicent Fawcett and the highly militant Women's Social and Political Union led by the redoubtable Emmeline Pankhurst.

Maude devoted an increasing amount of her time to speaking, often to crowded meetings, all over the country, and became editor of the NUWSS weekly journal *Common Cause*. She also joined the executive and in 1913 organized a massive nationwide pilgrimage designed to highlight the suffrage issue in the context of women's rights more generally. At a final service in St Paul's Cathedral no woman was allowed to take part, but Maude spoke on 'The Pilgrim Spirit' to a crowded congregation in the Ethical Church, not far away. A year later, she was one of the speakers when suffragists and Labour Party members joined forces to pack London's Albert Hall. She emphasized that women were part of humanity and that their humanity was a great and deeper thing than their gender.

The outbreak of war led to the suspension of all suffragist activity but the war itself brought some advance inasmuch as women over the age of 30 were in 1918 given the right to vote in parliamentary elections. It is generally believed that this *was* prompted by the very considerable contribution made by women to the war effort, though this had not been confined to those who were over 30.

The war, however, took Maude in two new directions. A convinced pacifist, she was totally opposed to the war and, having joined the Fellowship of Reconciliation in 1914, became its travelling secretary a year later. At the time she, along with some others, resigned from the executive of the NUWSS, which was backing the war. 'Militarism and feminism cannot be reconciled', she argued.

Her beliefs about this were expounded in *The Great Adventure: The Way to Peace* (1915), in which it was made clear that the pacifism and her feminism were both based on deep Christian convictions. The way of the cross required, she said, even greater heroism than that being displayed by the soldiers at the front line and it was the only way to true and lasting peace. Certainly it demanded considerable heroism in a woman who faced hostility, often of a violent kind, in almost every place where she spoke. At the first Conference of the Fellowship of Reconciliation held in July 1915 she appealed to the young people who were present, 'Go! Convert England to Christian Pacifism'. Leading the way herself, she organized a pilgrimage of peace with a large horse-drawn caravan in which literature was carried and sleeping space provided for a group of young women pilgrims. Other supporters joined them along a route that was planned to take them through the Midlands to London. From the outset, however, they were faced with violence, and on reaching Hinckley in Leicestershire were attacked by a mob. The caravan was set ablaze, and the police arranged for a London-bound express train to be stopped so that the women might be got quickly out of the way.

Several years earlier, in 1909, Maude had become the first chair of the Church League for Women's Suffrage (CLWS), of which Edward Lee Hicks, the radical Bishop of Lincoln and always one of her strongest supporters, was the President. The League had the uphill task of persuading church people, particularly the clergy, that women should have the vote, but Maude came to believe that this issue could not be separated from that of the leadership of women in the Church at every level, including the priesthood.

From 1913 onwards, and particularly after the end of the suffrage agitation, the women's ordination movement gathered pace. At a CLWS conference in 1915 a group within the League argued for women priests, bishops, archbishops and popes, adding the proviso that all should remain celibate. The *Church Times* responded with an editorial: 'that women be ordained is for any sane person so absolutely gross that he must refuse to discuss it'.

The National Mission for Repentance and Hope, launched by the Archbishops of Canterbury and York in 1916 in what proved to be a vain attempt to return the war-torn nation to a deeper Christian commitment, raised the women's issue from the theoretical to the practical. At the suggestion of William Temple, who was at the time Rector of St James's, Piccadilly, Royden was appointed to the Council of the Mission. At once she found herself in a divisive discussion about the possibility of women being allowed to speak at the Mission meetings. The ever-cautious Archbishop Davidson of Canterbury decreed that bishops should decide about this in their own dioceses, which led Bishop Winnington-Ingram of London to decree that women should be allowed to speak in churches only if there were no other suitable place. In this case, they should speak only to women and girls and this from the aisle in front of the chancel steps, not from the pulpit or the lectern. He later rescinded this by ruling that they should not speak in churches in any circumstances, a position taken also by the Bishop of Chelmsford. Whether, or how many, women became involved in the Mission is not known.

Soon after its ending, however, the way was open for Maude to begin her preaching ministry at the City Temple. This continued until March 1920, and during her three years there she conducted and preached at one service most Sundays, sometimes baptized infants and every Friday made herself available to anyone who wished to discuss her sermons or had pastoral problems. When, in 1918, women over 30 were given the vote she preached on her adaptation of a famous text from Ecclesiasticus: 'Let us now praise famous women and the mothers who begat us.' But she never became a Congregationalist and accepted only the title Pulpit Assistant.

Meanwhile Hudson Shaw had become rector of St Botolph's, Bishopsgate, in the City of London, and, while he did not believe that women should become priests, he believed strongly that they should be allowed to preach. Might, then, Maude be invited to preach in his own church? She started by reading Lessons at the Sunday evening services, and in his sermon on the first occasion Shaw informed the congregation that they had 'for the first time in this historic church heard a woman's voice proclaiming the glad tidings of Christ's Gospel'.

In September 1918 she gave an address to a packed Thursday midday congregation on 'The League of Nations and Christianity'. This was notwithstanding the Bishop's instruction that women were not to speak in churches until a committee, appointed back in 1916, had reported. When he heard of Maude's Thursday address, he told Shaw that on no account must she be allowed to preach on Sunday and that he should not start another series of Thursday addresses without consulting him. It was, nonetheless, arranged that she would conduct the Three Hours Service of the Meditation on the Cross in St Botolph's on the following Good Friday.

Learning of this somewhat late in the day, the Bishop despatched a letter on Maundy Thursday: 'Dear Shaw, I absolutely *forbid* you on your honour and your oath of canonical obedience to me to allow Miss Maude Royden to take the Three Hours Service in your church tomorrow.' He had in fact no authority to issue such a prohibition, since the service was non-liturgical and non-statutory. Shaw decided, however, to transfer it to the adjacent parish room which was full to capacity, with many others listening outside. On the following day the Bishop, who had actually come round to believing that women should be allowed to speak in church, but felt bound to await the findings of the committee, wrote to both Maude and Shaw: 'I was sorry to have to write such a letter but one has to hurt those you love sometimes for their good.' He was pleased the service had taken place in the parish room.

Soon after Maude had left the City Temple she received an invitation from Percy Dearmer, Vicar of St Mary's, Primrose Hill, not far from Hampstead, to join him in founding a new mission enterprise. He was already well known for his pioneering efforts to raise the standard of worship in the Church of England and for his editorship of the *English Hymnal*. Maude attended his church on Sunday mornings and usually had lunch at the vicarage afterwards.

Dearmer believed that she needed a place of her own to preach in, so Kensington Town Hall was hired for a Sunday evening 'Fellowship Service', with Maude as minister and he as her assistant. To emphasize that it was intended to complement rather than rival the established Church, it was called 'The Guildhouse'. The opening paragraph of a statement of aims began:

> Our feeling is that the Church of England, like other churches in this country, is at present appealing to that minority of English people who go to church on Sunday – a minority which appears to be decreasing. She ought to appeal to the public at large, by means of addresses and

informal gatherings for discussion, and to speak to the great body of people who are not at home in church, or who do not even know their way about the Prayer Book. Very probably there should be a centre of this sort in every district of our great cities, and certainly several in London.

Large numbers began to attend, and in June of the following year the redundant Eccleston Square Congregational Church, with a main hall holding 1,000 people, together with a smaller hall and ancillary rooms, became available to provide an independent home. An afternoon service was started under Dearmer's leadership to give scope for the use of poetry, orchestral pieces and solos, as well as an address.

When Maude was preaching in the evening, the building was packed almost entirely by women who regarded her as the leading champion of the feminist cause both inside and outside the Church. The Guildhouse never succeeded in attracting the intellectuals and artists, which had been the original hope, but by 1924 it was sufficiently well established for Dearmer to leave and return to his other interests. Many in the congregation became Maude's devotees and hung onto her every word, but she never succumbed to the temptation to play to the gallery, and her sermons ranged far more widely than the cause of feminism.

In general she sought to relate faith to the current issues of the day, of which there were in the 1920s and 1930s many of great importance. The coal miners' strike in 1926 found her firmly on the side of the miners and their families and she undertook a preaching tour of the country to plead their cause and to ask, rhetorically, 'Is there a Christian solution of the industrial conflict?' She believed there was: it was the way of justice, fair dealing and reconciliation, and she urged the many opponents of the strike, who lived far from the coalfields, to recognize that coal miners were not a special breed of men called to taxing and often dangerous labour but ordinary people like themselves. Frequent visits to Durham, south Wales and Yorkshire kept her up to date with their plight. She had joined the Labour Party in 1922 and been asked to stand as the Parliamentary candidate for Wirral, but she declined as she thought it best to concentrate on her religious work.

Although Maude left the Fellowship of Reconciliation in 1919 over a policy disagreement, her commitment to the cause of peace never wavered. She believed that the League of Nations offered the best hope of avoiding future wars, and the Guildhouse branch of the UN Union was the largest in the country. The Women's International League, another peace movement formed courageously during the war, continued to claim her time, and in 1923 she undertook a 9,000-mile tour of America in which she gave 75 speeches in 57 cities on 65 days, usually on the subject 'Can we set the world in order?' Many other tours of this sort were undertaken during the 1920s and 1930s and took her to New Zealand, Australia, India, Ceylon, China and Japan, as well as several return visits to America.

Back in England, Maude was elected to the Church Assembly, which met for the first time in 1920, and although she remained a member for only four years, she took the opportunity to join in a campaign for the revision of the Church of England's marriage service. Her proposal that the bride's promise to ' obey' be removed was, however, defeated, although it became optional in the 1928 revision of the Book of Common Prayer, which in spite of its rejection by Parliament became widely used. Her decision not to stand for re-election in 1924 was followed by the laying down of the Presidency of the League of the Church Militant. This was the successor body of the Church League for Women's Suffrage which, when the 1918 extension of the vote was passed, needed either to close down or find a new role.

Maude led the way by proposing that it should now embrace the cause of women's ordained ministry and, although this caused dissension among the members, the League maintained a vigorous life for many more years. Her resignation from the Presidency was prompted by the belief that her own extreme views had become a hindrance to its work. In her final message to the League she noted that in some places women were now being licensed to preach in churches, though only at non-statutory services. She accepted the presidency of the Society for the Ministry of Women, an ecumenical group that succeeded the League in 1930. In the same year she was appointed a Companion of Honour – a rare and high distinction.

The pleasure of this was, however, mitigated by the onset of a serious nervous collapse which surprised none of her friends who had marvelled at the stamina that sustained her multifarious activities. During the previous two years she had largely withdrawn from the Guildhouse, and it was not until 1931 that she was able to return. Mahatma Gandhi, who was in London for an historic Round Table conference, preached at the

Guildhouse, this requiring the police to control the crowds. Aberdeen University made her a Doctor of Divinity – the first woman to be so recognized.

The resurgence of militarism in the 1930s renewed her commitment to peaceful means of solving international problems. The immediate stimulus for this was the outbreak of war between China and Japan over disputed territory in Manchuria, and Maude, together with Dick Sheppard, the remarkable Vicar of St Martin-in-the-Fields, and Dr Herbert Gray, a Presbyterian minister, proposed the formation of what they called a Peace Army. The members of this would, literally, place themselves on the field of battle between the opposing armies, in the expectation that soldiers would not wantonly kill unarmed civilians. The cease-fire would provide an opportunity for negotiation. This proposal received a good deal of publicity and about 400 peace-lovers were quickly recruited. Fortunately, the Manchurian War was soon over and their services were not required. What is more, the government indicated that there would be no scope for a Peace Army in any future conflicts.

The rise of Nazi Germany and the 1938 Munich Agreement took Maude into the Peace Pledge Union and resignation from the League of Nations Union, which was not pacifist in either its beliefs or methods. She believed that the Agreement with Hitler might provide a space in which to promote, perhaps for the last time, the pacifist message and thus prevent another world war. When this failed, and Hitler's intentions became only too plain in 1940, she astonished her friends and many others by renouncing pacifism and declaring that she was sorry ever to have joined the PPU.

Three years earlier, the Guildhouse had come to an end. It was remarkable in many ways that it had lasted so long, since its life was wholly dependent on Maude's gifts and commitment. The 1920s were its best days, and it remained a place of significance during the first half of the 1930s. But the combination of Maude's increasing age and her other work which had become worldwide, brought recognition that the time had come to give it up. This was a great sadness to her, as well as a disappointment that the initial hope of a Guildhouse in every city had never materialized. Following the closure, she maintained contact with those who had been involved by means of a newsletter circulated until almost the end of her life.

The war years inevitably restricted her travel and this was exacerbated by the onset of rheumatism and the deterioration of her lameness. She now began to be used as a broadcaster and after the war this developed into a ministry to the many listeners who wrote to her. The ordination, albeit irregular, of Florence Li Tim-Oi to the priesthood in war-torn Hong Kong in 1944 greatly cheered her, but old age and its limitations became increasingly difficult for her to bear and for a time she turned to spiritual healing for help. A pilgrimage to Walsingham in quest of a cure for deafness brought no physical relief. She retained, however, a certain radiance until almost the end and died in her small cottage in Hampstead on 30 July 1956.

During the immediate post-war years, Maude had spent much time writing *A Threefold Cord*, which appeared in 1947. This intimate account of her relationship with Hudson Shaw aroused a great deal of interest, and many of her friends believed that she should not have published it. But in the foreword she explained, 'This book is written by my husband's wish, but our lives were very full and it was never even begun.' She went on to explain that in the book '"We" means three always: Hudson Shaw, Effie Shaw and myself.'

They were in fact married for eight weeks and three days, though they had by this time been together for 43 years. Long before Effie died in 1944, she made Hudson promise that if she went first he would marry Maude. When the time came, however, he lamented, 'My heart is broken: it is too late, it is too late.' Maude accepted this and thought it to be true, and assured him, 'It has always been hard, let it be hard to the end.' He was now 85, she 68.

Encouraged by many of their friends, however, and by Bishop Christopher Chavasse of Rochester, they were married by him in the village church at Weald on 2 October 1944. A few members of both families were present. That evening, however, he became ill and seemed to be dying and, although by the next morning he appeared to have made a good recovery, he lived for only another two months.

For both of them it had been love at first sight, though they had not immediately recognized this. Their sustained chastity, which was never easy, was grounded in strong Christian principles about right and wrong, as well as acceptance that their mutual love was even more powerful than their physical needs.

Not long after they had moved back in 1907 to the parish of Old Alderley in Cheshire, Shaw became uncertain about the rightness of their relationship and was also anxious lest it stand in the way of Maude meeting and marrying someone else. On this last point, her response was, 'For me there was only one man in the world. If he might not be my husband, no wish for children could make me give my love to someone else.' As to the 'rightness', she had not the slightest doubt about this; neither had Effie, who said they were mad even to contemplate separation. Nonetheless, at Hudson's request Maude went away, though it was not long before he wrote to ask her to return.

In 1912, when he moved to become Rector of St Botolph's, Bishopsgate, there being no Rectory, they lived first in a flat in Bedford Square. Then he and Effie moved to Hampstead Garden Suburb to care for an aged aunt. Since there was no room for Maude in the house, she moved to Poplar, leaving Effie lonely and desperately unhappy. Eventually, Hudson and Effie took an idyllic cottage in a village near Sevenoaks and, by a remarkable coincidence, another cottage next door became vacant and available for Maude to occupy with a friend crippled by arthritis for company. This was not unbroken bliss, since they had some sharp disagreements, even on the issues of women priests and pacifism, and some blazing rows. There were also times when he seemed to resent the love she shared with her close friends. But the relationship was rock solid and their love intensified with the passage of the years. In the end she was moved to write:

> Looking back on my own life I say with conviction, (quoting Robert Browning) 'I regret little, I would change still less.' In our threefold life each of us gave and each of us took. And all of us were the richer for the giving. Hudson and I by Effie's giving as well as Effie by ours.

Missing from this romantic and moving story, however, is Helen, Maude's adopted daughter who is not so much as mentioned in *A Threefold Cord* and, presumably for want of information about her, is given little attention in Sheila Fletcher's fine biography of Maude Royden. Helen was adopted in 1918, her mother having died a few days after her birth, and her father, it is believed, having been killed in the war. She was born prematurely and required careful attention in a nursing home, before Maude could receive her.

This was during the City Temple days, and Maude moved into an attractive house in Hampstead, where she was joined by Evelyn Gunter, a very close friend from Oxford days, and a resident nurse. Some additional domestic staff were recruited later, financed mainly by Maude's family trust. Helen did not call Maude 'Mother' but 'Minkie'. Hudson Shaw, her godfather, was Uncle Bill. And, since Maude was away from home so frequently and so busy when she was at home, Helen was largely brought up by Aunt Evelyn. In due course, she went away to a boarding school, and after her marriage Maude baptized her children. Helen was also present at the time of Maude's death, but it is not clear how close their relationship ever became. The striking omission of her existence from *A Threefold Cord*, even though this was not intended to be an autobiography, suggests that it was not at all close, and the pattern of Maude's life did not leave much space for its nurturing.

For more than 50 years, Maude felt that her vocation to the priesthood was being frustrated by an intransigent Church, but she always saw the ordination of women as part of the total transformation of the Church's life. During the later years of her life, when she recognized that such a transformation would not take place in her lifetime, the sense of frustration became less painful to bear.

14

The Power of the Spirit and of the Pen: Evelyn Underhill and Dorothy L. Sayers

Evelyn Underhill was one of the two foremost early twentieth-century Anglican authorities on Western mysticism, the other being the famous Dean of St Paul's, W. R. Inge. She wrote prolifically on the subject on a variety of levels and produced a classic study, *Mysticism*, which broke new ground and remains the standard work for serious students. At the time of her death in 1941 it was in its thirteenth edition, and it has never been out of print.

Her contribution to the revival of interest in and practice of prayer was strongly reinforced by the development of a ministry of spiritual direction and finally as a conductor of retreats – all previously unheard of from a woman. As a scholar of mysticism she was virtually self-taught, and her own deep spirituality enabled her to exercise a remarkable influence over the many who sought her help.

She was born towards the end of 1875 in Wolverhampton into a family of lawyers. Soon after her birth her father was called to the Bar, and they moved to London to a comfortable, upper middle-class life in a fine house in Campden Hill Place. Her father was interested in philosophy, but religion contributed nothing to her upbringing. When 13, she went to a small boarding school at Sandgate near Folkestone, and her confirmation three years later was little more than an element in the school's curriculum, though the local vicar, who undertook the preparation of the candidates, impressed her.

By the time she was 17, Evelyn was a sophisticated young woman with signs of literary gifts. Her favourite writers were Huxley, Carlisle and Matthew Arnold, while Shakespeare, Milton, Tennyson and Keats were her favourite poets. She confessed to believing in God 'in a general way' and best known through nature and one's fellow human beings. The Bible was an important book but not inspired, and religion called for special concern for the poor and needy. She also confessed to what became a lifelong love of cats.

For several years, travelling extensively with her parents in Europe stimulated an abiding love of art. She also attended King's College, London, which then had a separate women's department, to study botany, languages, philosophy and social science. This was, she thought, the moment to abandon religion, and her late-teens and early twenties were a period of atheism. During this time she also acquired considerable skill in bookbinding.

A near neighbour in Campden Hill Place was another law family, the Moores, and their son, Hubert Stuart, and Evelyn became close friends when they were still quite young. This friendship blossomed, and she wrote affectionate letters to him when on holiday with her parents. It became obvious that they would one day be married, but it was not until 1907 that they were. By this time he too was a very successful lawyer and had inherited the family house which became their new home and the centre of her ministry until the summer of 1939. With war looming, they moved to Highden. Although they had no children, and he was unable to share her religious beliefs as these developed, theirs was a very good marriage. They shared many interests and met each other's needs perfectly. He provided the stability and freedom from financial worry that enabled her to pursue her vocation as a writer and spiritual director, she provided him with the warmth of a loving home and much to stimulate his interests when outside his barrister's chambers.

Her career as a writer started in 1903–4 with the publication of several short stories, some of them in the magazine of the Horlicks company, and what proved to be a successful novel *The Grey World* (1904). But fiction did not provide the right outlet for the expression of her inner feelings which were taking her increasingly into the realms of the occult, magic and the mystical.

The Edwardian era witnessed a reawakening of interest in these matters and in middle-class circles it became a source of considerable fascination. There was nothing specifically Christian about it; instead it was viewed with suspicion and even hostility by the churches. Jacques Maritain, the French Catholic philosopher, said, 'One could not hear it spoken of without immediately being on one's guard against an eventual invasion of fanaticism and hysteria.' Evelyn was, however, drawn into it, and as she went deeper she discovered some of the riches of the Christian mystical tradition, as represented in the writings of great examples of the spiritual life whose work was largely unknown to Anglicans. Hence her writing of *Mysticism*, a task that occupied four years. Sub-titled *A Study of the Nature and Development of Man's Spiritual Consciousness*, the first part is designed to establish its subject as an authentic element in normal human life and experience and to separate it from the outlandish expressions that were giving it a bad name. Thus she examined it from the psychological, symbolic and theological points of view, explaining:

> The mystics are the pioneers of the spiritual world, and we have no right to deny validity to their claims merely because we lack the courage necessary to those who would prosecute such explorations for themselves. A certain type of mind has always discerned three straight and narrow ways going out towards the Absolute in religion, in pain, in beauty with the ecstasy of artistic satisfaction. Down these three paths as well as by many another secret way they claim that news comes to the self-concerning levels of reality, in which their wholeness are inaccessible to the senses – worlds wondrous and immortal whose existence is not conditioned by the 'given' world which those senses report.

It was evident that she had moved beyond the atheism of her earlier years and also that she was not merely an amateur, dabbling in subjects requiring the highest intellectual gifts as well as unusual insight and sensitivity.

The second, much longer part of the book consists of an examination of the lives and writings of many mystics in the Church's history, such as Julian of Norwich, Richard Rolle, Mechthild of Magdeburg, Jan van Ruysbroeck, Jacopone da Todi and William Law, with ample quotations from their works and particular attention given to their mystical experiences. From this she concluded that the traditional three stages in the development of the spiritual life – the ways of Purgation, Illumination and Union – could be more helpfully enlarged to five stages, starting with the Awakening of Self, moving on to the Purgation of Self, then to Illumination, followed by the Dark Night, and finally the Unitive Life, beautifully described by Ruysbroeck, her favourite:

> When love has carried us above all things into the Divine Dark, here we are transformed by the Eternal Word who is the image of the Father,

and as the air is penetrated by the sun, thus we receive in peace the incomprehensible Light, enfolding us, and penetrating us.

Aware that this understanding of prayer might encourage an inward-looking, self-absorbed contentment in its practitioners, she went on to emphasize that the state of Union is authenticated by more active involvement in the service of the Kingdom of God. True growth in the spiritual life, with its sometimes marvellous, radiant experiences, is linked inseparably with the day-to-day activities of ordinary men and women. The book ends with a valuable Who's Who of mysticism, demonstrating its continuity across the centuries.

The publication of *Mysticism* brought her almost instant fame, as well as a flood of letters and many invitations to address meetings of clergy. The fact that the author was a woman added to the sense of novelty. She was quick to point out, however, that, far from being herself a master of the subject, she was, a mere beginner. As she put it in reply to a correspondent who spoke of sitting at her feet, 'If you knew the real animal you would be provoked either to tears or laughter at the absurdity of the idea. I am not "far on" but at the very bottom.'

Among others who wrote to her about the book was Baron Friedrich von Hügel, whose close friendship became of the greatest significance to her, and she was largely responsible for making his work more widely known. He was a Roman Catholic layman of considerable erudition who was born in Florence, but after his marriage in 1873 spent the rest of life in London's Hampstead and Kensington, though he often travelled abroad. Sympathy with the 'Modernist Movement' in the Roman Catholic Church led to friendships with several of its leaders, and he also developed insights into the nature of mysticism and saw the institutional, the intellectual and the mystical as the three abiding elements in all religion. He became a significant spiritual influence in England's cultural circles, though mainly outside his own church, and was widely used as a spiritual director.

When he first contacted Evelyn, she had for several years been struggling with a decision whether or not to become a Roman Catholic. Movement out of atheism had been encouraged by friendships with several fellow-writers who were Roman Catholics and she was attracted by the combination of beauty and devotion she found in their churches. A visit, with one of these friends, to a convent of French Franciscan nuns in Southampton, this being known as a convent of Perpetual Adoration, had a profound effect upon her and after four days she fled, fearing that if she stayed longer she would be converted.

A serious obstacle to conversion was the attitude of her husband for whom the sticking point was that, if she became a Roman Catholic, she would be going to Confession. He felt that this secret disclosure of her sins and other spiritual problems to a priest would interpose a third person between them. During the course of her struggle, she consulted a number of wise Anglican and Roman Catholics who offered advice of a high order, and von Hügel joined them. None attempted to persuade her one way or another, and in the end she decided to throw in her lot with the Anglican Church, not so much because of the Confession issue but because the papal condemnation of 'Modernism' removed the only form of Roman Catholicism with which she could identify. In 1921 she became a regular communicant and thereafter was publicly known as a member of the Church of England. Nonetheless von Hügel, now her friend, was also her spiritual director until his death in 1925.

Meanwhile her own work as a spiritual director had grown rapidly, and the fact that she was a woman did not discourage many priests, and some bishops, from turning to her for counsel. She saw a very large number in her home in Campden Hill Place and advised even more by means of a voluminous correspondence. The depth of her spiritual insights and the caring humanity with which she shared these is to be seen in *The Letters of Evelyn Underhill*, edited by Charles Williams, published not long after her death and now a classic.

A retreat at Pleshey in Essex in 1924 proved to be another turning point in her life. She knew the warden of the retreat house and decided she needed a period of sustained prayer, not having had one since her visit to the convent in Southampton. This led to an abiding affection for the house which became her spiritual home. She helped to beautify it and before long was herself conducting retreats there. These continued until almost the end of her life, attracting over the years a very large number of grateful retreatants. Again, a woman retreat conductor had not been heard of before and retreats were themselves uncommon in the Church of England. In 1913 there was just one retreat house; by 1932 there were 22 diocesan houses and over thirty more belonging to religious communities.

Evelyn's literary output was considerable. Books, articles, pamphlets and translations poured from her pen and she had an attractive readable style, as well as an eye for illuminating analogies. She collaborated with Rabindranath Tagore in the translation of Hindu poetry and for several years was religious editor of *The Spectator* which in those days had a regular religious section to which theologians and leading churchmen contributed articles. Most of her writing, however, was concerned with various aspects of prayer and spirituality, and her last substantial work was *Worship*, written at the request of W. R. Matthews (Inge's successor at St Paul's) for the Library of Constructive Theology. Published in 1936, this is a wide-ranging survey of the nature of worship and the forms of worship offered by Jews and the main Christian traditions. The liturgy of the Orthodox Churches was of special interest to her as it expresses corporately what she regarded as the essentials of personal devotion. Her knowledge and value of liturgical worship increased greatly with the passage of time and she was among those who campaigned for a revision of the Book of Common Prayer in 1928.

While not creating the same excitement as *Mysticism*, *Worship* was welcomed as providing a study of its subject that was accessible to the non-specialist reader, not least to the clergy responsible for worship in parish churches. That it should have been written by a woman surprised many, and the book shows clear signs of a growing understanding of the central place of the Eucharist in the life both of the Church and the individual Christian. She concludes:

If Christianity be indeed the disclosure of the Eternal God to men, it follows that the Eucharistic principle, the free offering and consecration of the natural life, that it may become the sensible vehicle of the Divine life must radiate beyond its ritual expression, gradually penetrating and transforming all the actions of humanity. This will mean that every sacrificial life, whatever its apparent incentive, is woven into the garment of the Church's worship.

The years following the publication of this book were a time of declining health and activity for both her and her husband. However, she continued to receive many who needed her counsel, and wrote a number of small books – *Abba*, meditations based on the Lord's Prayer, and her last book, sold 5,000 copies within a few months of its publication in 1940. A pamphlet *The Church and War* was written for the Anglican

147

Pacifist Fellowship which she had joined shortly before the outbreak of war. Aberdeen University made her an honorary Doctor of Divinity, King's College, London, a Fellow, and she died on 15 June 1941. No one had done more to encourage greater concern for the spiritual life or to help others to pray better.

In the 1960s, however, there was a reaction against her and her methods, as there was against much else that was traditional and thought to be out of date. Liturgical change and increased social action were believed to be the highest priority. The charge was led by Valerie Pitt in the June 1959 number of *Prism* – the journal of the Church of England's new reform movement. Miss Pitt, a highly regarded literary critic, was an Anglo-Catholic and politically left wing. Her pen was both entertaining and devastating, and an article headed 'Clouds of Unknowing' used the publication of Margaret Copper's biography of Evelyn Underhill as the basis of a scathing attack on her approach to spirituality. The gist of this was that she spoke only to a cosy, comfortable middle-class coterie, and that her concern was only with the welfare of the individual soul and not with the physical needs of the poor and the homeless. Her work attracted 'the respectable Anglican ladies with their copies of *Mysticism*, the young clergymen describing through fumes of coffee the spiritual clarity which follows a retreat spent in fasting'.

Now it is true that Evelyn Underhill's influence was confined to clergymen and comfortably placed middle-class lay people. But virtually all spiritual leaders have had devotees of a particular kind, and there has yet to emerge one who is able to speak meaningfully of the spiritual life to the artisan classes who are, and have been for a very long time, alienated from the Church of England. What is not true is that she had no concern for social issues. Naturally these did not loom large in her letters to people seeking spiritual guidance, but there is much of them in her writing, and her concern was expressed with considerable force in a lecture on 'The Spiritual and the Secular' given to the first Anglo-Catholic Summer School of Sociology in 1925:

> The sacramental principle is operative over the whole range of life, in countless ways and degrees, and we are obliged to hold that God comes to many through and in natural means. We must therefore improve those natural means in every department of experience. And so we are bound to be personally active in these matters because our own

sanctification is only the first of two movements and is chiefly important in making us instruments with which the Spirit of God, indwelling in history, does his work.

The best short introduction to her thought is contained in *The Spiritual Life*, four talks broadcast and published in 1937. These still read freshly and have a timeless character. Her friend T. S. Eliot said, 'Her genius was that she understood the grievous need of her contemporaries for the contemplative element in their lives.'

*   *   *

The life of Dorothy L. Sayers was important and fascinating enough to have attracted several biographies, the titles of two of which – *Such a Strange Woman* and *Dorothy L. Sayers – A Courageous Woman* – suggest someone quite out of the ordinary. She certainly was. She applied her very considerable intellectual and literary gifts, in sequence, to the writing of classic detective stories, the communication of the Christian faith and the translation of Dante. Her fame was worldwide and, besides her writings, remains alive in a Dorothy L. Sayers Society, a portrait in the National Portrait Gallery and a statue outside the house in Witham, Essex, where much of her life was spent and where she died in 1957.

Dorothy L. Sayers was born in Oxford in 1893. Her father, a clergy-man and a Classicist, was at the time headmaster of Christ Church Cathedral Choir School, but when she was only four became Rector of Bluntisham in Huntingdonshire. This was the richest of the Christ Church livings, though the very fine Rectory had no running water and was lit only by oil lamps. Nonetheless it housed not only Dorothy's parents and herself, but also a grandmother and an aunt, as well as a large retinue of servants.

She was educated at home by her father and a series of governesses until she was 16 when she went to Godolphin School at Salisbury. Her two years there were not happy, but she was academically precocious and won a scholarship to Somerville College, Oxford. A somewhat flamboyant style and a sharp tongue led to an inauspicious start to her time as an undergraduate but she secured a First in Modern (that is medieval) French and the praise of her examiners who described her translation as 'unsurpassed in distinction of elegance, gaiety and style'. She also found time to sing in the Oxford Bach Choir, flirting with its distinguished conductor, and absorbed enough of college life to enable her much later to write *Gaudy Night*, generally regarded as her best novel and highly controversial at the time of its publication since several of the dons could be easily identified.

She left wartime Oxford in 1915 to become Modern Languages Mistress at Hull High School for Girls, where she was popular with her pupils but less so with her colleagues who found her, as did many others, opinionated and argumentative. After two years she returned to Oxford to learn from Basil Blackwell the skills of publishing, and it was while attending a social gathering in his house that she received her first proposal of marriage. This was from the Revd Leonard Hodgson, at that time Vice-Principal of St Edward's Hall but on his way to becoming a distinguished Regius Professor of Divinity at Oxford. She turned him down, which was, at least for Hodgson, probably just as well.

Instead she fell madly in love with Captain Eric Whelpton who had been invalided out of the Army in 1918 because of ill-health and returned to Oxford to complete a wartime degree. This achieved, he took a teaching post in Normandy and, although in love with another woman, invited Dorothy to join him as an administrator and fill-in teacher at the school. Before long, however, he moved to Florence to pursue another career, leaving her stranded in Normandy. Short of money, she returned to England, took a few temporary teaching posts in London before joining in 1921 S. H. Benson, the largest advertising agency in the country.

This was intended to be no more than a stop-gap job until she was successful enough to become a full-time writer, but the gap extended to ten years. During this time her gift with words and her wit were put to good use in the composition of arresting slogans and jingles, and she played an important part in advertising campaigns for Guinness and Colman's Mustard, which are said to have changed the face of advertising in Britain. But she had already started to collect the works of Arthur Conan Doyle and other leading writers of detective stories, and she decided, correctly, that it was in this field that she would be likely to make the most money. Her own first detective story, *Whose Body?*, appeared in 1923 after being rejected by several publishers on the grounds of its coarseness – the vital clue being whether or not the victim had been circumcised. But the public were less prudish and although the sales were not sensational they were good enough to encourage the publisher to contract her to produce another volume, *Cloud of Witnesses* (1926), which also enjoyed some success.

Among the admirers of her work was one of the publisher's young editors, Victor Gollancz, who decided to start his own publishing house and persuaded Dorothy to change her allegiance to him. In the end, she wrote 12 detective-story novels, most of which became world best-sellers, brought her international fame and established her as one of the best-ever authors in this field. They are marked by a vivid writing style, meticulous character portrayal, ingenious plots, the use of literary allusions and sometimes untranslated French and German; but most of all by their central character, Lord Peter Wimsey – an aristocratic amateur detective. The best of them, *The Nine Taylors* (1934), was prompted by a small book on the art of bell-ringing, which she picked up in a second-hand bookshop. The Rector of the parish which provided the scene of the plot bore a marked resemblance to her father, to whom she was devoted. In reality this godly priest, who had moved to a less well-endowed parish in rural Cambridgeshire, was the recipient of some painful shocks at the hands of his only child. Dorothy's arrival at the Rectory door, clad in trousers and smoking a cigarette, was, to say the least, unconventional in the 1920s and the cause of comment in the parish.

Much worse was to come: in June 1923 she revealed to her parents that she was pregnant. This was the consequence of a short-lived, almost casual encounter with a man whom she did not love and who quickly moved out of her life. She took six months leave from Bensons, ostensibly to write a book, and when the baby was born – a boy, given the names Anthony John – he was put in the care of a cousin who, with her mother, fostered children for a living. Dorothy was undoubtedly shocked by the moral, as well as the psychological and social aspects of this experience; but the suggestion sometimes made, that she carried a burden of guilt for the rest of her life, seems highly unlikely. As a High Anglican she went regularly to Confession and believed in the Grace of Absolution. Much later *The Other Six Deadly Sins* was a diatribe against the Church's apparent preoccupation with lust. Another suggestion – that she hated children and had no further contact with John (the name she used) – was certainly untrue. She visited him, wrote to him, provided financial support and gifts, and when he was grown up took great pride in his achievements. When she married, it was on the understanding that she and her husband would adopt him, but this never happened, owing it seems to her husband's reluctance.

This marriage proved to be a long way from satisfactory for her. Oswald Arthur Fleming, who was 12 years her senior, had served in the Royal Army Service Corps during the 1914–18 war, though he claimed a much more gallant record. He was now the motoring correspondent of the *News of the World* and a competent journalist, but lacked staying power. He had been previously married, but divorced for adultery, so their wedding had of necessity to take place in a registrar's office (another disappointment to her parents). Dorothy soon realized she had made a terrible mistake, but for some years she and Mac (as he was usually known) got on well enough and up to a point enjoyed their relationship. Yet he was unable to earn a living and relied entirely on Dorothy's income from writing. He turned to painting, for which he had good amateur skill, but did not persevere, then to the bottle with which unfortunately he did persevere.

Although the marriage survived until his death in 1950, the life had gone out of it much earlier as the gap between a weak character and his famously accomplished wife widened. Dorothy herself could hardly have been an easy companion. She had a good deal of the eccentricity that often accompanies genius and was not born to compromise or accommodate. She dressed in well-tailored suits, skirt and tie, short hair, a trilby hat – and her style was mannish. She argued, however, that women should be free to wear whatever clothes they felt most comfortable in, though not braces, 'those machines of leather and elastic' which she believed to be 'hideous beyond description'. For some years she rode a motor-cycle. Following the birth of John she indulged in over-eating and soon became grossly overweight – a condition in which she remained until the end of her days. She did not suffer fools gladly, but she was essentially a kind, generous Christian woman whom her friends loved. Her larger than life extroversion was really a cover for a deep shyness.

A turning point in her professional life came in 1936, when the Friends of Canterbury Cathedral invited her to write a play for their 1937 Festival. The two previous plays, written in verse, had been T. S. Eliot's *Murder in the Cathedral* and Charles Williams' *Thomas Cranmer of Canterbury*, but it was emphasized that she need not feel confined to verse, even though she had published some poetry. In the event, *The Zeal of Thine House* – an examination of the motives of William of Sens, the architect responsible for the rebuilding of the cathedral's choir in the twelfth century – proved to be hugely successful and a landmark in religious drama. This success was not easy to maintain and *The Devil to Pay* (Canterbury 1939), *The Just Vengeance* (Lichfield 1946) and *The Emperor Constantine* (Colchester, for the Festival of Britain 1951), while good enough, made much less impact.

Dorothy's evident skill led, however, to an invitation by the BBC to write a Nativity Play for radio, broadcast at Christmas 1938. *He That Should Come* attracted much praise, including a letter from Mrs Winston Churchill. It also marked the resumption of her relationship with the BBC, which had been broken four years earlier when she took umbrage, because the announcer of some of her frequent talks and appearances on Woman's Hour sometimes introduced her as Dorothy Sayers instead of Dorothy L. Sayers – always a cause of great offence.

The success of *He That Should Come* inspired the Head of Religious Broadcasting, James Welch, to ask her to write a 12-part series of 30 minutes on the Life of Christ designed for transmission in *Children's Hour*. She agreed on condition that she be allowed to have an actor (in the end Robert Speight) portray Jesus in person and also use the modern idiom for the language of the other characters. Both requirements were innovative, potentially highly controversial and, in the case of the portrayal of Jesus, thought to require the consent of the Lord Chamberlain – until 1968 the censor of all stage plays. Nonetheless James Welch told her 'not to spare the dynamite' and she added the demand that she should be consulted fully over the production and casting of the plays.

The challenge, as Dorothy saw it, was to create a dramatic narrative that would be believable by an audience that was essentially pagan, and at the same time remain faithful to the theology of the Gospels. It was imperative therefore that Jesus be presented as a real human being ('The Word was made flesh') and not as a sort of symbolic figure doing nothing but preach in elegant periods when all the people around him are talking in everyday style. The writing of the plays occupied her for most of the next two years, when she was greatly helped by Archbishop William Temple's recently published *Readings in St John's Gospel* and the work of the Cambridge scholar, Sir Edwyn Hoskyns, on St John's Gospel.

The production of the series, entitled *The Man Born to be King*, was fraught with problems. Most of these were related to the conflict between the views of Dorothy and those of the professional broadcasters over the details of presentation. James Welch and his colleagues received her scripts with great enthusiasm, but there were points at which minor adjustments were desirable in presentations for children. Dorothy would have none of this and after one disagreement withdrew from the project, returning her contract torn into many pieces in the envelope containing her resignation. That she was brought back into the fold and the series was ready for broadcasting on 21 December 1941 owed everything to the theological, broadcasting and pastoral skills of Welch who saw it as offering a breakthrough in religious broadcasting and a unique opportunity to present the Christian faith to a war-torn nation.

The expected controversy began before the first broadcast when, at a Press Conference, some of the dialogue was recited. The earthy language of this shocked a representative of the Lord's Day Observance Society who was present, and the journalists made hay with sensational headlines over exaggerated reports. The Central Religious Advisory Council, chaired since its inception by Cyril Garbett, soon to become Archbishop of York, was drawn into the controversy but, although he had a few reservations, the Council offered its strong backing.

As predicted by Welch, *The Man Born to be King* made broadcasting history. It was moved away from *Children's Hour* but was watched by innumerable children and young people as well as by over two million adults. The opposition was only marginal, otherwise there was widespread praise, and Archbishop William Temple of Canterbury described it as 'one of the great contributions to the religious life of our times'. It was repeated, either in full or in part, for several successive years and a printed version ran to over 30 editions.

There were a number of other books, of which easily the most important was *The Mind of the Maker* (1941), a short work of considerable erudition. This expressed her own Christian faith, which can best be described as radical orthodoxy (fundamental dogma, without frills) and it attracted a good deal of attention from other theologians. Of particular interest was her use of the concept of Creativeness as an analogy of the Trinity. The artist's work and the labour of others are all an expression of the creativity of the triune God – as true of the work of women as that of men. She also joined, in her characteristically pugnacious way, in the wartime debate about post-war reconstruction of society, but although her ideas were radical enough she was careful to disassociate them from any movement hinting of socialism.

Her devotion to Dante was stimulated by a review of his book *The Figure of Beatrice* written by Charles Williams in 1943 for the *Sunday Times*. Admiration for Williams, rather than Dante, made her determined to read *The Divine Comedy*, but she never got round to this until she grabbed a copy of the *Inferno* to read in an air-raid shelter one night in August 1944 when Hitler's V1 rockets were arriving.

Believing that she could improve on the translation, she set about producing one of her own and Dante became the last love of her life. The next three years were devoted to *Inferno*, the longest of the books, and she then moved on to *Purgatory*, which appeared in 1955. Only 20 cantos of *Paradise* had been completed when she died, and the remainder were taken on by an Italian scholar, Barbara Reynolds, a close friend of her later years and her best biographer. The translation in annotated English verse was in Dorothy's own vivid style and introduced *The Divine Comedy* to a wide readership through its inclusion in the new Penguin Classics series.

Besides this absorbing task, she remained busy about many other matters – writing essays, addressing meetings and dealing with a mountain of correspondence. Membership of the high-powered Christendom Group provided an outlet for her work as a moralist. For many years she had, whenever in London, attended the Anglo-Catholic All Saints, Margaret Street, but towards the end of her life became churchwarden of St Thomas's, Regent Street. The church had been severely damaged by wartime bombing and the parish was now absorbed into that of St Anne's, Soho, where the church, apart from its tower, had suffered destruction. Worship and meetings were held in the adjacent St Anne's House and it was there that her ashes were finally interred.

It was soon after the death of her father in 1928 that Dorothy and Mac bought a pretty Georgian house at Witham, in Essex. This was occupied initially by her mother and Aunt Mabel, but only briefly, since her mother survived for only another ten months. Thereafter it was Dorothy's main home and where, having spent the previous day Christmas shopping in London, she was found in the morning of 18 December 1957 dead at the foot of the stairs.

Dorothy tended to distance herself from the feminist movement of her time and believed that aggressive feminism might do more harm than good. In an address, *Are Women Human?*, to a Women's Society in 1938, she argued that men and women should not be classified as such in respect of their employment, but individual men and individual women should be judged only in regard to their capacity to do particular jobs. She did not, however, go on to suggest what reordering of society might be needed to allow this judgement to be made. She was nonetheless in no doubt that the Church's attitude to women was altogether wrong and she concluded an essay, 'The Human-not-quite-Human' in characteristically engaging style:

> Perhaps it is no wonder that the women were first at the Cradle and last at the Cross. They have never known a man like this Man – there never had been such another. A prophet and a teacher who never nagged at them, never flattered or coaxed or patronised, who never made jokes about them, never treated them as 'The women, God help us!' or 'The ladies, God bless them!'; who rebuked without querulousness and praised without condescension; who took their questions and arguments seriously; who never mapped out their sphere for them, never urged them to be feminine or jeered at them for being female; who had no axe to grind and no uneasy male dignity to defend; who took them as he found them and was completely unselfconscious. There is no act, no sermon, or parable in the whole Gospel that borrows its pungency from female perversity; nobody could possibly guess from the words and deeds of Jesus that there was anything 'funny' about women's nature.
>
> But we might easily deduce it from his contemporaries, and from his prophets before him, and from his church to this day. Women are not human; nobody shall persuade that they are human; let them say what they like, we will not believe it, though One rose from the dead.

During her lifetime the issue of women's place in the ministry of the Church had received little attention. When C. S. Lewis wrote to her in 1948, expressing his own concern and seeking her views on the ordination of Florence Li Tim-Oi to the priesthood in Hong Kong four years earlier, she responded by doubting that what he had heard could possibly be true. But if it was, 'nothing could be more silly and inexpedient than to erect a new and totally unnecessary barrier between us and the rest of Catholic Christendom'. She warned that he would find her an uneasy ally in any agitation against the ordination of women, and this for reasons that showed her to be well ahead of most of her contemporaries on the fundamental issue:

> I can never find any logical or strictly theological reason against it. Insofar as the priest represents Christ, it is obviously more dramatically appropriate that a man should, so to speak, be cast for that part. But if I were cornered and asked point blank whether Christ Himself is the representative of male humanity or all humanity, I should be obliged to answer 'of all humanity'; and to cite the authority of St. Augustine for saying that woman is also made in the image of God.

Her concern was with the ecumenical factor and in particular relations with the Eastern Orthodox with whom, at last, there seemed some prospect of understanding. So, 'The most I can do is keep silence in any place where the daughters of the Philistines might overhear me.'

15

A Sign of Hope from the Orient: Florence Li Tim-Oi

In June 1938 Florence Li Tim-Oi (known later, for convenience, simply as Florence Li) returned to her native Hong Kong, having just completed a course of training at the Union Theological College at Canton, in mainland China. The Bishop of Hong Kong, Ronald Hall, appointed her to minister to the Chinese congregation at All Saints Church in nearby Kowloon, and during the next two years she conducted Bible study and confirmation and marriage preparation classes for the church's regular members, together with pioneering work among the thousands of refugees who were fleeing across the border to escape the Sino-Japanese war then ongoing.

In 1940, by which time world war was gathering momentum, Florence was moved to Macao, a Portuguese colony some 35 miles away. Since Portugal was not at war with Japan, Macao was relatively safe, even though surrounded by Japanese forces. There Florence continued her ministry and after six months went back briefly to Hong Kong to be ordained deacon in St John's Cathedral. Deacon and deaconess were interchangeable terms in the Chinese Church, and, since there was no resident priest in Macao, she was authorized, among other things, to baptize and to conduct weddings and funerals. A priest travelled across once a month to celebrate the Eucharist.

Following the occupation of Hong Kong by the Japanese on Christmas Day 1941, this was no longer possible and Florence found herself ministering to the physical and spiritual needs of refugees who used Macao as a transit camp before moving on to what they hoped would be safety elsewhere. The priest who had normally celebrated the monthly Eucharist was no longer able to leave Hong Kong, so he wrote to the Chinese assistant bishop, Bishop Mok, who was located outside the colony at Pak-hoi, and said that in the exceptional circumstances of war 'It is good for you to authorize Florence Li to celebrate Holy Communion.'

Bishop Hall, who was away from Hong Kong when it was occupied, was now running the diocese from Chungking, not yet under Japanese control. Having heard from Bishop Mok, he issued a licence in 1942 authorizing Florence to minister fully to her congregation of 150 people – a move which they enthusiastically endorsed. A year later, however, he wrote to the Archbishop of Canterbury, William Temple, reporting this action, adding that if he had been able to reach her physically, he would have ordained her to the priesthood, since he believed that presiding at the Eucharist by a layman was 'more contrary to the tradition and meaning of the ordained ministry than to ordain a woman'. He went on to say that he was reporting his action and views to the Chinese General Synod and hoped that when the Lambeth Conference was able to meet again it would allow such ordinations wherever there was a shortage of priests.

The Archbishop could not agree, though he had long since reached the conclusion that there were no theological grounds for refusing ordination to women and that their common humanity might require this. It seems fair to assume that, given his national leadership responsibilities during the dark days of world war, this bombshell from an isolated part of the Far East was a most unwelcome distraction. He therefore wrote to Hall later that year advising him that in the serious state of emergency it would be better for Sister Florence to continue to celebrate as a deacon(ess) than for her to be ordained as a priest, since this latter course would give her a permanent status beyond the emergency.

Hall was not prepared to accept this advice. In his letter to Archbishop Temple he had described Florence's exemplary and courageous ministry. At Macao she was ministering to a congregation composed largely of schoolmasters, university lecturers and returned students in business and government posts:

We had no one else with the culture and ability to hold that congregation. Her work has been remarkably successful. My judgement is that only exceptional women can do this kind of work. But we are going to have such exceptional women in China and such exceptional need. Moreover, working as a minister in charge of a congregation, Deaconess Li has developed, as a man-pastor develops, and has none of that frustrated fussiness that is noticeable in women who having the pastoral charisma are denied its full exercise in the ministry of the Church. (Sorry if that sounds like a speech. I know you will understand.)

He now wrote to Florence to travel to Xingxing, which was also still under Chinese control, where he would ordain her to the priesthood. The journey, which involved crossing part of Japanese-held China, took about a week and was hazardous. She started travelling by bicycle and boat to a port on the mainland, where she was met by a family who provided her with a sedan chair and two male bearers. They carried her through mountains and villages, taking care to avoid Japanese guards and soldiers, to the home of the pastor in Xingxing. There she met Bishop Hall and, after a few days of talk and prayer, they went together to the small, old Anglican church at Zhaoqing, a few miles away.

The congregation, though small, filled the church. It included the local pastor and his congregation, together with a Baptist minister and members of the local institution for the blind. The ordinal was that attached to the Book of Common Prayer as used throughout the Anglican Communion. It was St Paul's Day, 25 January 1944, and a modest celebratory lunch was held afterwards.

Reflecting on the occasion many years later in a book *Much Beloved Daughter* (1985) written in collaboration with Ted Harrison, Florence said,

God had brought me through many dangers to the place, it strengthened my belief that it was his will that I become a priest. Here was I, a simple girl wishing to devote my life to his service. The wider issues of the ordination of women were far from my mind as I entered the little church. I was being obedient to God's call. The notion that this step I was taking would be controversial and have worldwide repercussions was something that never occurred to me until I had returned to Macao and the war was over.

Two days after the ordination, Bishop Hall wrote to Archbishop Temple to tell him of the steps he had taken. He said that he recognized that he had not acted as a bishop of the Anglican Church in China but only as one concerned to meet a need in his own diocese. He did not expect anyone else to recognize her orders at present, but at the first General Synod to be held after the war he would press for the ordination of women to be accepted and regularized. 'I have had an amazing feeling of quiet conviction about this – as if it was how God wanted it to happen, rather than a formal regularization first.'

Temple responded briefly to the effect that he would make no official comment until he had heard the reaction of the Chinese Church's House of Bishops. But wartime conditions made it impossible for Hall to communicate with his widely spread fellow bishops, and he decided not to tell any of his own clergy in occupied territory, since they would be arrested and interrogated if it became known that they had been in touch with him. Meanwhile Florence was back in Macao continuing her ministry and, with the end of the war coming into sight, in conditions somewhat easier for food and freedom than for several years.

The silence about the ordination was broken, however, when a short report of the event which had appeared in a New Zealand church magazine reached the eyes of Dr G. L. Prestige, the scholarly editor of the *Church Times*. He immediately wrote to the Archbishop to seek confirmation of the report. Temple was in a quandary and in a long letter told Prestige of the circumstances of the 'most grave pastoral emergency which induced the bishop to act as he did'. He expected the Chinese Church's bishops to refer the matter to the next Lambeth Conference in order that guidance might be offered to all the Provinces. He concluded by confessing that 'If we could find any shadow of theological ground for the non-ordination of women, I should be immensely comforted, but such arguments as I have heard on that seem to me quite desperately futile.'

Once the *Church Times* had published its report and comments there was no shortage of learned and unlearned readers ready to assure the Archbishop, whose health was now failing, that there could be no inch of theological ground to offer him comfort. Even Alec Vidler, the liberal Dean of King's College, Cambridge, maintained that there could be no assurance that the ministerial actions of Florence Li in relation to the Eucharist were actions of the Church. The 1920 Lambeth Conference had decreed that the order of deaconesses was the one and only order open to women, and the validity of actions taken by individual bishops who disregarded this was therefore open to serious doubt, no matter the circumstance which had motivated them.

At this point Temple's ill-health brought the Bishop of London, Geoffrey Fisher, into the picture. The Archbishop had drafted a long letter to Bishop Hall which he asked Fisher to take to the House of Bishops for approval. This was not given. Temple was anxious to separate the theological question, about which he had an open mind, from the ecclesiological issue of the regularity or irregularity of Hall's action. But Bishop George Bell and others thought that by doing this he was 'multiplying difficulties' for himself and that it was unnecessary to deal with the question of why notice of the ordination had not been taken earlier. All that was needed was a brief letter stating the irregularity and therefore the invalidity of the ordination.

Temple agreed to do this, but was unhappy with the negative tone of the resulting letter which now included the phrase 'High authorities have declared that a woman is incapable of receiving the Grace of Orders.' He toyed therefore with the idea of enclosing a letter of his own. The bishops somewhat reluctantly accepted this but asked that the official letter should include the phrase 'ultra vires', and Fisher wrote to the Archbishop urging him to add, also, 'I must say that this ordination cannot be recognized as such in the Church of England.'

But Temple never saw this letter as he died on the day it was written. The official letter was therefore sent on 3 November 1944, unsigned, to Hong Kong by the Archbishop's chaplain, who kept in touch with Bishop Hall until Geoffrey Fisher became the new Primate in January of the following year. Fisher read and endorsed it at his first meeting of the Convocation of Canterbury where there was general agreement with the contents, not least the emphatic sentence, 'I feel obliged to tell you that I do profoundly deplore the action you took and have to regard it as *ultra vires.*'

Hall returned on leave to England in July 1945 and had a long conversation with Fisher at Lambeth Palace, in the course of which the Archbishop, in his best headmasterly manner, sought to persuade him to change his position. But he lacked jurisdiction over the Bishop of Hong Kong and, when Hall said that he would abide by the decision of the Chinese House of Bishops (though he would resign if this went against him), he told him, firmly, that 'the proper course is for you to suspend this woman from all priestly functions pending the decision of your House of Bishops'.

It was some time (not until March 1946) before the Chinese Church's bishops, almost all of whom were at that time Westerners, could meet to consider the matter. Meanwhile Archbishop Fisher made another attempt, by letter, to persuade him, and to this Hall sent, in September 1945, a considered and moving reply:

> I write with intense personal regret to say that I am unable to accept your advice. I have only one reason. I acted in obedience to our Lord's Commission. I do not believe He wishes me to undo what I have done. That is my reaction to you as chairman of the Anglican Communion who have shown me such consideration and kindness, but I must try and say a little more. It was basically a pastoral situation out of which this ordination arose. Ecclesiastically I know – to quote Archbishop Temple – my action was *ultra vires.* Spiritually I know it was not. I beg you, my dear Archbishop, to have no anxiety about the future – or that the handling of this matter by our Synod and bringing it to the Lambeth Conference, will do harm to the church of God. What is wrongly done will perish; what is truly done will only strengthen Christ's church.

Meanwhile Florence Li was continuing her work in Macao, largely unaware of the controversy her ordination was causing until, with Bishop Hall away, his secretary, the Revd George She, who was also the Archdeacon, recalled her to Hong Kong for few days, as he had something very important to tell her. This was:

> The bishops at the Lambeth Conference (scheduled for 1948) will not accept your ordination. Bishop Hall is in a very difficult situation. Either he resigns as a bishop or you forfeit the title of priest. If you carry on as a priest he will have to leave his work in Hong Kong.

This was painful news, but her response was immediate. She wrote to the Bishop to say she supported him and had never claimed any fame or position in the Church – 'I want only to carry on my work for Jesus Christ . . . I would like to keep quiet to help the Church. You are an important man. I am a mere worm, a tiny little worm.'

When the Chinese Church's House of Bishops finally met, they had before them the advice they had sought from Archbishop Fisher. This was uncompromising. He warned that if they were to support Bishop Hall's action, this would be 'an overwhelming disaster' for the Anglican Communion, and he had no doubt that some Provinces would question whether they should remain in communion with the Chinese Church. It was their duty, therefore, to say to Bishop Hall, 'You are wrong . . . such a breach of Catholic precedent is only to be contemplated if the whole church were able to agree upon it.' He told the Presiding Bishop that 'it grieves me greatly to advise you to take this course, but I am perfectly sure it is right. Bishop Hall is so good and so glorious that to rebuke him in this way is beyond words grievous'. The bishops took this advice and passed a resolution that was then released to the public:

> This House regrets the uncanonical action of the Bishop of Hong Kong in ordaining Deaconess Tim Oi Li to the priesthood, and having understood that Deaconess Li has already placed in his hands her resignation from her priestly ministry this House requests the Bishop of Hong Kong to accept it. The Bishop of Hong Kong has acted in accordance with this Resolution.

This provoked a fierce reaction from the Synod of the diocese of Hong Kong, which issued a strongly worded statement:

> Members of this church find the attitude of the church in the West impossible to understand. The Reverend Tim Oi Li's ordination seemed to them natural and inevitable. She has shown in her life and work that God has given her the 'charisma' of the parish priest.
>
> It is our belief that the action by Bishop Mok in licensing Tim Oi Li to celebrate the Lord's Supper, and Bishop Hall's action later in ordaining her to the priesthood, were God inspired. We believe that God is using China's age-long respect for women and traditional confidence in women's gifts for administration and counsel, to open a new chapter in the history of the church. It is noteworthy that Chinese motherhood has been more remarkable in counsel and leadership than in nurture of babies, i.e. essentially pastoral rather than maternal. We believe that the Western churches should expect new things such as this to happen under God's providence, when Christianity really begins to take root in a civilisation as mature as that of China.

In the following year the bishops, prompted no doubt by Bishop Hall, resolved to submit to the forthcoming Lambeth Conference a proposal that for an experimental period of 20 years, suitably qualified deaconesses should be ordained to the priesthood in the Chinese Church. They were to be at least 30 years of age, unmarried and intending to remain unmarried. At the end of 20 years the provision would lapse unless renewed by the Chinese bishops, though women already ordained could continue their ministries for the rest of their lifetimes. Fisher protested against this but the bishops stood firm in their proposals. These were then remitted to a committee of the 1948 Lambeth Conference which included several Chinese bishops, but they were rejected by both the committee and the full Conference. So that was that for another 23 years when the Anglican Consultative Council finally agreed that Provinces might ordain women priests and Florence immediately resumed her own priestly ministry.

Back in Hong Kong it had by 1948 already been recognized that she could no longer continue to exercise leadership of the church in Macao, so she had been appointed to minister as a deacon of St Barnabas Church, Hoppo, near the Vietnamese border. There she led the building up of parish life after the depredations of war, taught in two high schools and become well known in the town. The Eucharistic elements were sent periodically from Pak-hoi.

China was, however, now engulfed in civil war. Following Japan's defeat by the Allied powers in 1945, China was governed by a Nationalist Party under Chiang Kai-Shek. But this was opposed by the Communists under Mao Tse-tung, who enjoyed wide support, especially from the peasant population, and the resulting war was seen by them and many others as one of liberation. Hoppo was one of the final places to be 'liberated' before the war ended in 1950, and since 1948 Florence had, with the authority of Bishop Hall, been regarded as a priest, though the Eucharistic element continued to be consecrated by a man.

This ended with the arrival of the Red Army, and after the new regime had announced that religious organizations would remain free, the outlook seemed promising. But the optimism was short lived. The pastors in the town were forced to live in one house, and on 25 January 1951 St Barnabas Church was closed. Later it was pulled down, and the assets of all the churches in the country were confiscated.

Communist ideology was partly the reason for this, but more important was the desire to rid China of all external influences, including the Christian missionary endeavours. The churches responded by promoting a non-denominational Three-Self Movement – self-support, self-government and self-propagation – which attracted widespread support from the Chinese pastors, including Florence.

From 1951 to 1953 she attended a special course of study at Yenching University in Peking, then went to the Union Theological College in Canton to study English, Church History and the principles of the Three-Self Movement. This occupied her for the next four years, during which she assisted at the city's Anglican Church, without functioning as a priest. On Christmas Eve 1957, however, the head of the college in which she had started to teach asked her to celebrate the Eucharist according to the Anglican rite.

The New Year marked the end of China's Five Year Plan and its replacement by the Great Leap Forward, which involved a radical departure from the previously dominant Soviet model. With the economy in poor shape, every citizen was required to contribute to the recovery by involvement in physical work. At the beginning of 1958 Florence was sent with a number of her students to work in the fields. She was put in charge of the chickens and rabbits, bred for food, and although the hours were long, the Christian group were allowed to meet briefly for prayer and Bible study. A memorable Easter Day service was held in the open air on a hillside.

After about a year the students were allowed to return to the college, but Florence stayed on for another six months before being sent to work in a Three-Self Movement factory. The authorities believed that intellectuals should learn about the conditions of the workers. The next eight years were therefore spent, on and off, in the factory, existing on subsistence wages but with occasional breaks including one of six months in the comparatively luxurious surroundings of a special college created for the study of socialism.

On completion of this course she was set the task of writing a history of the experience of the Chinese people during the Sino-Japanese War. This occupied her for the next five years and although it was a lonely life she was permitted to hold some low-key religious services. The Cultural Revolution (1966–70) quickly ended such deviations. Red Guards, some of them no more than teenagers, stormed her flat at midnight. All her books, including a Bible, were seized and burned in the church, where the services had been held, and she and the other pastors in the town were herded into the YWCA compound and set to work digging. They were subsequently returned to the Three-Self factory, now adorned with portraits of Chairman Mao. No church services were allowed, neither was any celebration of Christmas or Easter.

In July 1974, however, Florence was allowed to retire with a state pension and five years later freedom of religious faith was decreed. The church in Peking was reopened, contact with the outside world was re-established, and Bishop Baker, who had succeeded Ronald Hall at Hong Kong, paid a visit. On Advent Sunday 1971 some women had been ordained priest there.

In 1981 Florence was given permission to leave China in order to visit members of her family and friends who had emigrated to Canada from Hong Kong. She was persuaded to stay and, with the approval and warm support of Archbishop Ted Scott, the Primate of all Canada, ministered at the Anglican Church of St Matthew and St John in Toronto, which had both English and Chinese congregations. Those meeting her for the first time, and aware of her place at the centre of a controversy that shook the entire Anglican Communion, were invariably surprised to encounter a diminutive figure who seemed no one out of the ordinary, humble, quietly spoken and unmistakeably holy. Barely conscious of her international fame, she was, said a member of the Canadian congregation, 'very much like my grandmother'.

Born in 1907 in the small fishing village of Aberdeen, within the then British colony of Hong Kong, Florence Li Tim-Oi was the daughter of a doctor who had become headmaster of a local government-run school. Her grandfather, who had been chief cook to the Governor of the colony, supported eight wives; her father, who was a Christian, was content with two. The Chinese were at that time beginning to move away from their feudal past in which girls were generally undervalued, and he identified himself with the change by choosing the name Tim-Oi, meaning 'another much-beloved girl'.

She attended her father's school until she was 14, then, since there was no money to finance her further education in Hong Kong, remained at home for the next seven years to help with the upbringing of her two sisters and five brothers. Her father's chief wife, the 'Big Mother', had died; Tim-Oi was a daughter of his mistress. When she was 21, however, she persuaded her father to let her continue her education at the Public School for Girls. She was there for the next six years and during the evenings attended a teacher training college. She also went to St Paul's Anglican Church and in 1931 was present in St John's Cathedral when an English missionary, Lucy Vincent, was ordained as a deaconess. The preacher, a Chinese priest, said in the course of his sermon: 'Here today we have an English lady who is willing to sacrifice herself for the Chinese Church. Is there a Chinese girl who would willingly do the same?' Tim-Oi recounted later:

> I knelt down. Something came into my mind very clearly – the words of Isaiah chapter 6 which end 'I heard the voice of the Lord saying "Whom shall I send and who will go for us?" Then I said, "Here I am, send me."'

Haunted by these words, she wondered during the remaining years of her education if she might become a deaconess or a church worker, or possibly a nurse. She was greatly inspired by the story of Florence Nightingale – so inspired that she adopted the name Florence, partly in honour of the great nurse, partly because she had been born in May, the month of flowers. The Rector of St Paul's, Canon Tso Tze Fong, next took the initiative and spoke to her about the need for more women to serve in the Church – 'Only one girl has ever been to a theological college; one girl is not enough. The Church needs women.' So, although her father wanted her to teach in his old school for the children of poor fishermen, which she did for nine months, she decided to see the Principal of the Union Theological Centre.

Fifty years later she was in Westminster Abbey reading the Gospel, in Chinese, at a great service to make the fortieth anniversary of her ordination to the priesthood. The Archbishop of Canterbury, Robert Runcie, was not present but sent a message which was read by the Dean of Westminster: 'It is with a deep sense of gratitude for your Christian witness and ministry that I send greetings to you on the 40th anniversary of your ordination to the priesthood.' Later she went to see him at Lambeth Palace. She died in Canada in 1992.

16

Mission and Unity:
Florence Allshorn and Kathleen Bliss

William Paton, who was secretary of the International Missionary Council in the 1930s and one of the founders of the World Council of Churches, said of Florence Allshorn, 'I think she has the greatest spiritual insight of anyone I have ever known.' Many others shared his view, and she had an enormous influence on many individuals during the mid-twentieth century.

After four tough years as a missionary in Uganda, she spent the next 13 as principal of a training college for women missionaries, then devoted the remainder of her life to the founding and development of the St Julian's Community at Coolham in Sussex. This women's community was unique. Its corporate life had a spiritual framework and a degree of devotional discipline, but it was in no sense a religious order. Its sole purpose was to provide those who had become wearied by their missionary labours overseas or by other forms of stressful service with a beautiful, peaceful and prayerful environment in which they could recharge their physical and spiritual batteries before moving on to another spell of demanding Christian witness.

Florence was the spiritual powerhouse who made renewal possible for so many. Assisted by the fact that she lacked training in academic theology, her own personal faith was the sole determinant of her teaching and of the relations with others that created dynamic Christian communities. The basis of this faith was grounded in the commandments – Love God and love your neighbour – and it was her application of them that was important, and her embodiment of them in her own personality that made her so influential.

She welcomed the remarkable scientific and technological achievements of the twentieth century but came to see, with particular clarity, that these were ceasing to be the handmaids of human development but were now dictating the direction which this development must take. The result, she believed, could only be dehumanizing and destructive. It was therefore the task of Christians to reassert the priority of life's spiritual element and of human beings over machines. This required in Christians serious attention to worship and prayer.

She often pointed out that, while obedience to the command 'Love your neighbour as yourself' had, over the centuries, found expression in many admirable humane movements, it had much less frequently led to 'fellowship one with another' in small communities that shine like light in dark places. It was, she believed, a fundamental failure on the Church's part to create such communities, and this often fatally undermined the Church's witness to the Christian gospel. And it was her own special empathy with others and skill in resolving conflict that made the communities she led such beacons of Christian life.

Florence Allshorn, the daughter of an East End of London homeopathic doctor, was born in 1887. Her mother came from a prosperous Sheffield business family. Four years after their marriage, however, he died leaving three children. These were taken to Sheffield by their mother, but she too died when only 26. A Miss Jackson, who had been a governess in the mother's family for many years, assumed quasi-guardianship of the three children and brought them up in her own home. This was sacrificial on her part, and she was a caring woman, but the home was colourless and drab and a long way from providing the children with a free and joyous environment in their early years.

Florence attended a day school in Sheffield and went from it to the School of Art, but she had to abandon her training because of a serious sight problem that required six months of almost complete darkness. Nonetheless she retained a great love of the arts, expressed later in the impeccable taste and sometimes adventurous initiatives that made her college and the St Julian's Community houses places of beauty and harmony.

Once her sight was sufficiently recovered she embarked on a four-year course at the Sheffield School of Domestic Science. While this did not lead to a catering or teaching career, its practical skills proved to be invaluable in the ordering of the institutions for which she became responsible. Moreover it imbued in her what was probably an innate disposition to seek practical solutions to profound problems.

In the event she first threw her energies into Sheffield's parish church which had recently become the cathedral of a new diocese. The Vicar, Dr Gresford Jones, who was also Archdeacon of Sheffield, and his wife befriended and influenced her considerably, as also did other members of the cathedral's staff. She started a club for factory girls, which had about 80 members, and related to these in a way that no one else had ever found possible. She also became superintendent of the girls' Sunday School and became greatly loved by the children.

During this time she had earned a living by working in a coal office, but in 1918 became a full-time member of the cathedral staff, adding a girls' Bible Class to her responsibilities and the visiting of parishioners and hospitals. Two years later came a critical turning point in her life. She offered for missionary work overseas and contacted the Church Missionary Society. Bishop Wells of Uganda, who was on furlough at the time, travelled to Sheffield to talk to her about this and succeeded in convincing her that she was called to serve in Uganda. He also persuaded Gresford Jones to join him as Assistant Bishop of Kampala.

Florence was now 32 and in Uganda her first assignment was that of head of a high school in Iganga for 100 daughters of chiefs. These knew no English and she knew nothing of their language, but she was not daunted: 'I am in the soup. But it's a great job, because it's the place on which the raising of the status of the women of this region depends. Isn't that a gorgeous bit of work to tackle? I'm jolly glad of it. Thank God for something absolutely impossible.' She coped by loving the children, and they responded by loving her – giving a party for her birthday. And besides the academic work, for which she often needed a translator, she introduced practical subjects such as cooking and gardening. There was also a teachers' training course which provided practical skills by taking classes in village schools. A high-powered Education Commission visited the school in 1924 and described it as 'a first-rate girls' boarding school' and 'a particularly good piece of work'.

The chief problem for Florence involved her relationship with a senior colleague on the mission station who spoke the local language and on whom she was dependent for many things. A few weeks after her arrival she wrote to a friend:

My colleague is a dear in many ways, but the fact is that Iganga is a hopeless sort of place. Of the people who have had my job before no one has stayed for more than a few months, because it is so unhealthy and made them all ill. My colleague has stuck it; it just happens not have affected her health but it has absolutely rotted her nerves, and she has the most dreadful fits of temper. Sometimes she doesn't speak at all for two days. Just now we've finished up three weeks of never a decent word or a smile.

Florence felt this to be affecting the life of the school, and a point was reached when she thought she could take no more and might as well return to England. But one day the situation suddenly changed. As she sat on the veranda of her house, crying her eyes out, an old African matron came to sit at her feet and after a time said, 'I have been on this station for 15 years and I have seen you come out, all of you saying you have brought us a Saviour, but I have never seen this situation saved yet.'

Florence was, as she put it, 'brought to my senses with a bang' and recognized that she was the problem herself – 'I knew enough of Jesus Christ to know that the enemy was the one to be loved before you could call yourself one of his followers. I prayed, in great ignorance as to what it was, that this same love might be in me, and I prayed as I have never prayed in my life for that one thing.' Slowly things changed. She and her colleague came to fashion a good working relationship and gradually the whole atmosphere of the place altered. When, after four years, it became time to return to England on furlough, she was able to say, 'This has been the first "home" I have ever known. My colleague has made it that for me this last year.'

Florence had in her moment of despair undergone a profound spiritual regeneration that influenced her attitude and her relationships for the rest of her life. Earlier she had already expressed in a letter to a friend on holiday something of the depth of a faith that had non-traditional implications, and also remained a lifelong characteristic:

Don't worry your head about theological problems. Read books with only half-a-dozen lines on a page, mostly sloppy. It will do you a world of good. Also don't think about yourself at all, I mean your moral sense. Just be a pagan, loving the sky and the sun and the smell of things and let yourself expand that way a bit. It's no end healthy . . . Do you know I think one of the best things you can do on holiday is to ask nothing, want nothing, but just praise God for everything.

After four years of continuous work in Uganda, she was herself in need of just such a holiday. It was her firm intention to return to Uganda after a good break, but she was suddenly unwell and medical investigation revealed she had tuberculosis. The consultant proposed to remove the infected lung and she reluctantly agreed, but while on the way to the hospital on the day fixed for the operation, she called it off. Instead she went, financed by friends, to spend the winter in a sanatorium in Switzerland and then returned home more or less cured. A further three months of rest was, however, required. These were spent at Storrington in Sussex where a married couple were creating experimentally a community which they called 'The Sanctuary'. Anyone was free to join and live in their own hut. They included artists, homeless, worn-out nurses and drop-outs of every kind, about 30 in all. Florence flourished in the bohemian lifestyle, helping considerably in the developing community life, turning her hand to most things – playing the piano for dancing, baking bread for local gypsies, leading discussions and prayer.

'I adore this simple way of life,' she told a friend, 'it is quite the best way of all.' The only thing that troubled her, and it troubled her greatly, was the attitude of the congregation of the nearby parish church. This was, she said, 'Dead against the community because it worked through friendship – the way Christ worked – with all who came to share its life. I do want someone to put me in love with the Church again.'

Her stay at 'The Sanctuary' ended in 1928, when she was asked to fill a temporary gap by becoming Warden of St Andrew's Hostel – one of the two Church Missionary Society's colleges for training women missionaries. She was surprised by this, since she had no academic qualifications and no idea how colleges of this sort were run. But she felt she owed the CMS something in return for their kindness to her since she became ill, so she took the post on. She stayed in it for the next 13 years, and when in 1934 the other women's training college, Kennaway Hall, was amalgamated with her own, she became principal of the combined institution.

There were inevitably some problems with the CMS hierarchy during her early years. Having appointed such a free spirit, it was hardly likely that she would conform to the established methods of missionary training, and in the end there was nothing quite like what she devised in any other educational institution in the country. For most of the time she was single-handed, but visiting lecturers were imported to deal with academic matters, while she handled the practical missionary subjects, together with spirituality and worship.

The library was a special concern and she built up a remarkable collection of novels, poetry, biography and books about art which helped to enlarge the outlook of the students. No detail of the college's life escaped her attention. The diet was changed to strengthen the students for their arduous life abroad. The furnishings of the college were far from austere – everything had to be in good taste, bright and cheerful – students were expected to dress for dinner. There was plenty of fun, too, but above all a community life in which love of God and love of neighbour ruled.

Not all were able to cope with this and an 18-month course was too short for all that she wished for the students. She could be tough if necessary and believed it to be important to 'Help the student to cope with the girl she dislikes.' Her remedy was 'Put them at a job together, interpret them to each other. Don't let her off till she knows how to refuse defeat.' This had more than domestic value – 'since only two forces drive the world – love and hate –missionaries must be people with some fire of love who have achieved some positive success in living with other people in real Christian friendship'.

The students were devoted to her, and her influence on women's missionary work was enormous. She became increasingly aware, however, that their training needed to be continued, albeit in different ways, after they had completed their first spell of work overseas. A letter to former students in February 1940 outlined what she had in mind:

> I want to do something where I can still go on serving you with what I have of experience and real caring for you. I have a dream of a house in some lovely quiet place where you could come and be quiet and rest and read and talk – where things could be refreshed and recreated before you went off to your new courses and your other furlough adventures. And I should like it to be open for home people as well who needed to stop and know God again.
>
> It is a dream and there is no material hope of it happening, but perhaps it may because I think it would fulfil a need, and I feel it so very strongly. I visualise a central house and one or two warm cosy huts in the garden, far enough away from each other to be really alone, and where you could play the gramophone if you wanted without

disturbing others. And there would be a Quiet Room for you to use as you liked, and nothing forced so that you could be a pagan for a bit if you needed that! And lots of books, all kinds, and a place where you could do handwork. I believe that as the need for spiritual leadership becomes more and more urgent, as it is doing, we shall have to keep times of quiet and re-creation and being still to know God, not only on first furlough but on every furlough. Also for church people at home who go on and on and on in the same rut.

This dream was quickly turned into reality with the founding in 1941 of what became the St Julian's Community – Julian being a local Sussex saint noted for her hospitality.

Florence and three other women who had been involved in missionary training secured a large house, 'Oakenborough', in Haslemere which an old lady had left in her will for some sort of community life. At first, wartime conditions stopped most missionaries from returning home, so war-tired British people were welcomed, and meetings and conferences were held. The harmonious atmosphere was just as she had envisaged and so relaxed that visitors could, if they wished, be served breakfast in bed.

After the war, when the missionaries returned, the accommodation soon became insufficient and in 1950 a much larger property was purchased at Coolham on the South Downs of Sussex. This had 460 acres, including a five-acre lake with swans and ducks, two farmhouses with outbuildings and 13 cottages. The foreman of the farm was retained to develop this as an important part of the community's life. One of the farmhouses became a place where children whose missionary parents were overseas could have holidays.

Missionaries staying at St Julian's appreciated their surroundings and valued their encounters with its founder. A frequent visitor was Max Warren, the General Secretary of the CMS and one of the great missionary statesmen of the twentieth century. For him, it was an essential place of renewal in a highly pressured life, and he served as chairman of the Council for 20 years. In an article in *Theology* (May 1962) he wrote:

Here was a place where you could let quietness and peace do its healing work. No one would ever intrude upon your stillness. But always available was the little 'Society', part of whose serious responsibility it was to keep mentally alert, widely read, in touch with the wider world, and to be ready to meet the troubled and perplexed should they ask for guidance.

The community eventually grew in number to become an apostolic twelve, and although Florence always hoped that some men would join, the few that came to test their suitability never quite fitted in and did not stay. Members of the community received board and lodging and a little money for personal use.

At least 300 young people came every year, about 40 of whom stayed for four long weekends, forming study circles and making use of Bible study notes, which they were challenged to apply to their personal circumstances.

It was a mere six months after moving to Coolham, however, that Florence became ill, and on 3 July 1950 she died of Hodgkin's disease. Her death was a great shock to the many who had come under her influence, but the measure of her greatness was demonstrated by the fact that St Julian's not only survived but continued to develop in the spirit of its founder for another 50 years. By the end of the century, however, the pattern of overseas missionary work had changed so radically that St Julian's was no longer able to fulfil its founding purpose. It was therefore entrusted to the Roman Catholic diocese of Arundel and Brighton which re-named it St Cuthman's Retreat Centre. A few lightly organized retreats are held there, but it continues mainly the St Julian's tradition of catering for individuals who are in need of physical and spiritual refreshment. It is fully ecumenical and attracts some of those who still value the legacy of Florence Allshorn.

*   *   *

Kathleen (Kay) Bliss was an educationalist who became deeply and influentially involved in the ecumenical movement, both nationally and internationally, during the 1940s and 1950s. These were the pioneering years of hope and expectation when many of the leaders of the churches devoted their time and energy to what was sometimes described as 'The Coming Great Church'.

The main thrust of the movement, which had a powerful missionary imperative, was not so much concerned with schemes for reunion, which had of necessity to be left to member churches, but rather with the re-shaping of the Church to meet the changed post-war world and to discern how the Church could creatively engage with a world that was becoming increasingly sophisticated and secularized.

It was this that drew Kay into the ecumenical realm, and in it she was profoundly influenced by J. H. Oldham – a layman who had been closely involved in the formation of the World Council of Churches and brought wide vision and acute intelligence to the gargantuan task of awakening the Church to the importance of the laity's ministry in the world and of the need to equip them for this ministry.

Kathleen Bliss, the daughter of a local government officer, was born in Fulham, London, in 1908. She was brought up as a Congregationalist and went from the local high school to Girton College, Cambridge, where she took a First in Theology and a Second in History. During her time at Cambridge she became much involved in the then flourishing Student Christian Movement which helped to widen her Congregational outlook. She then undertook a number of temporary teaching posts before marrying Rupert Bliss, a marine engineer, in 1932.

Together they went, under the auspices of the London Missionary Society (predominantly Congregational), to South India where they spent the next seven years involved in a number of educational projects. On their return to England, soon after the outbreak of war in 1939, they had a year's leave before Kathleen became assistant to J. H. Oldham who was then editing his *Christian Newsletter*. Paper rationing demanded a modest format, but the quality of the content was consistently high, Oldham having formed a Christian Frontier Council – a 30–40-strong think-tank for the consideration of public affairs in a Christian context.

Kay's own contributions so impressed Oldham that after 12 months he made her assistant editor, and in 1945 she took over the editorship. Publication continued for another four years until the churches' in-creasing pre-occupation with their own internal affairs seriously reduced the circulation. Meanwhile Kay had joined the staff of the British Council of Churches to organize 'Religion and Life' weeks held in most of the main towns and cities and which brought Christians of all denominations together in ways they had never before experienced. She was also instrumental in forming many local Councils of Churches. During this time she became an Anglican, and later her husband became an Anglican priest.

In 1948 Kathleen went as a delegate to the First Assembly of the World Council of Churches held in Amsterdam. Her intellectual and literary reputation went ahead of her, and she was recruited to help with the drafting of resolutions and reports. She coined the phrase 'We intend to stay together', which became the watchword of the historic gathering. Afterwards she was appointed part-time Secretary of the Council's Commission on Women in the Church and wrote a book on *The Service and Status of Women in the Church* (1952):

> Women have wielded influence with very great skill over the centuries and many prefer it to any form of responsibility which brings them out into the open. But the choice between influence and responsibility is one that women have to make, and the Churches have to make in relation to women.

This was still a voice crying in the wilderness, but three years earlier the importance of her work was recognized by Aberdeen University with the award of an honorary DD, and in 1954 she was elected to the Central Committee of the WCC and membership of its Executive Committee – further signs of her growing influence in the ecumenical movement.

In 1950 she had joined the staff of the BBC's Religious Broadcasting Department as a producer of programmes. After the end of the 1939–45 war questions began to be raised about the Christian monopoly of religious broadcasting. Since the foundation of the BBC in 1922, control had been exercised by a Central Religious Advisory Council consisting of nominees of the main churches and chaired by an Anglican bishop. Nothing critical or even questioning of the Christian faith was permitted. Fringe Christian groups were denied broadcasting opportunities and the proponents of atheism or secular philosophy were absolutely excluded. The time of a Sunday evening broadcast service was regulated to avoid conflict with the normal time of church services.

Although they feared conflict with the churches, the new BBC management were acutely aware that the monopoly could not continue. For one thing it breached the Corporation's code of impartiality (propaganda had become a very dirty word), for another it threatened the maximizing of programme ratings. Successive Heads of the Religious Broadcasting Department recognized the validity of the objection and also pointed out to alarmed, and sometimes angry, church leaders that the Christian cause was not best promoted if religious programmes were unable to discuss the kind of questions that non-churchgoers frequently asked.

In 1947 the Governors decided that change was essential, though it took another three years of discussion, including protracted negotiations with the British Council of Churches, before steps were taken to see what the practical implications of their decision might be. Kathleen and J. H. Oldham had been involved in some of these discussions and their expressed views on the matter led to an invitation to join the staff in order to do something about it.

Kay's 'frontier' outlook made her ideally suited to this task, though it proved to be an exceedingly difficult assignment since so many conflicting interests had to be placated, and new-style programmes were bound to attract howls of protest. She was herself convinced that if religious programmes were to engage the serious attention of people who were beyond the normal reach of the churches, they must be of a high quality and carry no hint of propaganda.

Her intellectual approach was useful, though it soon led to clashes with some potential programme makers, who were naturally wary of anything that suggested a university seminar. There was much to hammer out. J. H. Oldham was roped in to lend a hand with the continuing of what had become the Fundamental Debate and the preparation of a series of four programmes under the title *Encounter of Belief*. These preparations were not superficial. Nearly all the heavyweight thinkers in the country were consulted and, predictably, there was little agreement among them. A weekend conference at St Julian's in Sussex in July 1952 suggested, however, that it might be possible to find sufficient common ground to enable four programmes to be devised. The participants were Karl Popper, a well-known London School of Economics philosopher, John Baillie, a highly regarded Presbyterian Principal of New College, Edinburgh, James Drever, a Professor of Psychology, also at Edinburgh, Harold Blackman, the secretary of the Ethical Society, and Alasdair MacIntyre, a Manchester University philosopher.

Four papers were circulated on four chosen 'attitudes' – Humanism, Behaviourism, Marxism and Christianity – and during the three-day conference Bliss and Oldham were in their element. She was convinced, and the nervous BBC agreed, that, in order to prevent the programmes from becoming slanging matches between irreconcilable adversaries, they should be fully scripted and that the responses to the introductory talks should be made by well-informed commentators, rather than by representatives of totally different viewpoints. The Light Programme was in no one's mind, and the discussions were constructive enough to enable Karl Popper to say that it was one of the best conferences of its kind that he had ever attended.

But recruiting the right people to take part in the programmes was an altogether different matter. Most intellectuals were at that time suspicious of broadcasting and did not wish to expose themselves to a means of communication over which they did not have ultimate control. Others did not like the format, and the BBC's Governors were fearful that the Marxists might win the minds of some listeners.

Kay approached a huge number of potential participants before the four pairs of programmes could be put together. Even then some of the contributors let her down at the last minute, when the first of the series had actually been broadcast, and the project was not considered a success. Church leaders had displayed little interest in it. But it was an important milestone and opened the way to a more liberal approach to religious broadcasting which flourished for a time until intense competition between radio and television and different broadcasting authorities led to a serious scaling down of all forms of thoughtful programming.

By the time she left the BBC, Kathleen had become an Anglican, and in 1958 she was appointed the first General Secretary of a newly constituted Church of England Board of Education. This was a formidable challenge, involving the co-ordination and overall direction of activities as diverse as primary schools, teaching-training colleges, as they were then called, university chaplaincies, Sunday Schools and the educational work of the Mothers' Union. She responded with her customary energy, wrote a book *We the People* (1963) about the Christian Society, and gave special attention to the setting up of Anglican chaplaincies in the many new universities that were being founded. It was, in fact, an impossible assignment for one person to handle and in 1966 she resigned, utterly exhausted.

A period of recovery was followed by appointment in 1967 as a Senior Lecturer in Religious Studies in the University of Sussex. This suited her much better. The new university was pioneering different approaches to higher education and Kay was more than ready, as well as ideally equipped, to pursue this in the field of religious studies – a wider territory than that of traditional theology.

During her time there she accepted an invitation to contribute a volume, *The Future of Religion* (1969) to the otherwise secular New Thinkers' Library. It was reprinted in 1972 as a Pelican paperback and is a work of considerable erudition, displaying in fewer than 200 pages a sharp theological mind grappling with the issues arising from the intersection of religion and modern culture. A necessary and valuable analysis of the fundamentals of Judaism, Hinduism, Buddhism and Islam, as well as Christianity, is followed by pointers to adjustments required of each if an adequate response is to be made to a world so different from that in which they originated.

Most space is allocated to Christianity, and the pointers bear the marks of the 1960s, emphasizing the ecumenical imperative, the urgency of liturgical change, the re-shaping of the Church, and constructive engagement with the secular. Re-reading the book half a century later is bound to cause disappointment that so little significant progress has been made in these fields. And even Kathleen Bliss, like virtually every other 1960s reformer, failed to discern the desperate need for women to be enabled to take their proper place in the Church's worship and mission.

On the main subject of the book, however, she had no doubt that religion still has a vital part to play in a changing and often bewildering world, and that without the insights of religion there can be no fulfilment for either individuals or society. It is by no means outdated. Kay's husband, Rupert, followed her into the Church of England and, following his ordination, held several educational and rural parish appointments. Theirs was a long and happy, even if somewhat unusual marriage. They had three daughters who were largely brought up by their father, and his private income facilitated a degree of flexibility in their home life. Kay was herself highly strung, a perfectionist and, when under pressure, sometimes displayed violent outbursts of exasperation and temper at home. These tended to be absorbed by her close friend from Cambridge days, Margaret Bryan, who shared the family home from 1946 to 1974, as well as a shared interest in music and dressmaking.

After Rupert's retirement from parish ministry they moved from Dorset to London where Kathleen remained in demand for lectures, speeches and sermons until shortly before her death from cancer on 13 September 1989.

17

Radical Social Action:
Janet Lacey, Diana Collins and
Margaret Kane

Janet Lacey was the first woman to preach in London's St Paul's Cathedral, as she was also in Liverpool Cathedral and St George's Cathedral, Jerusalem – all in the late 1960s. But although a powerful speaker, her great achievement was the creation of Christian Aid, now one of the world's largest and most respected charities involved in the battle against poverty, hunger and disease in the developing world. When, in 1952, she was appointed Secretary of the British Council of Churches Inter-Church Aid and Refugee Service, the income of the organization that year was £20,000; when she retired from the post of Director of Christian Aid, as it had become, in 1969, this had risen to £2.5 million; in 2010 it was £104.6 million.

The origin of the charity lay in the decision of the embryonic World Council of Churches to mobilize relief for the millions of starving people, including a vast number of refugees, in devastated post-war Europe. Efforts for both started in 1945 and led in 1948 to the formation of a Division of Inter-Church Aid and Service to Refugees, a branch of which was established in Britain a year later.

Janet Lacey was at the time the British Council of Churches Youth Secretary and gaining something of a reputation for her flair and vigour in the promotion of youth work on an ecumenical basis. Inter-Church Aid had been less fortunate in its leadership and when the post of Secretary fell vacant in 1952 she was drafted in to revive its fortunes and develop it into a significant part of British church life. It proved to be an inspired choice. Having experienced at first hand the devastation and human misery in Europe and become acquainted with many of the church leaders there, she was only too well aware of the magnitude of the problem.

She became closely involved with Alec Dickson in the setting up of Voluntary Service Overseas which became, and remains, an important agency for young people willing to serve for a year or more in a developing country. In 1957 the first Christian Aid Week took place in 200 British towns and villages and raised what was then the substantial sum of £26,000. A replica of a refugee camp was erected at St Martin-in-the-Fields in London's Trafalgar Square. Two years later she became a prominent member of a United Kingdom World Refugee Year Committee, one of 97 such committees worldwide. The United Kingdom target was £2 million, but in the event £7.3 million was raised, together with £1.8 million in kind – clothing, houses, etc. For her part in this she was appointed CBE.

'Need not Creed' was her constant motto, and she would work with anyone who was ready to respond to the plight of the poor and dispossessed. During her time at Christian Aid the money raised was channelled to particular projects through the World Council of Churches' Division and, since she was on the committee and the British contribution to the international effort was by far the largest, her influence at Geneva was enormous and became determinative of policy. Short and stocky in build, Janet was autocratic, formidable and often infuriating. Her north country bluntness was not to everyone's liking, neither was her tough approach to problems, but she was a skilled manager and was held in great affection by most of those who worked with her.

As the post-war years advanced, the emphasis of Christian Aid's work gradually turned away from Europe to the developing nations of Africa, Asia and Latin America. Janet had, of necessity, to become a global traveller – visiting places where the human suffering was heartbreaking in order to assess need and returning often to ensure that projects were delivering relief. This sometimes involved journeys to countries beset by civil war and hindered by incompetent, often corrupt governments. It was a demanding responsibility in which satisfaction and frustration were just about evenly matched.

Her first visit to Africa was to Kenya in 1955 at the time of the Mau Mau uprising there. The flight to Nairobi took 18 hours, and two hours after her arrival she was involved in discussions with the first of several groups of Kenyan church leaders. The next day she was taken to visit some of the detainee camps and prisons. On a day of pouring rain she had what she said was the unforgettable sight of hundreds and hundreds of African men huddled together in groups in large wire-netting compounds, with grey blankets held tightly round their bodies. The grey sky, the grey faces and the grey blankets reminded her of L. S. Lowry's paintings of 'stick people'.

Over the course of a fortnight Janet visited many more such camps in different parts of the country, as a result of which an initial list of needs, of both workers and money, was produced. On her return to London it was decided to raise £100,000 over the next two years for the financing of this project. Five community centres were built in the urban areas of Nairobi. A house was opened for 500 children in need of care, and attached to this was a training centre for African women who attended courses then returned to their villages to open and supervise infant welfare centres.

Projects of this sort were to occupy her throughout her time at Christian Aid with special efforts for the victims of war in Vietnam and Nigeria. But it was not long after she had become Director that she discerned the need to look more deeply into the causes of world poverty and the economic re-ordering of international trade and finance necessary to its elimination. In 1969 she tackled the British government over its aid and trade policies, though the charitable status of Christian Aid required her to tread carefully in the field of politics. Her book *A Cup of Water* (1970) indicated the scope of her work and also its limitations.

Janet Lacey was born in 1903 in Sunderland, where her father was a property agent, and her grandfather a local Methodist preacher who went every Sunday in pony and trap to conduct services in surrounding villages. She attended local schools and was fortunate enough to have a mistress who gave her a fine introduction to English literature – something for which she said she was 'eternally grateful'. Thespian interests also led her to produce her first play, presented in a crowded Methodist chapel, where the minister described her as 'a gifted and imaginative child'.

Her father having died when she was only ten, her mother decided five years later that it would be best for her to go and live with an aunt in Durham. This turned out to be an unhappy experience as she disliked the aunt, and for the next seven years they fought. Nonetheless Durham widened her experience usefully. After taking courses at the Technical School, she obtained a job that required her to travel to many pit villages where she saw at first hand the dire poverty in which the miners and their families lived. This aroused her interest in politics and later to membership of the Labour Party.

Most of the money she earned was spent on drama and elocution lessons with the wife of the leading tenor of Durham Cathedral choir who also ran a small drama school. This led to membership of a concert party which took her again to the mining villages to give performances, and at the time she wondered about the possibility of a stage career. But she soon came to realize its hazards, and when 22, turned in another direction, though something of the actress was never lost in her and she had an abiding love of the theatre.

Her family background was Methodist and in 1925 she applied for work with the Young Women's Christian Association. A year later she was sent to Kendal to train as a youth leader and remained for six years, using her drama skills to good effect and becoming interested for the first time in theology. Her faith was, nonetheless, always of a practical, ethical kind and she had no time for the tenets of doctrine and the divisions these created.

In 1932 Janet moved to Dagenham to join the staff of a mixed YWCA and YMCA community centre in the vast housing development created for over 200,000 people moving out of London's East End. The breakdown in social cohesion caused by this movement of population led to many social problems. These were exacerbated by the outbreak of war in 1939, and Janet devoted 13 years of her life to this work until in 1946 she went to Germany for the YMCA to develop an educational programme for soldiers who were awaiting demobilization.

There she witnessed the desperate suffering of the German population, and also, in Hamburg and Hanover, the arrival of thousands of refugees in the worst European winter in living memory. They came in goods trains and, of those who had not died on the journey, many were in a pitiable condition due to frostbite. It was this experience that made her determined to undertake work for refugees. Meanwhile, she had extended her educational work to include German people, and when Sir Robert Birley arrived in Berlin in 1947 as Educational Adviser in the British Zone of Germany, he said that she seemed to be involved in so many different posts at once that it was not at all easy to tell which one she was filling at any one moment. He added that she did not appear to take him very seriously, but he became one of her great admirers and noted that it was rare to find in one person the combination of energy, unorthodoxy and efficiency. The work brought contact with some of the great ecumenical leaders of the post-war era, especially the Lutheran Bishop of Hanover Hanns Lilje and Bishop George Bell of Chichester.

It was during her time in Germany that Janet became Education Secretary of the British Council of Churches, combining this role for a time with her other responsibilities, and when in 1952 she moved across to its Inter-Church Aid Department, her experience and qualities for the new task could hardly have been bettered.

Given the magnitude of her responsibilities for Christian Aid, as it became known, most other appointments open to her after her resignation from this were bound to be less demanding and apparently less significant. The Family Welfare Association, of which she became the Director in 1969, was well within her interests. A national charity, which has government support, it provides a wide range of support services designed to keep families together and improve the well-being of the most vulnerable.

Janet devoted four years to this and did much to stimulate its activities and streamline its organization. But she was essentially a pioneer rather than a consolidator, and her personal style was not really suited to the FWA's tradition, so her time with it was only partially successful. More successful were the next four years, 1973–7, which she spent reorganizing the much smaller, less complex, Churches' Council for Health and Healing.

One of the curiosities of her personal life was that, although she could manage large organizations, she was incapable of boiling an egg. Generous to a fault, she delighted in entertaining her friends in good restaurants, and in retirement she took them not only to her beloved theatre but also to music concerts and sculpture exhibitions. Later in life she was prepared for confirmation by Father St John Groser, a renowned socialist East End parish priest.

*   *   *

John Collins, one of the most notable and controversial canons ever to have occupied a stall in St Paul's Cathedral, died at the end of 1982. Ten years later his widow, Diana, published a fine book, *Partners in Protest: Life with Canon Collins*, and the title was apt. For, although her husband's activities had attracted massive national and often international attention, she was equally involved in all that he achieved through Christian Action, the Campaign for Nuclear Disarmament, and the Defence and Aid Fund's campaign against apartheid in Southern Africa. She drafted many of his speeches and sermons as well as some important policy documents.

Diana was, in fact, more intellectually able than John and combined this with a persuasive charm which helped to smooth situations made more difficult by his impetuous decision-making and somewhat abrasive style. Yet, in spite of her considerable gifts and total commitment to their shared concerns, she was always ready to take a subordinate place on the public stage and remained totally loyal in her support of his leadership.

Towards the end of her own life, by which time she was actively involved in the Movement for the Ordination of Women, the earliest meeting of which had taken place in her home, she reflected on this role and said,

> John's and my marriage began in a traditional way. I accepted that my role would be to support John in all that he did; that was what I wanted to do, and what I would want to do again. It might have been difficult had I already had or had wanted a professional career; as it was, I was exceptionally fortunate.

She might have added that she played the larger part in the upbringing of four sons, one of whom was tragically killed in a motoring accident not long after his father's death.

Diana was born on 13 August 1917 at Stutton Hall, Suffolk, the home of her grandparents. Her father was at the time serving with the Suffolk Regiment in France, and, until his demobilization and settlement at Putney after the war, she was accustomed to a household that supported a butler, a nanny and a cook. Her years at a girls' boarding school were less than happy, and she was asked to leave. A church boarding school proved to be more to her liking and, having ended as head girl and captain of games, she was sent to a finishing school in Paris. A London season followed and she was one of the few young women to be presented at Court during the brief reign of King Edward VIII, who she said looked sad as well as very bored.

At Lady Margaret Hall, Oxford, she won a lacrosse Blue, but her academic progress was hindered by her engagement to Ronald Lunt, who later became a distinguished Chief Master of King Edward's School, Birmingham. When he broke the engagement, she became involved with his friend John Collins, then Dean of Oriel College. They were married in October 1939, she being only just 22.

The following summer, after Dunkirk and with German invasion threatened, John joined the RAF as a chaplain, and Diana returned to Stutton Hall, where she lived until the end of the war. He had hoped for a dramatic, demanding chaplaincy at an RAF bomber station in East Anglia but spent almost all of the war at Yatesbury, Wiltshire – a training camp for technicians, and reported to be the worst run and most unpopular in the RAF. Although they got together from time to time during the war years, Diana and John decided to share the experience of most other couples in their position by living apart.

During his RAF years John found opportunities to express some of the socialist convictions he had acquired from his former pupil and friend Mervyn Stockwood, who became a notorious Bishop of Southwark. A series of high-profile public figures, including Archbishop William Temple and Sir Stafford Cripps, were invited to give lectures at Yatesbury on political and social issues. These created controversy not only in the RAF but nationally, and the Prime Minister, Winston Churchill, minuted, 'The chaplain at Yatesbury must be either a Communist or a dupe.'

The encounter with Cripps had important consequences when, after the war, John, reunited with Diana, returned to Oriel College. By this time both had been appalled by the dropping of nuclear bombs on two Japanese cities and by the Church's lack of concern at this action. Together with a number of friends they therefore convened a public meeting in Oxford Town Hall under the slogan 'A call to Christian action in public affairs'. In spite of appalling weather, the Town Hall was filled to capacity, as was the university church, used for an overflow meeting, and it was estimated that some 3,000 people had turned out for an event that caught the mood of the immediate post-war years.

A small organization named Christian Action, and based on Oriel, came into being with John Collins as both Chairman and Secretary. He got various notables to become patrons or to serve on the committee, and these included Sir Stafford Cripps who was now Chancellor of the Exchequer in a Labour government. He valued John's outlook and gifts and, when a London base was needed for the development of Christian Action, persuaded the Prime Minister, Clement Attlee, to appoint him to a vacant canonry of St Paul's Cathedral.

Diana, who was enjoying married life in a college house in rural

Bartlemas, and had just given birth to a second son, was not at all keen to move to London. Neither did the prospect of being dragged into the lobby of ecclesiastical politics with its envy and back-biting appeal to her. But, after much heart searching and a letter of refusal that was never posted, they moved to the official large house, 2 Amen Court, where they remained for the next 33 years. It was a move that neither of them ever regretted, and Diana wept when they left in 1981.

The basement of the house provided ample space for the infant Christian Action in which Diana became increasingly involved, taking on, among other things, editorship of its journal. A 'Homeless in Britain' campaign was launched, and over the next four years 19 housing associations were established. Houses for unmarried and deserted women were opened, together with a shelter for vagrant women in Lambeth. There were several houses for the rehabilitation of alcoholics and other addicts. During the 1950s, an Anti-Capital Punishment Campaign was run from Christian Action's office, and a feature of the Collins's work was the provision of financial and administrative support, including office accommodation, for other small projects dealing with special problems.

In 1950 there was little concern in Britain about the rapid development of racist rule in South Africa. But John and Diana were profoundly influenced by their reading of Alan Paton's *Cry the Beloved Country* which exposed the true nature of the regime. This led to the setting up of a Race Relations Fund, designed initially to help black students and immigrant workers in London but soon extended, at the request of Bishop Trevor Huddleston, a close friend, to provide money for the families of men who were being imprisoned for their non-violent resistance to apartheid. Lasting friendships with Nelson Mandela and other African leaders followed, and those who were free to visit London usually stayed at 2 Amen Court.

In 1956 Christian Action launched a Treason Trial Defence Fund and raised £170,000 for the defence of 156 black and white South Africans whose opposition to government policy had led to their trial on charges of high treason. The fund's terms of reference were extended to cover support for Rhodesian rebels, and eventually it became the International Defence and Aid Fund through which the Swedish and several other governments channelled their money for the legal humanitarian assistance of apartheid's victims. The fund became too large to shelter under Christian Action's umbrella, so a separate Defence and Aid Fund was started, and although John remained at the helm and was always the public face of this opposition to apartheid, Diana was no less closely involved at every level. After John had been banned entry into South Africa she went incognito in his place.

But South Africa was not their only major concern. Still shocked by the use of nuclear weapons to end the war in 1945, they convened a meeting at 2 Amen Court in January 1958. Among the 50 people present were Bertrand Russell, J. B. Priestley and Michael Foot, and it was decided to launch a Campaign for Nuclear Disarmament (CND) with John as Chairman.

This soon became a mass movement, the chief rallying point of the campaign being an annual march at Easter from Trafalgar Square to the nuclear research centre at Aldermaston in Berkshire. This was later reversed to enable the event to end with a mass meeting in Trafalgar Square. The number taking part sometimes reached 20,000. Diana chaired and spoke at one of the earliest of these meetings, and she also served on the campaign's women's committee. She and John believed that CND spread among the public a wider perception of the danger and horror of nuclear weapons and helped to create the atmosphere in which the signing of a Test Ban Treaty in 1963 became possible.

Their various campaigns, which included John's utterances from the pulpit of St Paul's, exacted a heavy personal price. On one occasion their house in Amen Corner was daubed with the slogan 'Hang Canon Collins', he was frequently denounced as a Communist, they were ostracized both within and without church circles, and at St Paul's their words and actions were rarely appreciated. John inevitably bore the greatest burden of this, but it was shared, and it was their sharing, allied to her never-failing love and affection, which enabled him and the campaign to continue. This was needed increasingly after he suffered a severe heart attack when he was 70. Thereafter he was never quite the same, and although they remained at St Paul's and were still active in many ways, he died 12 months after his retirement at the end of November 1981.

Diana lived for a further 21 years and, although life for her was never easy, she remained her sparkling, energetic self and continued to be an outspoken advocate of justice, freedom and peace until the end of her days in May 2003. She had been made a Dame in 1999 – a fitting recognition of the great contribution she had made in the field of Christian social action.

*   *   *

Margaret Kane was the first woman industrial chaplain in England and the pioneer of systematic industrial mission work in the mining industry. She also spent 12 years as consultant on industrial and social affairs to successive Bishops of Durham – the distinguished Ian Ramsey and John Habgood. All these roles were undertaken as a laywoman, and it was not until she was almost 80 that she was ordained to the priesthood, having become a deacon seven years earlier.

Margaret entered the industrial mission field in the 1950s – the time when Ted Wickham was developing the Sheffield Industrial Mission into the most serious and substantial experiment in engaging the alienated working classes ever undertaken by the Church of England. Unlike other efforts involving chaplains who conducted services in works canteens and engaged in pastoral work in factories, the Sheffield Industrial Mission was concerned to create lay-led initiatives that would bring together groups of workers to consider, in the light of the biblical revelation, some of the moral, economic and political issues they faced daily in the steelworks. Over a period of 21 years this was attended with considerable success and aroused international interest and emulation, but, in common with most experimental work in the Church, it was never sufficiently incorporated into official structures. Thus a change in leadership led to a catastrophic collapse parallel to, though different from, the worker-priest movement in post-war France.

In 1952, after a period of study of Church and society issues at William Temple College, Rugby, Margaret was invited by Leslie Hunter, the visionary Bishop of Sheffield, to work in the coalmining parish of Maltby, near Rotherham. Over the next seven years she went down one of its pits every week to engage in pastoral work among the colliers, but chiefly to get men together to discuss various issues arising from their work. She also took part in the training of apprentices. This work brought her into partnership with the nearby Sheffield Industrial Mission, and in 1959 she left Maltby to join its large full-time staff. Her work remained in the Rotherham area, where she continued to go down mines and was also involved in the steelworks. She described one wet Saturday in the autumn of 1959:

> There were about 40 of us present and the room seemed packed to capacity, as piles of raincoats on the tables grew higher, and the group around the fire continually opened up to squeeze late-comers in.

Manual workers can often be distinguished by their build. Alf, with his shock of greying hair and rough outbursts of comment, was an outsize man in every way, and Sam, another roller, was over six foot tall. Between them, George and Henry looked slight and wiry. Several of those present were clerical workers and there were a few managers, not yet of much seniority.

All the subjects were introduced by laymen. First came reports – Bernard, a clerical worker, described a new venture in which a group of people who lived and worked in the same district were studying 'The Problem of Youth at Shedbridge'.

From the other extremes of industrial mission's spread, George reported on a conference held for 20 industrial mission supporters from his own firm. Then David, a young man with a keen political concern, gave a report of work being done by a small group on 'Social Problems of the Recession'. The second half of the evening consisted of Bible Study – one of a series on 'The Parables of the Kingdom' – and Geoff, a small man with heavy lines on his face, introduced the parable for the evening: the Strong Man Bound. Discussion was lively and the laymen approached the Bible with freshness and simplicity.

Mission work was always undertaken with the consent of trade unions and management, and the collaboration of shop stewards. This was not always forthcoming, as union leaders were sometimes suspected of left-wing agendas. Margaret's involvement in the establishing of a branch of the British Iron Steel and Kindred Trades Association (BISAKTA) in a large engineering tool works caused some problems, but patient negotiation usually opened doors. The appearance of a woman chaplain in a steelworks was in itself little short of sensational.

Another aspect of her work in the coal-mining district involved the encouragement of local clergy of all denominations to engage with their pits. A six-monthly meeting of the clergy in the area facilitated the exchange of ideas and a consistency of approach which management found helpful.

The days of this dynamically creative mission were numbered when, at the end of 1959, Ted Wickham left Sheffield for the much less important post of Suffragan Bishop of Middleton in Manchester diocese. He was succeeded by Michael Jackson, who had been on the staff of the Mission for the last few years and was believed to be in full sympathy with its aims.

This turned out not to be the case and he initiated, without consultation, a change of policy that shifted the emphasis from the Kingdom of God to the Church, and from the laity to the clergy. There was at this time an almost complete turnaround of chaplains, and Margaret joined the staff from Maltby. Calm prevailed for the next two years but the arrival in 1962 of the evangelical John Taylor as successor to Bishop Leslie Hunter accelerated the Mission's policy change. Most of the staff, including Margaret, left in protest and she went to Hong Kong for two years to advise on the starting of a mission in a rapidly developing industrial community.

Margaret Kane, the eighth of nine children, was born in Cork in April 1915. Her father, a naval chaplain, was a friend of Captain Robert Scott and would have accompanied him on his ill-fated expedition to the Antarctic had he not been prevented at the last minute by an attack of flu.

On leaving Queen Anne's School, Caversham, where she was head girl, she was expected to take up a place at London University to read Mathematics and Chemistry, but to the chagrin of her parents decided at the last minute to go instead to the Regent Street Polytechnic School of Art. Making good progress as a painter, she one day chanced to go into All Souls Church (not then in Conservative Evangelical hands) across the road, where in the silence she had an intense spiritual experience and felt called to be a missionary. An interview with the Church Missionary Society followed, but she soon abandoned the idea of work overseas and joined instead the Peace Pledge Union, becoming involved in the running of a club for working girls. Her eyes were thus opened to the wide gulf between such girls and any expression of the Christian faith. So in 1940 she went to St Christopher's College, Blackheath, for training as 'an accredited church worker'.

Two years later she began to minister in a tough parish on the London–Essex border, then became a chaplain's assistant with the armed forces – both experiences reinforcing her awareness of the detachment of the Church from the working classes. After the war, she worked briefly in a Birmingham suburban parish and became greatly influenced by the French worker-priest movement. It was this that took her to William Temple College and on to industrial mission.

Her return from Hong Kong in 1966 coincided with the appointment of the Oxford philosopher Ian Ramsey to the Bishopric of Durham. On his arrival in the north east, he found himself handicapped by his lack of knowledge about industrial matters and the social problems of a diocese of coalmines, shipyards, engineering and chemical industries. He therefore appointed Margaret as a consultant – the first such in any diocese – and her brief was to provide a background of theological thinking to support new attempts by the Church to present the Christian faith in ways that would speak to the specific needs of the north east and its people.

This was a challenging assignment, not least because of the high intellectual level from which it came, but for the next 12 years Margaret responded with unusual skill, combining a sharp mind with theological insight and her considerable experience. She also had a deep conviction that the Church had got its understanding of God wrong and that this was the primary cause of its alienation from England's working classes. The failure of all but a small minority of the clergy to recognize her diagnosis was, for her, a cause of endless frustration, but it was fortunate that Ian Ramsay, who died prematurely in 1972, was followed by a bishop who also valued her work. The extension of her responsibilities to include parts of the dioceses of York and Newcastle did, however, create some problems.

It was also fortunate that on her arrival in the north east she found on Teesside a flourishing industrial mission, founded on Sheffield principles, another on Tyneside, and chaplaincy work in Sunderland. She spent four weeks as a worker in a calculator factory to see how industrial chaplains could meet the needs of women in industry, and the appointment of a woman chaplain resulted. The fruits of her insights and experience were powerfully expressed in three books: *Theology in an Industrial Society* (1975), *Gospel in Industrial Society* (1980) and *What Kind of God?* (1986). There was also an unpublished *Out of Sheffield*.

On her retirement in 1981 Margaret became a freelance consultant, and her specialism was the linking of frontier theology to the liberation theology of Latin America, as well as the bringing together of academics and leaders in management and trade unions to discuss the implications of this for their decision-making. She also engaged in a more traditional form of pastoral ministry in the parish of St Aidan, Billingham-on-Tees – a post-war housing development to accommodate workers at the huge local ICI factory.

It had never been her intention to seek Holy Orders, but, when the ordination of women became possible, she offered herself primarily to support the other women priests. Many believed that the final phase of her work was enriched by this step. She died on 13 May 2003.

18

Synodical Stateswomen:
Betty Ridley and Christian Howard

For much of the second half of the twentieth century, the Church of England was fortunate to have in its central councils two women of outstanding ability. Neither Betty Ridley nor Christian Howard (both of whom became Dames) felt called to the priesthood; had they done so and had ordination been possible for them, it is impossible to doubt that each would have risen to a high place in the episcopate. Instead they found a vocation as laywomen to inject life and purpose into the Church Assembly and its successor General Synod. Foremost among their concerns was the ordination of women which, during their time and thanks to their efforts, came to occupy a serious place on the Church's agenda.

By the 1970s Betty Ridley had become the *grande dame* of the Church of England inasmuch as she was a leading figure in its central councils and also a senior member of its administration. She believed passionately that the health of the Church and its obedience to the Christian gospel required the freedom of women to exercise their gifts in its service. This conviction dated from 1930, and six decades of struggle were needed before the General Synod's decision to embrace the ordination of women brought tears to her eyes.

Born in 1909 in the East End of London where her father, Henry Mosley, was Rector of Poplar, then Bishop of Stepney, Betty Ridley was educated at the North London Collegiate School and Cheltenham Ladies' College. Her interest and skill in music secured her a place at the Royal College of Music but she also felt called to be an overseas missionary. Both possibilities were swept aside, however, when, still only 19, she fell in love with Michael Ridley – chaplain to her father, who by this time had become Bishop of Southwell. They were married in the same year and went to a parish in Hampshire.

In 1930, when pregnant, Betty went to stay with her parents at Bishop's Manor in Southwell, and while there a meeting of the Central Council for Women's Work, of which her father was chairman, was held in the house. In informal conversations before the meeting she told members of the Council that they were wasting their time and would be better employed working for the ordination of women to the priesthood. They responded by inviting her to become a member of the Council, having decided that a revolutionary voice was needed in their ranks.

A few years later her husband was appointed Vicar of St Gabriel's, Pimlico, and she joined the London Diocesan Board for Women's Work. By 1939 she was bringing up three children and during the years of the wartime blitz was much involved in social and relief work among the victims of the bombing.

Before this, she had become an early and active member of the Anglican Group for the Ordination of Women. This came into being in 1930, first as an *ad hoc* group to prepare material on the ordination of women for the Lambeth Conference of that year. When this was flatly rejected by the Conference, an ongoing organization was formed with the aim of upholding the Christian principles of spiritual equality between men and women, and calling attention to the growing need for admission of women to the ordained ministry. While fully supporting these aims, Betty had decided that she ought not to be too strident in the voicing of her opinions, lest she be written off as a crank. She also believed it to be important, as a first step, to secure for women the freedom to undertake all the other offices that were open to laymen in the Church.

When the worst of the blitz was over, Michael Ridley became Rector of Finchley in north London. Many church people had moved out of the capital, and Betty found herself in demand by several church bodies, as well as the St Hilda's East Settlement at Bethnal Green, of which she was soon the very active chairwoman. The recently founded British Council of Churches claimed her, and in 1945 she was elected to the Church Assembly, becoming one of its youngest members.

The death, from cancer, of Michael in 1953 was a severe blow; theirs had been a close partnership in work as well as in the nurturing of four children. Betty decided to return to Pimlico to facilitate her increasing central church responsibilities. These involved becoming the first woman member of the Central Board of Finance, on which she served for 25 years, and also the first woman member of the Central Advisory Council for the Training of the Ministry. In 1954 she became Vice-President of the British Council of Churches at a time when its influence was growing rapidly, and she was elected chairwoman of its administration committee, whose members included the leaders of all the Free Churches as well as the Secretary of the Church Assembly.

This proved to be just the beginning of her responsibilities. Still in her mid-forties she was appointed chairwoman of a committee established to rationalize a multitude of Church Assembly Boards and Councils which had reduced the Church's central government to near chaos. Her report streamlined the various bodies into four main boards, together with a central board of finance and a general secretariat. The speech commending it to the Assembly occupied two hours, but it provided a framework also for the General Synod when it was formed in 1970. Achieving this had been far from easy, since many rival interests required reconciliation, and at one point Betty crossed swords with Archbishop Geoffrey Fisher who, she said, 'Treated me like a schoolgirl on the mat, being told off.'

Appointment to the Church Commissioners in 1959 had taken her on to some of its committees, and she confessed to being 'one of those tiresome but useful people who are always being put on things to link up with something else'. But there was more to it than that, since her unusual ability was widely recognized, and she was a popular figure whose no-nonsense style was tempered by warmth and kindness, and a great sense of humour.

These qualities were needed in fullest measure from 1968 onwards when Betty joined the salaried staff of the Church Commissioners as chairwoman of a new committee set up to deal with redundant churches. This was a very tricky assignment. In the case of churches of historical or architectural importance an alternative, suitable use had to be negotiated. For almost all of the churches local opposition had to be overcome and the demands of lawyers faced. Under Betty's leadership, however, problems were overcome and a procedure established that continues to serve the Church well. Even heavier responsibility awaited her. In 1972 she became the first-ever woman Third Estates Commissioner, responsible for dealing with the amalgamation, reorganization and sometimes closing of parishes. Much travelling was involved and rarely was a scheme carried through without stirring local opposition. Again, clarity of purpose and sensitivity were prime requirements, and of the 40 decisions that led to appeals to the Privy Council, the Church Commissioners lost only five.

Combined with this was the responsibility for the housing of the clergy, including that of the bishops. Although she always regretted the sale of a Georgian rectory or any other valued parsonage house, Betty knew from personal experience that the clergy no longer had the financial resources to live comfortably in very large houses, neither did the Church have the money needed to keep them in good repair.

The bishops' houses presented, in her time, a different problem. On appointment to a diocesan bishopric the new bishop and his wife often found their new abode and its furnishings not altogether to their liking and requested changes that were very expensive. Betty was sympathetic up to a point. She had, after all, spent her early years in none too comfortable episcopal houses, but she did not believe that the Church's diminishing resources should be used extravagantly and, if subjected to what she regarded as unreasonable pressure, would say, with a smile on her face, 'You don't have to accept this bishopric.' This usually settled the matter.

During these years she never lost sight of the women's ordination issue and took every opportunity in councils and committees to press the claims of women. In 1966 the Church Assembly debated a report on *Women in Holy Orders*, in which Betty affirmed once again her belief that women should be eligible for ordination and went on to wonder why the commission responsible for the report had taken three years to do no more than set down the pros and cons of the issue. She added:

> Experience of the past 30 years convinces me that the failure of the Church to find a real ministry for women goes deep down to a feeling that a woman can never be ordained. The real problem here is that the Church thinks of women as women, not as persons.

Membership of the Standing Committee of the successor General Synod provided further opportunities. A critical moment came in 1975 when, with her strong support, Synod passed a resolution of the greatest importance declaring there to be no fundamental objection to the ordination of women. This was followed by another resolution calling for the immediate preparation of legislation to enable women to be ordained whenever the Synod decided to authorize this.

To the surprise of everyone and the dismay of those pressing for such a decision at the earliest possible date, Betty voted against the resolution. During the debate she confessed to surprise at finding herself taking this line after so many years of hard work for the cause, but she believed that, if serious division in the Church were to be avoided, more time was needed for the truth of the first resolution to be widely absorbed – 'I cannot be sure that it is the will of God that our Church should be torn apart by going ahead nów.' She was aware that when the second resolution had been debated in the dioceses, only 15 of the 44 synods had accepted it. The General Synod voted against, and some believed that Betty's own decision had been critically influential, thus delaying the ordination of women by several years.

Betty received letters from some of the other campaigners expressing their bewilderment and, in some cases, anger at her action. It is, however, by no means clear that the General Synod would have voted otherwise had she not declared her mind or that it would have authorized the ordination of women any earlier. There were other hurdles to be overcome. Nevertheless Betty was for the rest of her life anxious about the step she had taken and not long before her death some thirty years later asked a priest friend, 'Has the Church forgiven me?'

Although it took some time before the most militant of the campaigners felt able to do so, Betty was by no means alone in advocating caution as most likely to achieve ultimate success. The Movement for the Ordination of Women, of which she had been a founder member, was divided over the timing of this issue. For others involved in the leadership of the Church, respect for her integrity increased even more.

Her circle of friends was immense, she was quite without 'side' and, a rotund, bustling figure, she brought a maternal presence and influence to even the grandest occasion. Her appointment as a Dame in 1975 was widely acknowledged to be a fitting recognition of a remarkable contribution to the life of the Church. But she still had four more years to serve before laying down her responsibilities, and was asked by the newly appointed Archbishop Runcie to stay on while a successor at the Church Commissioners was found. In retirement she chaired the Crown Appointments Commission responsible for nominating a new Archbishop of York – the choice falling on John Habgood.

Underlying all her burdensome work was a strong faith and a disciplined life of worship and prayer. For most of her life she was a member of the Bach Choir, and her love of music took her on to the

Council of the Royal School of Church Music. During an active retirement in Winchester she became governor of King Alfred's College and chair of the Hampshire Churches Preservation Trust, and presented a moving television programme on Evensong in the village church where her husband had 60 years earlier been the Rector. She died in 2005, aged 95.

*   *   *

In his address at the Memorial Service for Christian Howard held in York Minster in 1999, the Archbishop of York, John Habgood, said, 'It is to her perhaps, more than anyone else, that the Church of England owes the ordination of women.' The insertion of 'perhaps' may well have been due to the Archbishop's natural caution, but it might also reflect the fact that, although Christian Howard played a highly significant part in the debates on this subject in the Church Assembly, then in the successor General Synod, she was never among the most vociferous advocates of change.

By 1992, when the final debate was held and the historic decision was made, she had retired from the General Synod but, in recognition of her outstanding advocacy, was allocated a special seat in the public gallery. And she played a full part in the nationwide celebrations afterwards, later attending the ordinations of her many young women friends. She always asserted, though, that the issue was not primarily about what was good for women, but what was good for the Church, and again this distanced her somewhat from those who saw it also as a matter of justice and a recognition of the vocation to Holy Orders that some women undoubtedly felt.

Of the greatest value were the reports she compiled in 1972, 1978 and 1984 which were based on painstaking research and laid out the theological and ecclesiastical issues that must inform serious consideration of the ordination of women. Included was evidence of the role of women in the religions of the ancient world as well as much information about their place in the leadership of other Christian churches ancient and modern – all presented with objectivity and scrupulous fairness.

That she was born into one of England's great aristocratic families and spent much of her life in one of the country's finest stately houses, Castle Howard, was, in the circumstances of the time, no hindrance to her contribution not only to the Movement for the Ordination of Women but also to the affairs of the Church of England more generally. She belonged to its central councils for a quarter of a century, was an influential force in the British Council of Churches, and from 1961 to 1975 a member of the World Council of Churches' Faith and Order Committee, becoming its first woman moderator.

Christian had a natural authority and made her presence felt in any company. An acute mind, a mature political sense and an ability to think on her feet made her a formidable debater. She liked to be called fairly late in debate, so that she could demolish earlier arguments and pick up points that had been missed. Her temper in committees could be terrifying, but more than most she had sympathy with her serious opponents, and a generous way of apologizing when she felt that she had gone too far. She was always heard with serious attention.

Christian Howard was born in London in 1916. Her father was a son of the 9th Earl of Carlisle and held office in Asquith's Liberal government. Her mother was a daughter of Field Marshal, the 3rd Lord Methuen and her paternal grandmother, Lady Carlisle, was a leading suffragist who had one of her houses burned down for her pains.

Christian spent the first five years of her life in London before spending six months of the year at Castle Howard. A series of governesses, one of whom was dismissed because of her support for Mussolini, was respons-ible for her early education before she went to Westbourne House School at Folkestone. In common with most of her aristocratic contemporaries, she attended finishing schools in Florence and Paris, and said later, 'They could not seem to understand that I was not in the least interested in my appearance.' This deficit remained, and she always wore what seemed to be the same tweed suit.

She felt, and sometimes said, that she had never had a proper youth. Her mother died in 1932 and her father three years later. Two of her brothers were killed in the 1939–45 war and the third wounded. Thus when she was only 19 she found herself more or less running Castle Howard. This did not daunt her, and in November 1940 she played a vital part in the rescue of the family treasures when much of the house was destroyed by a disastrous fire.

A year earlier she had taken the London University Certificate in Religious Knowledge and in 1943 obtained a First in the Lambeth Diploma, having been tutored by Michael Ramsey, the future Archbishop of Canterbury who was at that time a Professor of Divinity at Durham University. This equipped her to teach Divinity at Chichester Girls' High School for a couple of years.

She then became secretary of the York Diocesan Board of Women's Work, a post she held from 1947 to 1979 and which turned her mind towards the true role of women in the Church and the need for their emancipation. Membership of other diocesan bodies and election to the Church Assembly soon followed.

When in 1967 the Church Assembly accepted that there were no theological reasons why women should not be ordained to the priesthood, some of those who rejected this attempted to introduce a diversionary measure requiring further study of the subject. Christian would have none of this and told the Assembly plainly that it could make no sense of the role of women until it had decided whether or not they might be admitted to the priesthood.

She was elected Vice-Moderator of the Movement for the Ordination of Women when it was formed in 1979. While warning its members that they faced a 'long haul', she never ceased to press the urgency of the case. She nonetheless always opposed any action that might be deemed illegal, and when an American woman priest accepted her invitation to celebrate the Eucharist in the chapel of Castle Howard, she explained that the chapel was outside the Church's jurisdiction and therefore beyond the reach of ecclesiastical law.

Christian herself never felt drawn to Holy Orders, though she often conducted services and preached in Yorkshire churches. She also devoted much time to the pastoral care of women parish workers and deaconesses who felt called to ordination and who were experiencing frustration at the long delay in their acceptance by the Church. Among her other contributions to the Church's life were membership of two commissions on Synodical Government and the executive of the British Council of Churches. When she attended her first meeting of the World Council's 119-strong Faith and Order committee, held in Montreal in 1963, she was shocked to find that there were only two other women members.

Christian's interests outside the Church included active support for the Liberal Democrat Party and the Girl Guide Movement, as well as the various schools of which she was a governor. When her brother George (later Lord Howard of Henders), having served as Chairman of the governors of the BBC, assumed responsibility for Castle Howard, she moved into the Gatehouse, then into a house at Coneysthorpe on the estate. Her love of the great house and delight in introducing visitors to it history and contents never faded, though ill health limited her activities during her final years.

Like her father and his mother – who is said to have had the contents of Castle Howard's cellar poured into the lake – she was a lifelong teetotaller. She became a Lay Canon Provincial of York Minster, was given a Lambeth MA, and in 1986 appointed Dame of the British Empire.

19

Impatient Feminists: Una Kroll, Monica Furlong and Bridget Rees

On 8 November 1978, at the end of a heated General Synod debate on a motion to remove the legal obstacles to the ordination of women, the Archbishop of Canterbury, Donald Coggan, asked that after the announcement of the result, a period of silence should be kept. When a negative result was announced, the silence was almost immediately shattered by a plaintive voice from the public gallery – 'We asked for bread and you gave us a stone.' It was that of Una Kroll, a diminutive figure wearing a T-shirt carrying the slogan 'Ordain Women Now', and her action is now seen as a significant, symbolic moment in the history of the twentieth-century movement for the ordination of women. Television and press cameras conveyed it round the world and it was often resurrected when the ordination of women was under discussion. She said later, 'I didn't want to do it, but for over two hours God kept saying, "Go on, get up there".' But no one who knew her was surprised when she did, for she was the most courageous, colourful and prophetic of the campaigners and was also deeply committed to the movement for improving the status of women more generally.

The daughter of a distinguished soldier, Una was born in 1925 and, having lost her father when she was only two, was brought up in Paris and Latvia, as well as in London, becoming fluent in three languages. The outbreak of war in 1939 interrupted her education at St Paul's Girls' School, which was completed at Malvern Girls' College. She went on to Girton College, Cambridge, to read Medicine, and while there had a Christian conversion experience which included a call to be a priest.

Since response to this was not possible, she decided on completion of her medical training at the London Hospital, to become a nun. Her missionary order sent her to Liberia to work in a hospital as a surgeon from 1953 to 1960. This led to her first clash with male ecclesiastical authority in the person of Father Leopold Kroll, an American monk, who was in charge of the hospital.

Their disagreement was over policy, but it led to them falling in love, and they decided to marry. This caused a good deal of scandal. Leo, who was older than Una, was expelled from his order and suspended from the priesthood. The Archbishop of Canterbury, Geoffrey Fisher, informed him that he would do his best to ensure that he would never again work in any part of the Anglican Communion under his jurisdiction, and he never did while Fisher was alive.

Back in London, and starting a family which grew to include three daughters and a son, Una spent the next 21 years in General Practice in south-east London. But the call to the priesthood would not go away, and in 1967 she persuaded Bishops Mervyn Stockwood and John (*Honest to God*) Robinson to let her join the recently created Southwark Ordination Course. This was designed to provide part-time training for men who would exercise their priesthood in secular employment. It was not intended for women, who could not be ordained.

At the end of her training no one knew what to do with Una, and in the end it was decided to ordain her as a deaconess in the parish of St Helier, Morden. The dynamic Donald Reeves, who had just become Vicar of this huge pre-war housing estate parish, was an enthusiastic supporter of women's ordination, and Una and Leo both became members of what became a large team engaged in many new forms of ministry. Una combined this with her medical work, to the advantage of both.

But she was not a priest, and her growing frustration extended to include discrimination against women in many other spheres. She therefore founded 'In Love and Anger', the Christian Parity Group. An immediate issue was a government proposal that Family Allowances, which had always been paid directly to mothers through the Post Office, should be taken away from them and given to the fathers. Una's approach to 20 well-known churchwomen's organizations to enlist support for a petition to Parliament failed, the most common excuse being that respectable churchwomen ought not to ally themselves with the 'disreputable' Women's Movement.

Nonetheless, she and her group joined in a protest march and various other lobbies related to discriminatory tax laws, social security provisions and, most notably, pressure to secure in 1975 the passage of a Sex Discrimination Bill. A year earlier she had stood for Parliament as a Women's Rights candidate for Sutton and Cheam, the first in the country since Christabel Pankhurst, when women were granted the vote. In this safest of Conservative seats she won only 298 votes but gained much valuable publicity for her cause. In the same year she joined 156 women from 46 countries in Berlin at a World Council of Churches consultation on sexism.

The basis of her campaigning was the conviction, much influenced by her medical experience, that at the most fundamental level the true relationship between men and women is not being properly expressed in the modern world, and that men as well as women need to be liberated from that which inhibits them from living life to the full. She does not believe that the Genesis myths offer any guidance here, and in her book *Flesh of My Flesh* (1975) she said:

> In assuming human flesh Christ accepted his mother's flesh as his own. Within this one person Jesus incorporates all the elements of humanity. The union of these elements of humanity is so perfect in Christ that it is impossible to distinguish in him elements which can be labelled 'feminine' or 'masculine'. It is, I think, important to understand that Christ is the pattern for wholeness for women and men alike.

Although Una and the Christian Parity Group, which was never large and more of a networking organization, were specially concerned with the wider issue of women's rights, they pressed increasingly for women to be ordained to the priesthood. They helped to make two television programmes on the subject and sponsored a tour of England by Mary Michael Simpson, the first nun-priest to be ordained in America. The presence in London of another American priest, who was employed by a bank, provided the group with a priest who for some time presided at celebrations of the Eucharist when they met.

Of special importance was its provision of a supportive haven for a number of women whose vocations were being frustrated, and some of these were given financial help to enable them to go to America for training and ordination. Una's pastoral insights and skills were of the greatest value within the group and beyond it. Although uncompromising and sometimes fierce in her promotion of the cause, she brought to everything considerable spiritual depth and compassion. Her first book was *Transcendental Meditation: A Signpost to the World* (1974), and congregations at Westminster Abbey, where she sometimes preached, found themselves listening to sermons on the spiritual basis of humility and reconciliation, rather than the expected fireworks and calls to the barricades.

Inevitably Una was drawn into the formation of the Movement for the Ordination of Women (MOW) and was present at the initial meetings. Neither was her support for it anything other than wholehearted. But she believed that nothing short of a revolution was needed for the overcoming of sexism in the Church and the liberation of men as well as women from its destructive thrall. Such a revolution was hardly likely to be ignited by the placation of worried bishops and the long-drawn-out debates and compromises of the General Synod.

The Christian Parity Group therefore continued to highlight the fundamentals but persisted with its own guerrilla tactics designed to indicate the need for radical and urgent action. Homosexuals and transsexuals were also taken onto its agenda. Una was now a household name in the Church of England and a hate-figure for many, but nothing could deter her and, besides the group's campaign and participation in theological dialogue, it became involved in the setting up of a Christian Women's Information and Research Service. This was to raise money for women in all the churches and to co-ordinate the efforts of many other small groups who were working for the abolition of sexist oppression in their churches.

From 1980 onwards she conducted her work from Fairlight Cove in Sussex. Leo, who always provided a strong emotional and domestic anchor, was becoming old and frail, so she gave up General Practice and for the next seven years was a Clinical Medical Officer in the Hastings Health District. She also helped in local parishes and was content for MOW to wage synodical warfare.

Following Leo's death in 1987, Una went 'bruised and battered' (as she put it) to the house of the Order of the Sisters of the Sacred Cross at Tymaws in south Wales. She now believed that only prayer could bring about the necessary change, but went also to test her vocation to the solitary life within a contemplative community. She emerged in 1988 to join the deaconesses who were being ordained to the diaconate. Three years later, she was professed as a solitary in the Order, though she left in 1994 in order to live entirely on her own.

The Church in Wales did not ordain women to the priesthood until 1997, and when the time came Una, now 71, hesitated before taking the final step to fulfil a lifelong vocation. 'After all the opposition over the years, I find it hard to accept', she said. She was also fearful that women priests were in danger of becoming absorbed into the culture of a still male-dominated Church. In the end, she decided that priesthood could only be experienced 'from within', so she was ordained by Rowan Williams, then Bishop of Monmouth, to live as a priest-solitary close to St Mary's Church, Monmouth, and to assist in the parish. There she remained until 2004 when she moved into a retirement flat in Bury in Lancashire, from where she continues to exercise a personal ministry, though some years ago she returned her Licence to Officiate to the bishop because of the way the Church of England treats gay people. She has written about a dozen books with titles such as *Sexual Counselling* (1980), *The Spiritual Exercise Book* (1985), *Growing Older* (1988), *Vocation to Resistance* (1995), *Forgive and Live* (2000) and, in her eightieth year, *Living Life to the Full* (2006).

*　　*　　*

Monica Furlong, the most radical of the Movement for the Ordination of Women's four Moderators and founder of the St Hilda Community, was one of the foremost religious writers of her time. She had a considerable following among those who found the Christian faith interesting and possibly significant but had difficulties with its orthodox presentation. Although deeply involved in the religious reform movement of the 1960s and a friend of most of its leaders, she did not remain anchored there. Her faith, expressed powerfully in her writing, had a deeply personal element and there was an element of the mystic in her.

Making full use of her already mature religious and psychological insights, Monica devoted her first book, *With Love to the Church* (1965), to an impassioned plea that the Church should move out of its established ways of approaching faith and morality. The language of the book was fiery and expressed her bitter disappointment that a vision of God she had experienced in Lincolns Inn Fields bore scarcely any relationship to the life of the Church in which she was attempting to live out its implications.

Her next book, *Travelling In* (1971), was banned from Church of Scotland bookshops because of its favourable reference to the drug LSD which she had herself experimented with under the supervision of R. D. Laing, a controversial psychiatrist in the 1960s. Then came *Contemplating Now* (1971) and *The End of our Exploring* (1973), also digging beneath the surface of human experience and again making use of Freudian and Jungian insights. She was, however, primarily engaged in journalism at this time as a long-running columnist on the *Daily Mail* and the *Spectator*. Her frequent excursions into the religious field, in which her sharpness of language, wit and compassion were unequalled, invariably brought hostile response, thus confirming her negative analysis of current opinion in the Church.

Born in Kenton, Harrow, part of north London's fast developing suburbia, in 1930, Monica developed a serious stammer at the age of four which affected her for much of the rest of her life. Soon after learning to write, she started to compose stories and announced that she intended to become an authoress. At Harrow County Girls' School she displayed considerable academic promise, but her parents were not of the sort to encourage her to persevere with entrance to Oxford, believing that she would do better to go to a secretarial college. This she did and always regretted her lost opportunity.

Her schooldays had been punctuated by the wartime bombing of London and many nights spent in air-raid shelters. The blast from a V1 rocket in 1944 caused her to be knocked unconscious by a trapdoor which fell from the ceiling of her house. The blast from another blew the doors and windows out, the ceilings down and all the tiles off the roof. Not surprisingly, she considered the war to have been the chief influence on her adolescence.

There were other influences at work, however, for as a child she was sent with her sister to the local parish church, where the high-church ritual edified as well as amused her. But after a time she migrated to the nearby St John's, Greenhill, where she liked the vicar and readily agreed to be prepared for confirmation. The somewhat conventional life of the church changed considerably after the war when the Vicar was replaced by a recently demobilized Army chaplain, Joost de Blank.

Of Dutch extraction, he was among the large cohort of returning warriors who were bent on making the world a better place and regarded a reformed Church as one of the key instruments in bringing this about.

The Parish Communion was adopted as the main focus of Sunday worship and this was accompanied by a variety of activities that made it one of the most dynamic parishes in the country. De Blank went on to be Bishop of Stepney, then a notably courageous Archbishop of Cape Town, before being driven by ill-health back to London and a Canonry of Westminster Abbey. During the Greenhill years Monica became aware of the pain caused by his repressed homosexuality, and the close friendship that developed between them was always important to her, as well as to him, and remained so until the end of his life.

On completion of her secretarial training, Monica applied for a job on the *Church Times* but failed to convince the formidable editor, Rosamund Essex, that she knew the difference between a chasuble and a cope, so she went instead to the BBC as secretary to a talks producer. This did not last long as her stammer made it virtually impossible for her to answer the telephone. Demoralized by the impediment, she was driven to take a much less interesting job as a typist with a Fleet Street publishing group. By this time she no longer believed in God, but one lunchtime, while sitting in Lincoln's Inn Fields, she had a visionary experience as a result of which 'I knew myself loved, accepted, accused, forgiven, laughed at, laughed with, touched, held, set free. It was the most important moment since I was born. I became a Christian.'

The immediate consequences of this were not happy. Compassion for a nice but lonely man, Bill, led her to accept his proposition of marriage. She knew before the wedding this to be a mistake, but felt unable to pull back. The mismatch brought much emotional suffering, and her life and outlook were scarred by this, but the birth of a son and a daughter was a great blessing.

Freelance journalism, including contributions to *Truth* – a weekly magazine akin to the *New Statesman* and the *Spectator* – brought her to the attention of Bernard Levin, who was to become one of the late twentieth-century's leading journalists, as well as a lifelong friend. He secured for her a regular column in the *Spectator*, and this in turn led in 1956 to her recruitment by *The Guardian* for regular feature writing.

Five years later, she moved to the *Daily Mail* for a five-year stint producing two or three articles a week on a variety of topics, all approached from a feminist angle and written in a lively style that attracted many readers. It was hard work, but earned a high salary which supported both her husband and their family.

It was about this time that Monica came into contact with a group of Oxford-educated high churchmen who had launched a monthly magazine, *Prism*, designed, they said, for Anglican graduates. She became one of its star contributors, and when the magazine evolved to become the house journal of the 1960s reforming movement, was drawn into the company of Bishop John Robinson, Eric James and other radicals, though there was no serious discussion during that decade of the possible ordination of women to the priesthood. Her contract with the *Daily Mail* having ended, she continued to write for the *Spectator* on religious matters and also for the *New Christian*, when it succeeded *Prism* in 1965.

She then decided to move with her family to a house in a fairly remote part of Norfolk. One of the effects of the LSD experiment had been to make her think that having a job was unimportant. She wanted a quieter existence and the opportunity to write more books. The next few years were another important period in her life. Attendance at Norwich Cathedral, as an occasional relief from the trying local church, led to friendship with its Dean, Alan Webster, and his wife Margaret, with whom she would later share in the leadership of the Movement for the Ordination of Women. The space afforded by life in the country, and the fact that her children were now reasonably independent, enabled her to see that divorce, however painful for all concerned, could no longer be delayed.

She therefore set this in train and returned back to London to become a producer in the BBC's Religious Broadcasting Department. The nuts and bolts of radio production were not really to her liking, but she was, as always, full of ideas and drew the best from her contributors. After four years, however, she went back to full-time writing and for a couple of years combined this with the study of Philosophy at University College, London.

A major project, which required extended visits to America, was a biography of Thomas Merton – an investigation of the life of a Trappist monk who had been a best-selling author on the spiritual life but then became a radical social and political reformer. This was a sympathetic study, but not without serious questioning of his motives and methods. It was highly acclaimed in Britain and America and won the Winifred Mary Stanford prize for biography in 1982. *Genuine Fake* (1986) was a similar examination of the life of the Californian Alan Watts who oscillated between Anglicanism and Buddhism and became renowned in the 1960s for his advocacy of free love. Another biography, *Thérèse of Lisieux* (1987), portrayed the young French saint as severely neurotic but courageous in making the most of her limitations.

Altogether different had been her earlier *Puritan's Progress* (1975), in which she suggested that John Bunyan is best regarded as an artist and a genius who voiced universal aspiration and need. There were also a few novels. The first, *The Cat's Eye* (1976), was about psychological projection, the next, *Cousins* (1983), concerned a sculptress whose love for a married theologian ended in disappointment but illumination for her. *Wise Child* (1987) was a mythology – a subject to which she became increasingly attached in her later years. In *God's a Good Man* (1974) she tried her hand at poetry.

For much of her later life, Monica found it helpful to consult a psychoanalyst on a regular basis. Then, during a short period of physical ill-health, she chanced to be treated by Dr Una Kroll. A friendship blossomed, and Una's commitment to the feminist movement was a constant topic of conversation. But although Monica had always had feminist sympathies, she was unmoved by the increased concern and activity that developed during the 1970s. She infuriated Daphne Hampson, a theologian, by telling her that she did not particularly care about women's ordination, since she believed there to be more important questions needing attention. And when she remarked to Una Kroll that she did not feel discriminated against as a woman she was told that she sounded like Queen Victoria inveighing against the wicked folly of women's rights. 'You may not suffer from discrimination,' Una added, 'but what about making an act of solidarity with all the women who do?'

Thus challenged she went with Una to the meeting at 2 Amen Court, the home of John and Diana Collins, in 1978, which led in February 1979 to the formation of the Movement for the Ordination of Women. Gradually she was drawn into its activities and led a small group in a silent demonstration at an ordination in St Paul's Cathedral in July 1980. During the singing of a psalm, immediately after the ordination itself, Monica and another member of the group walked across the huge space under the dome, holding up a banner saying 'Ordain Women'. Others held up their banners on each side of the nave until all were hustled out by stewards.

This demonstration, which was widely reported on television and radio, as well as in the press, created a great deal of anger. The Archbishop of Canterbury, Robert Runcie, asked her to go to see him at Lambeth Palace and take with her a few other women. They were received with charm and courtesy but there was no meeting of minds. Though the ordination of women might be right, there was no pressing need to do anything about it. Monica, who never herself felt called to be a priest, was appalled by the Archbishop's apparent insensitivity to the feelings of those who did. 'For the first time since I became a Christian,' she wrote later, 'I caught a glimpse of something I would come to see much more clearly in the years to come – that in the Church women are not quite real people, or at least not as real as men.'

The more cautious members of MOW also had reservations about the demonstration, believing that activity of this sort might well be counterproductive. Nevertheless, Monica, who had been the founding editor of the Movement's magazine, became Vice-Moderator in 1981 and in the following year succeeded Bishop Stanley Booth-Clibborn as Moderator. During the next three years her influence within and beyond the Movement was enormous, and the need to attend the General Synod's debate on the issue had the effect of driving her in an even more radical direction. *Feminism in the Church*, a volume of essays edited by her in 1984, and her own *Dangerous Delight* (1991), added to the ammunition.

The General Synod's refusal to allow women who had been lawfully ordained abroad to exercise their priesthood when visiting England led Monica to found in 1987 the St Hilda Community. Consisting initially of a group of eighteen men and women, this started to meet on Sunday evenings in the ecumenical chapel of Queen Mary College in London's East End. Its primary aim was to defy the General Synod by inviting women priests from abroad to preside at their Eucharists and to advertise these services in the church press. A sufficient flow of such priests made this possible, though eventually the presiding priest was usually an American woman working in London. Attendances grew rapidly and before long the congregation was comparable in size with that of a typical parish church. Most had temporarily forsaken their own churches as a way of protesting against the General Synod.

When, however, the *Sunday Times* reported on the Community's existence, the Bishop of London, Graham Leonard, immediately ordered them to cease meeting in the chapel. Initial resistance to this edict had to be abandoned when it turned out that the London diocese owned the land on which the chapel stood and that proceedings for trespass were to be started. They were, however, warmly welcomed to a joint Anglican–Methodist church where they flourished until no longer needed.

The Community quickly discovered that even the new forms of worship emanating from the Church of England's Liturgical Commission were not suitable for their purpose. Something much less formal and more inclusive was needed, and Monica began, as she said, 'to study liturgy in depth for the first time'. Although she remained the acknowledged leader, other members took it in turn to devise the liturgies, producing a rich variety. For Monica, as doubtless for many others, it was 'the most profound experience of a community at prayer that I ever experienced'.

On the day of the General Synod's decision that women might be ordained, Monica was among the large number of MOW supporters who, having failed to gain admission to the Church House public gallery for the debate, gathered outside to await the verdict. She was in a wheelchair, with a leg in plaster – the result of a walking holiday accident. She was nonetheless able to take a full part in the celebrations and was treated as one of the heroes of the hour. It turned out, however, that the battle was far from won, and Monica was among those first to see that the subsequent provisions for the dissidents represented a betrayal. Much of the rest of her life was spent seeking to get the Act overturned. *Act of Synod – Act of Folly?*, edited by her in 1998, included a wealth of plain speaking on the subject by others too.

There was still time for three more important books of her own. In 1984 she had gone to Australia to help start a MOW there, and during her visit was taken to see the outback in New South Wales. The experience of a vast territory largely untouched by human hand had a profound effect on her. She returned several times to other remote parts of Australia to stay with Aboriginal communities. This resulted in a study of their spirituality, *The Flight of the Kingfisher* (1996).

The place of myth in their spirituality turned her mind towards a study of the place of myth in religious experience. This did not materialize in the way she had hoped but developed into a revealing and unsurprisingly candid autobiography, *Bird of Paradise*, which related her personal experiences to a deeply religious and unconventional view of life. More than one important personal relationship had ended in tears, but for her the Bird of Paradise symbolized those flashes of truth that light up a world previously unseen and 'sometimes the capacity of others to love me – to

214

perceive me or understand me without a wish to clutch me or possess me – has had the same effect. "Jesus" is shorthand for those moments when, like the Bird of Paradise, religious truth becomes present to us.'

Before cancer intervened and demanded of her the same courage that had characterized the whole of her life, she completed *C of E: The State It's In* (2000). This substantial volume was in a sense a return to beginnings, with a large-scale analysis of the Church's condition. She concluded by suggesting that instead of worrying about the members it lacks, the Church should instead concentrate on ensuring that the members it does have experience the best quality of Christian life that can be managed.

When she moved from fashionable Notting Hill to a small house in less than fashionable Penge in south London, she played a full part in the life of the local church and ended her career as a writer by editing the parish magazine. She died on 14 January 2003.

*   *   *

Much less well known than either Una Kroll or Monica Furlong, but an important contributor to the campaign for women priests, is Bridget Rees who, in June 2011, became a Lay Canon of Bradford Cathedral – the kind of recognition that for most of her life would have seemed unthinkable.

Although proud to be following in the footsteps of her father and grandfather, both of whom were canons, she diverted to a path that has made her one of the most radical Christian feminist reformers. Within the Movement for the Ordination of Women, in which she played a full part, she was unashamedly among the so-called 'rockers of the boat' who argued for women priests, ordained overseas, to be invited to preside at its annual conference Eucharists and on other occasions. Many were opposed on the grounds that the ensuing controversy would harm the cause, but Bridget defended her position with passion.

She was also a leading figure among those who demonstrated at ordinations by standing silently inside cathedrals during the services or holding placards outside. After one ordination at Southwark in 1983 she preached at a 'Wilderness Liturgy' when milk and honey cake were shared, symbolizing a journey through the wilderness to the promised land. Similar liturgies were held elsewhere as a form of protest, and Bridget joined Monica Furlong in the forming of the St Hilda Community, which welcomed women priests from overseas. The use of inclusive language was a related concern, and an attempt to introduce new methods of teaching theology at Mirfield's monastic college proved to be unacceptable. For six years she refrained from receiving Holy Communion in churches that did not ordain women.

Her prophetic stance was not without personal cost, for she was often reviled for her witness. But her earlier years were quite different. Brought up in Jerusalem at the time the state of Israel was being established, she belonged for some years to the Church of England's Anglo-Catholic tradition. Having read Theology at Durham University, she became a lay worker and children's work adviser in Southwell diocese, at the same time lecturing at the Society of the Sacred Mission's theological college at Kelham.

This was followed by seven years (1973–80) as a licensed lay worker and education adviser in Carlisle diocese, when her outlook changed and she became involved in MOW. At its first conference held in Birmingham in 1980, Sue Hiatt, one of the American priests who had been irregularly ordained at Philadelphia, was among the guests, and some suggested that she should preside at the Eucharist. When the Bishop of Birmingham took this role, Bridget was among those who walked out and joined Una Kroll, who was praying outside. At the next annual conference, a woman priest from New Zealand presided.

The encounter with Sue Hiatt led to an invitation to stay with her in America – the first of several visits during which she met Carter Heywood and other radical Christian feminists. As a result she was able to encourage the British activists to engage with the processes of feminist theology and the books that were still by and large being read only by academics. The consequences of this were of considerable significance, providing MOW with a firmer theological base.

In spite of her singular stance, Bridget works collaboratively, and in her diocesan work has always had a special concern for the recognition and development of the ministry of the laity. She has also worked for Christian Aid, and a longstanding recognition of the link between feminism and other liberation movements took her for several years into the chair of the Friends of a Liberation Theology Centre in Jerusalem.

20

Transatlantic Explorers:
Elizabeth Canham, Kathleen Burn and
Susan Cole-King

Elizabeth Canham's pilgrimage to priesthood, described by her in a book with that title, was both circuitous and painful. It included a radical change of spiritual direction from a markedly conservative evangelical position to the catholic tradition of Anglicanism, and she is now exercising her priesthood in America as a freelance retreat conductor, spiritual counsellor, leader of pilgrimages and writer.

She was born in Old Hatfield in Hertfordshire and spent her early years in a terrace house until her father succeeded his father as licensee of the local Gun Inn. As a child, she attended the parish church Sunday School for a time, then migrated with a friend to that of the Congregational Church, before settling in a Brethren Assembly. There she eventually underwent baptism by immersion and embraced a narrowly conservative approach to the Bible and the closed community life of a sect. Sometime later she moved to a larger Evangelical Free Church, which met her spiritual needs for several years.

Meanwhile she had trained as a Religious Education teacher and taught the subject for six years in a number of comprehensive schools. During this time she also attended the London Bible College to study for a London University external BD. This exposed her to the tension between the academic requirements of the university and the conservative teaching of the college's lecturers.

Elizabeth then spent a year teaching and travelling in South Africa at the time when apartheid was being applied uncompromisingly. She accepted the privileges of a white woman but became increasingly uneasy at the plight of the black majority. On her return to England she became

Head of RE at a London comprehensive school, where she experienced at first hand the problems of race and poverty and the difficulties of teaching RE in this environment. She was, however, fortified by her involvement in the life of St Andrew's, Chorleywood – a lively Anglican evangelical parish in Hertfordshire – where she experienced a revitalizing of her faith and, after a few months was confirmed in St Alban's Abbey.

In 1975 she was appointed as a Lecturer in Biblical Studies at Wilson Carlile College where men and women are trained for ministry as Church Army officers. At the same time she enrolled at King's College, London, to work for a Master of Theology degree in the New Testament and also became a Lay Reader responsible for conducting services and preaching in Southwark diocese.

She now began to move out of the evangelical tradition and to embrace the Catholic emphasis on the sacraments and an incarnational approach to theology. Whenever possible she attended All Saints, Margaret Street, and was enriched by its worship and teaching. Her duties as a Lay Reader gave some satisfaction, but she felt that she wanted to do more, recognizing, however, that because she was a woman she could never be a priest. This was a tradition she had never questioned and for most of her life firmly upheld. With some reluctance she decided to seek ordination as a deaconess, her reluctance mainly due to the confusion that then existed over the history and status of this order. By this time, however, women had been ordained to the priesthood in America, Canada and New Zealand, and the pressure for the same in the Church of England was greatly intensifying.

Bishop Mervyn Stockwood, nearing the end of his lively Southwark episcopate, was a strong supporter of this move, and at Elizabeth's ordination he deliberately used the word 'deacon', rather than 'deaconess', thus suggesting that, as in the case of men being ordained with her to the diaconate, this was to be seen as preparation for the priesthood. As with certain of the Bishop's other actions, this was irregular, since there was nothing in the Church of England's canons that provided for women to be ordained even to the diaconate. The anomalous nature of his action was clearly indicated by the fact that when subsequently Elizabeth attended diocesan and deanery synods she was regarded as a lay person.

Nonetheless Stockwood's action was highly significant, and Liz, continuing to teach at the Church Army's College, became an honorary curate of St Luke's with Holy Trinity, Charlton, in south London. There she was regarded as a deacon, and the Rector, Tony Crowe, who was involved in the Movement for the Ordination of Women (MOW), provided for her to take a full part in the worship of the two high church parishes. She later acknowledged that she owed a great deal to him, but was feeling increasingly drawn to the priesthood and found it more and more difficult to attend male-dominated services. Her three years in Charlton, during which she also lectured on the diocesan Readers' course were, she said, 'years of struggle and joy, of frustration and fulfilment'.

Her experience beyond Charlton led her to discover painfully the high degree of suspicion, and often outright rejection, that a woman in her position felt when moving in circles opposed to their ordination. She joined in an MOW-organized silent protest at a Southwark Cathedral ordination, and in 1980 went to the United States to meet some of the women priests there and Bishop John Spong of Newark, in New York – the most radical of the American bishops.

She raised with him the possibility of transferring to the Episcopal Church so that she might fulfil what she now clearly felt to be a vocation to the priesthood. He was entirely sympathetic but felt that he must first consult the Church's House of Bishops. It would also be necessary to have the approval and commendation of the Bishop of Southwark. This proved to be no problem and, in a letter to Spong, Stockwood informed him that she was 'a properly ordained deacon of the Anglican Church' and added, 'I wish it were possible for me to ordain her to the priesthood but as you know it is forbidden for the time being.' He went on to outline the good work she had done in Southwark diocese and concluded, 'I hope you will receive her into your diocese and in due course ordain her to the priesthood.'

Meanwhile, she had formed a support group in London to provide 'a much-needed sense of solidarity', and when Bishop Spong, having consulted his fellow bishops, invited her to return to Newark to test her vocation, the Church Army granted her two months' sabbatical leave. These were spent as a deacon at St John's Union City, preparing for an examination in American Church History, polity and Canon Law and undergoing medical and psychological screening. On 28 January 1981 she was formally received as a deacon in the Episcopal Church.

It was, however, necessary for her to return to London to complete her service with the Church Army, and during this time she had an interview with the Archbishop of Canterbury, Robert Runcie. She explained to him how her vocation had grown and that, although she felt very positive about ministry as a priest in America, she hoped that it might be possible to return to England quite soon in order to help during the period of transition where the Church reversed its position on women priests. She suggested that when people had an opportunity to see women priests in action, they usually abandoned their opposition.

The Archbishop listened sympathetically but restated his opposition to women priests at the present time, because of the effect this would have on ecumenical relations. But he went on to say that he believed the Church of England would before long have women priests and asked Elizabeth to keep him informed of her movements. A visit to Colin Winter, the exiled Bishop of Namibia, was different. He had been one of her strongest encouragers and was now in a London hospital, having had a third heart attack. As she was leaving he said, 'Liz, give me your blessing before I go.' Coming so soon after her meeting with the Archbishop, she was stunned by his request, but was reassured when Bishop Winter added, 'Look, you are a priest. Soon the Church is going to affirm your vocation and I'm just a worn-out bishop who needs your ministry now.' He died later.

Elizabeth was back in America in May 1981 and three months later became Associate Rector of St David's Episcopal Church at Kinnelon, New Jersey. She spent four and a half days in the parish and two at the General Theological Seminary in New York, where she was being supervised for a Master in Sacred Theology degree in Spiritual Direction.

On 5 December 1981 she was ordained priest in the cathedral at Newark. Mervyn Stockwood, now retired, was the preacher, a letter from his successor at Southwark, Ronald Bowlby, was read, and among the large congregation was Tony Crowe from Charlton, and several other friends and supporters from England. The media were also present in force and the ordination was widely, and sometimes sensationally, reported on both sides of the Atlantic. Those who had not been able to travel to Newark formed a large congregation in St Michael and All Angels, Camberwell, for a celebratory service at the same time as the ordination.

A month later, Elizabeth was in London again and accepted an invitation from Alan Webster, Dean of St Paul's, and his wife Margaret, who was General Secretary of MOW, to preside at a celebration of the Eucharist in their Deanery. Women priests ordained overseas were still not permitted to minister as priests in the Church of England and the decision to hold the Eucharist in the Deanery rather than in the cathedral was an attempt to circumvent this regulation. During her stay, Elizabeth presided at five other House Eucharists – one of these in the Rectory at Charlton – and she was besieged with requests from the media for interviews.

It was not, however, until the day of her arrival back in America that objections to her actions were voiced, and the Bishop of London, Graham Leonard, spoke most loudly. He was leader of the opposition to women priests and obviously irritated by the fact that an 'illegal' Eucharist had been celebrated within the precincts of his own cathedral. In a four-page statement to the London Area Bishops' Council, quoted in many newspapers, he concentrated mainly on the legal position:

the law both of the church and of the land leaves us in no doubt that anyone who has been legally ordained abroad is not allowed to perform any ecclesiastical function in the Church of England and, whether privately or publicly, without, first, the authorization of the Archbishop of Canterbury under the Overseas Clergy Measures and, secondly, the authorization of the bishop of the diocese.

While this was, and remains, the case, it settled nothing since, as Elizabeth was quick to point out, there is a constant flow of overseas men priests to England. These often exercise priestly functions during their stay, but rarely, if ever, seek permission from the Archbishop of Canterbury or a diocesan bishop. Seeking to apply the rule only to women priests was therefore clear evidence of Bishop Leonard's sexual bias. There was the further question of whether or not a Eucharist celebrated in a house by a small group of friends could legitimately be described as 'an ecclesiastical function'.

On receipt of the statement, Bishop Spong responded with a no less lengthy document in which he noted that Elizabeth had responded to an invitation from the Dean of St Paul's who might reasonably be presumed to know the legal position concerning House Eucharists. He added that the description of such a Eucharist as 'an ecclesiastical function' stretched the concept of the Established Church to breaking point.

Spong raised, however, an altogether more substantial point related to a comment by Archbishop Runcie who, on his return from a visit to the

United States coinciding with Elizabeth's stay in London, stated that no one had tried to 'embarrass' him by forcing him to function sacerdotally with women priests. Spong reminded Runcie that he was the spiritual head of an Anglican Communion in which the United States, Canada, New Zealand and Hong Kong had women priests. If therefore it was an embarrassment to function with any of these priests then 'the fibre of integrity that holds that Communion together has been ripped asunder'. He added that the Archbishop's attitude also called into question the bishops who had ordained the women priests as well as the General Convocation of the Episcopal Church which had authorized the ordinations. He concluded by calling, unrealistically it seemed, for the issues to be discussed in a public dialogue and addressed in 'a sensitive, open and caring manner'. In spite of the powerful advocacy of Archbishop Ted Scott of Canada, the issue of women priests ordained overseas was never resolved until 1992, when General Synod authorized the ordination of women in Britain.

St David's, to which Elizabeth returned, was a parish of considerable affluence, situated in a beautiful rural area, surrounded by hills and lakes. She had a comfortably furnished apartment on a gated estate – all of which were some way removed from the kind of urban mission area with its immense social problems in which she had expected her priesthood to be exercised. There was also the problem that an eye affliction prevented her from driving a car and, since the parish was widely spread, she had to rely on lifts from other people or hire a chauffeur-driven car to get from place to place. She nonetheless contributed much to the church's life and gained valuable experience. Her ministry was greatly appreciated, but she felt increasingly drawn to spiritual direction, and in September 1982 moved from the parish to an apartment in the General Theological Seminary to complete her degree in this subject and also to teach in the Centre for Christian Spirituality. Later she completed a Doctorate in Ministry.

She moved in 1986 to South Carolina to become a cloistered oblate of an Episcopalian Benedictine community at Pinewood and director of its retreat ministry. Five years later the monastery closed and she founded Still Point Ministries at Black Mountain in North Carolina, where she now lives with two cats. From there she exercises a wide-ranging, ecumenical ministry that involves organizing pilgrimages (often to South Africa), retreats, training of retreat conductors and workshops, together with much spiritual counselling. She has written several books, including *Heart Whispers: Benedictine Wisdom for Today*.

*   *   *

Kathleen Burn's way to the priesthood was no less circuitous and in many ways more painful than that of her contemporary Elizabeth Canham. The obstacles standing in the way of the exercising of her vocation were formidable, and perseverance required considerable courage as well as a profound sense of divine calling.

She was born in 1948 in St Helens, Lancashire, but when she was only three months old the family moved to Wallsend, the shipbuilding town on the Tyne from where her father originated. He joined a small self-build housing partnership and constructed a bungalow at nearby Whitley Bay for himself and his family.

Kathleen attended the local grammar school and, initially, a Methodist Sunday School, but a friend took her to the high Anglican St Paul's Whitley Bay. There she was much influenced by the curate, was confirmed and, besides regular attendance at the Sunday services, was often present at weekday Eucharists. Involvement in diocesan youth pilgrimages took her to Lindisfarne, Hexham, Durham and the Yorkshire abbeys.

Having failed to qualify for university entrance, she went to a college of education, not because she felt specially drawn to teaching but because it would facilitate the continuation of her piano and organ studies. Nonetheless, she embarked on a teaching career at a small school in the village of Seaton Sluice where she taught seven- to nine-year-olds, and specialized in music. At St Paul's she was on the Church Council and the Diocesan Synod, and also found time to help with the work of Shelter.

After three years, however, she was accepted for missionary service by the United Society for the Propagation of the Gospel and went for training to the College of the Ascension at Selly Oak in Birmingham. Outside the college she was influenced by the charismatic renewal movement.

In 1972, Kathleen went to St Denys School at Muree on the Pakistan side of the Punjab, 8,000 feet above sea level in the foothills of the Himalayas. This was Muslim territory and most of the Christian minority belonged to the recently formed United Church of Pakistan. St Denys was a boarding school for the sons and daughters of Pakistan's upper classes.

It provided a traditional English education – formal, oppressive and totally unsuited to a teacher of Kathleen's background and outlook.

Visits to a nearby school run by American evangelicals provided a degree of relief and led to a conversion experience. Contact with Roman Catholics returned her to the world of charismatic renewal, all of which increased her sense of isolation from St Denys and led after a year to a move to become secretary/personal assistant to the Bishop of Lahore. She found worshipping with a Roman Catholic women's community more congenial than the services in the Anglican cathedral.

In 1975, she returned to England and spent a year at home readjusting and dealing with some health problems. She also began a course of preparation for reception into the Roman Catholic Church, but then changed her mind and decided to remain an Anglican. The United Society for the Propagation of the Gospel (USPG) employed her in its London headquarters for a few months, which she enjoyed, and she next planned to test her vocation to the religious life with an Anglican Franciscan community in Somerset. At the last minute, however, she changed her mind and went instead to the Roman Catholic Little Sisters of Jesus – an order founded by Charles de Foucault for work among the poorest of the poor.

Her contact was with the Order's house in Fulham, but it was decided that she should test her vocation in another house, in Dublin, to which she went at the beginning of 1977. There she was required to earn an income for the community, so she worked for a time as an orderly in a maternity hospital. The Archbishop of Dublin's decision that she could not receive Holy Communion with the Sisters left her 'angry and hurt', and when, after three months, it was mutually decided that she had no vocation to the life of the Order, she returned to the USPG in London.

It was about this time that Kathleen became aware of her vocation to the priesthood, and after a meeting with Una Kroll started to attend the Christian Parity Group, sharing its concern with the wider issue of the disparity between men and women in society. She also moved into a house in Notting Hill, in west London, shared with a Franciscan friend. Together they provided a welcome to ex-prisoners, unemployed and others in need.

When the bishops attending the 1978 Lambeth Conference went for a service in Westminster Abbey, she was among those who demonstrated outside in favour of women, and when she applied to Southwark diocese to attend an ordination selection conference, this was refused on the grounds that she was interested only in becoming a priest, not a deaconess. The Christian Parity Group then asked her to go to the United States as its representative at a conference in Baltimore organized by Roman Catholic women who were seeking ordination.

This proved to be a turning point in her life. The joyful expectancy of those she met at the conference and afterwards contrasted sharply with the somewhat depressed outlook of those in England who were in the process of forming the Movement for the Ordination of Women and planning for a long campaign. With the encouragement of Canon Mary Michael Simpson, with whom she had stayed in New York, she applied for admission to the General Theological Seminary. This was announced at a Press Conference in London organized by the Christian Parity Group, and an article in *The Guardian* brought her many letters of support including over £1,000 in donations to assist in the cost of the course.

The Bishop of Southwark, Mervyn Stockwell, sent a letter of support to the Dean of the General Seminary but warned Elizabeth that if ever women were to be ordained in England it would not, he thought, be for several years. Meanwhile he hoped that she would find a suitable outlet for her ministry in the United States and perhaps, in the years to come, in England. Much more than £1,000 was to be needed to finance her Master of Divinity course and the Christian Parity Group set about raising the balance required. But not everyone thought that she should go, arguing that it would be better for her to remain in England to continue the struggle in her own church. Nonetheless she went, after a service of blessing in St Botolph's, Bishopsgate, in the City of London.

Studying in an American seminary was not as easy as she had initially supposed it to be. The 'hothouse' style was not to her liking and integration into its community life took about two years. The traditional forms of patriarchal worship were especially difficult, and at one point she considered leaving. In a draft letter to the Christian Parity Group, which fortunately was never sent, she said:

I am becoming almost totally disenchanted with priesthood . . . In no way can I see myself part of the priest model in the church as most people see it today. The subordination of the laity; the way theology is kept in the hands of an elite; priest garb (especially that dog collar) – all these and more are more than just passive feelings in my attitude and responses to priests.

This explosion of frustration and anger acted as a catharsis, and the remainder of her time in the seminary was much more constructive and actually enjoyable.

It was, however, necessary for her to return to London for two months to undertake, as part of her training, a course on Clinical Pastoral Education at St George's Hospital. This went well and allowed time for involvement in a demonstration at a Petertide ordination at St Paul's Cathedral, as well as an interview with a *Guardian* journalist, which led to a half-page article in which she was described as 'a time bomb ticking quietly away in the Church of England'.

A three-months spell as a student minister at Christ Church, Oberlin, in Ohio, led her to apply to the Bishop of Ohio for ordination. Her ordination to the diaconate took place in 1982, with Elizabeth Canham present as a lesson reader, and the opportunity of further service at Oberlin and also in an inner-city, mainly black parish in Cleveland. On Ascension Day 1983 she was ordained to the priesthood. This was a time of joy and fulfilment, in spite of some problems with the Rector of the Cleveland parish who was not always sensitive to the role of a woman priest.

Much more serious than this, however, was the problem of her immigrant status. Up to this point Kathleen had stayed in the United States on a student visa, and when this expired it was explained to her that, since she had not been a Christian minister for at least two years before entering the country, she had no claim as a recently ordained priest to remain. Various representations to the authorities were made by the two parishes, and a judge extended by one year permission to stay.

The only course now open to her was to seek an appointment in Canada, where the immigration rules for clergy were much less strict. The Anglican Church there had, however, few vacancies, and she was driven to accept a three-church parish in upper-south west Ontario, which had been without a priest for over two years. Ministering in the three small farming towns involved a 45-miles round trip, the winters were hard, church life was traditional and stuffy, the congregations were resistant to change. Not surprisingly, Kathleen was both lonely and frustrated, and in a letter to her friends, sent shortly before Christmas 1985, she said, 'I'm hovering on the charred edges of burn out', and added:

> I have found that working without the support and companionship of colleagues is soul destroying. It only perpetuates the hierarchy of clericalism which needs congregational dependency, and it gives the wrong theological message about the nature of God, who lives in community.

Shortly after this she sent a letter of resignation to the Bishop of Huron who was not at all sympathetic and thought she was lacking in persistence.

By this time she had served as a priest long enough to qualify for re-entry to the United States. There she was offered accommodation to enable her to write a book about her life and experiences, which appeared in 1988 under the title *The Calling of Kate Burn*. She also became the Rector of St Mark's, Cleveland, a run-down parish in which, once again, she found herself battling against resistance to change. But church life was revived under her leadership, and she concluded, 'For the first time in my ordained ministry I feel deeply committed to ministry within a parish community.'

*   *   *

Susan Cole-King, the daughter of the legendary Bishop Leonard Wilson, who was tortured by the Japanese during his wartime years as Bishop of Singapore, devoted two decades to the care of the poorest of the poor in Africa before her ordination to the priesthood in New York in 1986.

Born in 1934 at Eighton Banks in County Durham, where her father was the Vicar, Susan moved to Hong Kong in 1938, he having been appointed Dean of the Cathedral there. Following the outbreak of war 12 months later, she was sent with her mother and her brother to Australia for safety. On Leonard Wilson's appointment as Bishop of Singapore in 1941, however, they elected to rejoin him, only to experience the arrival of the Japanese army a few months later and the need to return hurriedly to Australia.

The family was reunited when the Bishop was released from prison, and they returned to Britain in 1948, when he became Dean of

Manchester. In 1953 he was appointed Bishop of Birmingham, by which time Susan had enrolled as a student nurse at St Thomas's Hospital in London. Soon she was accepted for training as a doctor and, having qualified in 1962, went to Malawi to undertake primary health care in the villages.

In 1971 she took a diploma in Tropical Public Health and later studied Third World Development at Sussex University. Thus equipped, she joined the staff of the World Health Organization in Geneva, but did not find the administrative work satisfying, so she went as chief health adviser to UNICEF. Based in New York, this involved extensive travel in the developing world to advise on health care as an integral part of social and economic development.

It was during this time that she came to recognize even more clearly the importance of the spiritual dimension of healing and also felt called to be a priest. This was now possible in America so, after spending two years at the General Theological Seminary, she was ordained in 1986 to join the staff of the Church of All Angels on 80th Street, off Broadway in New York. This provided ample opportunity for ministry to the poor, and during the next three years her medical skills as well as her spiritual insights enabled her to make an important contribution to the Church's work among the homeless.

In 1989 Susan attended the service of celebration for women's ministry held in Canterbury Cathedral, and decided that she ought to return to England to join and support those women who were struggling to be accepted as priests. From 1989 to 1992, she served at Dorchester Abbey in Oxfordshire, and then spent two years as deacon-in-charge of St Peter's, Drayton, in Berkshire.

Although a priest, she accepted this role, believing it to be right to accept a responsibility that would not allow her to exercise her priestly ministry until the Church of England had changed its mind about this issue. Neither would she preside at Eucharists elsewhere, which disappointed the more militant elements in MOW who urged her to break the rules.

Her limited ministry in the parish was nonetheless greatly valued, and she also conducted retreats and addressed meetings on the subject of women priests. Her spirituality led her to become an oblate of the Society of the Sacred Cross at Tymawr, near Monmouth.

Following the ordination of women priests in England in 1994, she resumed the exercising of her own priesthood and, such was the esteem in which she was held in Oxford diocese, that in 1995 she came top of the poll in the election for the General Synod. Her experience soon led to appointment as vice-chair of the Board of Social Responsibility's international and development committee. She also became the first woman Honorary Canon of Christ Church Cathedral.

She officially retired in 1997, but her concern for the poor and suffering often took her back to Malawi, whose leaders she tried to persuade to tackle AIDS more effectively. At the 1998 Lambeth Conference she preached a memorable sermon on suffering, and three years later she died. Her marriage in 1955 to Paul Cole-King was dissolved in 1980; they had three sons and a daughter.

21

Guiding the Campaign to Success: Margaret Webster

In any assessment of the factors that led eventually to the ordination of women to the priesthood, it would be impossible to overestimate the contribution made by Margaret Webster. From 1979 to 1986, she was the Executive Secretary of the Movement for the Ordination of Women and effectively the leader of the campaign that secured change on 11 November 1992. This required unusual qualities of leadership, administrative skill and dogged determination, bound together by a spirituality which ensured that the campaigning took place on a plane higher than ecclesiastical politicking.

Margaret shared the reforming zeal of her husband Alan, who had been Principal of Lincoln Theological College, Dean of Norwich and in 1978 became Dean of St Paul's. It was not long after they had moved into the Deanery that Margaret was invited by John and Diana Collins, also at St Paul's, to attend an informal meeting in their home close by. Others at the meeting included Una Kroll and Monica Furlong of the Christian Parity Group, and Kathleen Burn, an aspiring priest.

They discussed how influence might be exerted on the vote at a forthcoming General Synod when the Bishop of Birmingham, Hugh Montefiore, proposed that its Standing Committee should 'prepare and bring forward legislation to remove the barriers to the ordination of women to the priesthood and their consecration to the episcopate'. The chief outcome of this meeting was a declaration of support signed by eight churchmen and women prominent in public life and also by Diana Collins and Margaret.

Shortly after the defeat of the Montefiore motion both were invited, in February 1979, to a consultation chaired by the Bishop of Newcastle, Ronald Bowlby, the then chairman of the Anglican Group for the Ordination of Women. Attended by the representatives of several organizations concerned with the issue, as well as some sympathetic members of the General Synod, it was decided to set up a national organization to be known as the Movement for the Ordination of Woman (MOW). This was officially launched on 4 July of the same year.

John and Diana Collins offered the use of a Christian Action office in Blackfriars, and Margaret undertook to 'look in to check the post'. Little did she realize what this would lead to and how significant it would turn out to be. Within a month, however, Christian Action found it necessary to vacate its office, and St Stephen's, Rochester Row in Westminster came to MOW's rescue with the offer of space in its Napier Hall, which is where it remained until its work ended, enjoying easy access to Church House and Parliament.

The launch was timely. Pressure for the admission of women was growing rapidly and soon MOW had active supporters' groups in 40 of the 43 dioceses. These included many men, and a threefold programme of study, prayer and action was adopted. This remained the central core of the movement's life at every level. Later it turned out that MOW had an important role in providing support and encouragement for the not inconsiderable number of potential women priests who were experiencing painful difficulties in their parishes and dioceses.

Doubling of the membership made increasingly heavy demands on Margaret's time and energy, until she was joined in the office by the highly competent Margaret Orr Deas to form a creative partnership which was extended over the next seven years. The first Moderator of the movement was Stanley Booth-Clibborn, a descendant of the founder of the Salvation Army, who had just become Bishop of Manchester. An unusually courageous Bishop, who was unwilling to compromise over what he believed to be right, his leadership during the early years was of the utmost importance.

Money was a constant problem. The office had only basic furniture and Margaret continued to keep costs to a minimum, but members' subscriptions were hardly sufficient to meet the requirements of a rapidly expanding movement. It proved impossible to reclaim the income tax on subscriptions since MOW was campaigning for something that would require a change in the law. It could not therefore be regarded as a charity.

A public meeting held in Church House, Westminster, in 1980 was addressed by the forthright Ted Scott, the Primate of Canada, where women had already been ordained. This provided encouragement as well as welcome publicity, and an imaginative Festival of Women, held in the same year at St James's, Piccadilly, helped to heighten confidence. Vigils and silent demonstrations now began to be held outside certain cathedrals at the time of ordinations. These were carefully organized and the demonstrations consisted of no more than the exhibition of placards and the handing out of leaflets.

This and other campaigning activity led, however, to accusations that MOW was shrill, strident, aggressive and infected by secular feminism. Opponents of women priests spread this about, but there were others of a more generally conservative outlook who did not welcome anything that might suggest radical extremism. For some years this was a problem for the movement, but it was in part solved by the evident centrality of prayer in all its activities, and also by the good humour that was never far from the surface. Again Margaret's influence was crucial.

The spiritual emphasis was reinforced from 1983 by the annual observance in May of Juliantide commemorating Julian of Norwich, a fourteenth-century anchorite, mystic and probably the first woman to write a book, *Revelations of Divine Love,* in English. In the north of England, Hilda of Whitby was added to a great celebration in Durham Cathedral. At St Paul's, Alan Webster preached at a special service attended by 500 members of the Anglican and Roman Catholic women's religious communities. New liturgies and forms of prayer were also devised, and in January 1984 special services were held in Westminster Abbey and Sheffield Cathedral to commemorate the fortieth anniversary of the ordination to the priesthood of Florence Li Tim-Oi by the Bishop of Hong Kong. She was involved in both services.

The regular arrival in England of women priests who had been ordained in other parts of the Anglican Communion now raised the issue of whether or not they might preside at the Eucharist during their visits. The Church of England's laws forbade this and an attempt to persuade the General Synod to relax them in 1986 failed. But four years earlier the Revd Janet Crawford, a New Zealand priest, presided at a Eucharist held on the Sunday of MOW's second annual conference at Swanwick in Derbyshire. The Bishop of Derby, Cyril Bowles, preached a welcoming sermon and the event went largely unnoticed outside MOW circles.

There had been no such episcopal welcome for the Revd Elizabeth Canham when she presided at a Eucharist held in the Deanery at St Paul's in January of the same year. She was an Englishwoman who had gone to

America to be ordained, and her action in the home of Margaret and Alan Webster provoked a four-page statement condemning the event by the Bishop of London, Graham Leonard – the arch-opponent of women priests. The resultant publicity did no harm.

Neither did it four years later when the Revd Joyce Bennett, who had been ordained in Hong Kong and was now ministering to a Chinese congregation at St Martin-in-the-Fields, presided at a Eucharist held in Church House, Westminster. This was on the occasion of MOW's annual general meeting, when 200 members were present and widespread reporting led to a considerable uproar. Letters of protest poured into the MOW office, Archbishop Robert Runcie, who was visiting America at the time, was reported to be dismayed, and a letter of explanation signed by Margaret and others brought a hostile response from virtually all the bishops.

Dismayed but not cast down by the reaction, MOW continued to invite women priests to officiate during its AGMs. When later in 1986 the General Synod approved the ordination of women to the diaconate, thus removing any ambiguity about the status of deaconesses, this was welcomed, though not without some concern since opponents of women priests regarded the diaconate as an alternative to the priesthood for women. MOW now had its own widely read journal *Chrysalis*, expertly edited by Monica Furlong, the Vice Moderator. An advertising agency also offered its services for free for other promotional work.

At this point Margaret gave up the position of Executive Secretary after seven strenuous and often exhausting years, though she remained very active in the movement's leadership. She was succeeded by Margaret Orr Deas and Caroline Davis, who became joint Executive Secretaries.

The 1988 Lambeth Conference required another major publicity effort, and this included an exhibition 'Women of God' in the Canterbury Centre, a converted church which became a meeting place for bishops, their wives and many women from overseas. So the pressure for change continued, with more younger people joining the movement, and close collaboration with the much smaller Priests for Women's Ordination, which provided important male support. By the early 1990s MOW had 6,000 members and another 4,000 more loosely attached. A special appeal to finance more literature brought in £20,000.

On 11 November 1992, the day of the momentous vote, Margaret had a seat in the gallery at Church House. Although it was by no means certain that the required two-thirds majority would be achieved in each of the General Synod's three Houses, she had an inner conviction that it would. She brought a candle to light at the hoped-for celebrations afterwards. These lasted for one-and-a-half hours outside Church House and were echoed by MOW groups, with many other supporters in every diocese.

One of Margaret's most important contributions had been to hold together in the movement those who believed that success would come only through patient, persistent pressure on the Church's Synodical government, and others who believed that unless a loud noise were made, and positive, even illegal steps taken, the long-practised opponents of change would always win. These different beliefs were represented by successive Moderators – Monica Furlong, radical, high profile and heroine of the younger, impatient women; and Diana McClatchey, a deaconess and outstandingly able member of the General Synod, whose debating skills were influential. The parallel with the Suffragette and Suffragists movements 80 years earlier was obvious and now, as then, both were needed and both shared in the celebrations.

Her book *A New Strength, A New Song* (1994), which gives an invaluable account of what she called 'The Journey to Women's Priesthood', Margaret concludes with an expression of her conviction that the ordination of women brought something new to the life of the Church – 'The important questions about ministry can no longer be put into trays marked "Too Difficult" or "Not Yet". The windows are open, the papers are blowing about, we have to work in a different way.' But, in spite of the valiant campaigning efforts of Women and the Church (WATCH), MOW's successor organization, another 20 years would be needed before women could become bishops.

22

First-Fruits of the New Order

Between 1994 and 2009 (the latest available figures), 4,714 women were ordained into the priesthood of the Church of England. During this period 4,451 men were also ordained. Of the women, 3,247 were ordained to self-supporting ministry, while 1,927 men were similarly ordained. Every year since 1995 the number of women entering self-supporting ministry has exceeded that of men, often substantially, and in the years 2008 and 2009 the proportion was 300 to 208.

In 2009, the total number of priests in the provinces of Canterbury and York in full-time stipendiary ministry totalled 8,228, of whom 1,649 were women. Those in part-time stipendiary ministry were 330, of whom 166 were women; in self-supporting ministry 2,522, of whom 1,270 were women; in ordained local ministry 578, of whom 316 were women. There were also 7,472 Licensed Readers, of whom 3,723 were women.

The attractions of part-time and self-supporting ministry include, obviously, greater compatibility with family responsibilities, as well as the opportunity to combine priesthood with a secular profession. But there are other factors, which include the shortage of stipendiary posts for women and their preference for spheres of ministry in which there is no sex discrimination.

Nonetheless a large number of women are now engaged in traditional pastoral ministry – about 100 are Area or Rural Deans – and it is difficult to see how the long-established pattern of parochial organization could have been maintained without their contribution to it. Their absence from leadership in major town and city parishes is, however, noticeable.

By 2010 there were four cathedral Deans, 11 Archdeacons (now 19) and 22 Cathedral Residentiary Canons – figures that are seriously disproportionate to the number of women in the priesthood. Until 2000 it was possible (just) to explain that women priests were not sufficiently experienced to be considered for senior posts, though it was not unknown for men of similar experience to be preferred. Such an explanation is no longer possible, since a large number of women priests had long experience as deaconesses and deacons before ordination to the priesthood became possible. It is evident that some dioceses offer more possibilities to women than others do, and the attitude of their bishops is decisive.

Research carried out by Canon Jane Hedges of Westminster Abbey indicates a marked unwillingness on the part of women to apply for senior posts when, as is now normal, these are advertised. There is evidence that many able men priests are similarly reluctant which also suggests that alternative methods are needed. Admission to apostolic leadership should not depend on the ability to complete a form more impressively than sister competitors.

The brief examples that follow of ministries exercised by women priests since 1994 is intended to indicate the rich variety of work being undertaken in different spheres. The contribution being made by the other 5,000 is no less significant.

Joanna Stoker

Joanna (Jo) Stoker became Rector of the Basingstoke Team Ministry in 2003. Before the 1939–45 war, Basingstoke was no more than an old Hampshire market town, but during the 1960s it expanded rapidly to accommodate part of London's post-war overspill. Today it has an affluent population of 80,000 employed in major pharmaceuticals, electronics and insurance companies as well as at the headquarters of the Automobile Association. A frequent 45-minute rail-link with London Waterloo makes it popular with commuters.

The Team Ministry serves the busy town centre from the ancient St Michael's Church, and the large urban housing estates from four modern churches. It normally has six or seven ordained ministers and four licensed lay ministers, working in their local areas, co-ordinated and led by the Rector from St Michael's. Four of the Team Vicars are women, as is the self-supporting curate.

Jo sees an important part of her responsible role as keeping up with and reflecting on changed social patterns and attitudes in order to plan a strategic approach to mission. The developing of collaborative patterns of work and encouraging the professional development of the team clergy is also a prime concern.

She brought to Basingstoke much relevant experience, having been from 1997 to 2003 a Team Vicar, then the Team Leader, of the large ecumenical parish of Stantonbury – an urban priority area on the edge of the new town of Milton Keynes. There Anglicans (of Anglo-Catholic heritage), Methodists, Baptists and members of the United Reformed Church worked in partnership, ministering to a highly mobile population from seven church buildings. Jo led a team of nine ordained ministers and ten licensed lay ministers.

She was born in Somerset, educated at Frome Grammar School, spent a gap year in Brussels as an au pair, then took an Honours degree in English Literature at Leicester University. A year as a clerical assistant with Leicestershire County Council was followed by three years at Lincoln Theological College preparing for ordination as a deaconess in 1983.

From 1983 to 1989 she was at Farnham Royal with Hedgerley – three villages on the edge of Slough. Next came five years as deacon, then priest-in charge (incumbent) of Seer Green and Jordans – an affluent, one-church parish in south Buckinghamshire. She also became involved with the Quiet Garden Trust (eventually as chair of the trustees) – a non-denominational ministry of hospitality and contemplative prayer in private homes. Leading Quiet Days and helping to run a Quiet Garden at Stoke Poges was part of this.

Beyond Basingstoke Jo is an Examining Chaplain to the Bishop of Winchester, an adviser on ministerial selection and a governor of Winchester University. She is an Honorary Canon of Winchester Cathedral. Married to Ian, she has two grown-up sons.

Vivienne Faull

Vivienne Faull has ministered in three very different cathedrals – first Gloucester, as Chaplain, then Coventry, as Canon Pastor and Vice-Provost, and since 2000 Leicester, where she was the first woman to be appointed as a Provost (this title was changed to Dean in all the so-called parish church cathedrals in 2002).

Leicester is not the easiest of cathedrals to lead and it required courage to take it on at the beginning of the new millennium. When the diocese was formed in 1927 and the not particularly attractive parish church of St Martin designated as its cathedral, there was no money for the endowment of a Chapter of clergy or indeed for anything else. Since then it has been one of the two poorest English cathedrals. Lacking also the historical ambience and support attracted by an ancient foundation, it has in the past struggled for recognition and affection.

Vivienne's appointment was designed to signify a new approach and not therefore welcomed by the senior canon who was a member of Forward in Faith. The last 11 years have nonetheless vindicated the Bishop of Leicester's decision, and today the cathedral houses a vibrant community reflecting the ethnicity and social diversity of what is described as Europe's first plural city. A £2 million Millennium Appeal enabled a Cathedral Centre, providing meeting space and offices, to be established and, working in partnership with the city authority, a Visitors' Centre was opened.

Another partnership, this time with the diocese, has led to the purchase and refurbishment of an adjacent redundant grammar school building, which is to become a major centre for new approaches to mission. The Cathedral's Christian Education programme has already won national acclaim and other faith communities in the city are being helped to develop their own educational programmes.

All this in addition to raising £350,000 for the rebuilding of the organ, £800,000 for the restoration of stonework, and something more for the installation of an exciting 'Burning Bush' window by Amanda Ford. Vivienne's time has also been claimed by chaplaincy to two Lord Mayors, of no faith, and now to a High Sheriff, who is a Sikh. She is also chair of the Association of English Cathedrals and the vice-chair of the Deans' Conference.

Before her ordination as a deaconess in 1982, Vivienne went from St Hilda's College, Oxford, to teach in north India. This was followed by three years of youth work in a tough area of Everton in Liverpool. Preparation for ordination at St John's College, Nottingham, where she took a degree in Theology and a diploma in Pastoral Studies, led to a curacy at Mossley Hill Parish Church in Liverpool. While still a deaconess, she became chaplain of Clare College, Cambridge, and after five years went from there to Gloucester Cathedral, joining the first of those who became priests in 1994.

Rose Hudson-Wilkins

Rose Hudson-Wilkins' appointment as Chaplain to the Speaker of the House of Commons in 2010 attracted a good deal of publicity, this being the first time a woman had been chosen for a unique historic office. It also created a certain amount of fuss, because it had been separated from the Canonry of Westminster and the Rectory of St Margaret's, with which it had in recent times been combined. Now she is responsible for conducting the traditional prayers before the daily meetings of the House and also the pastoral care of the 650 MPs and 2,500 members of the staff.

Rose was born in Montego Bay, Jamaica, and as a child attended the local St Faith's Mission run by the Church Army. When only 14, she felt drawn to serve God in some form of ministry and four years later went to England to train as a Church Army Sister. On her return to Jamaica she began to ask, 'Why not women priests?', but her application for training just as a deacon in England was not immediately successful. She was told that her chief task was to care for her husband and children. But the Bishop of Lichfield, Keith Sutton, eventually accepted her and, after attending the West Midlands Ministerial Training Course, she was ordained to a curacy at St Matthew's, Wolverhampton.

Outside Church House, Westminster, during the decisive debate in 1992, she held a banner bearing the words 'Women Beautifully and Wonderfully Made in the Image of God', and was herself ordained to the priesthood two years later. Soon afterwards she became Lichfield diocese's Officer for Black Concerns, combining this with the post of associate priest of the Church of the Good Shepherd in West Bromwich.

In 1998, Rose became Vicar of the united parish of Holy Trinity with St Philip, Dalston and All Saints, Haggerston, in London's East End. Ideally suited for this toughest of challenges, she has built up a vibrant church life and tackled head-on the considerable social problems of the area. Time has also been found for service of the General Synod, as one of the panel that chair its meetings, on the Broadcasting Standards Commission, in the chair of the National Committee for Minority Ethnic Anglican Concerns, and the World-wide Committee of SPCK. Altogether, a very considerable handful of responsibility. Her husband Kenneth is a prison chaplain, and they have three children.

Sheila Watson

Sheila Watson became Archdeacon of Canterbury in 2007 and in this historic office has, besides responsibilities in the diocese, the unique duty of enthroning in their cathedrals the newly appointed diocesan bishops in the Province of Canterbury. In this, she is acting on behalf of the Archbishop of Canterbury in a custom that dates back to the thirteenth century, and the irony of having a woman in this role is, for the moment, inescapable.

Sheila was born in Scotland and, after education at St Andrew's University (MA, MPhil), Corpus Christi College, Oxford and Edinburgh Theological College, was ordained as a deaconess in 1979 to serve churches at Bridge of Allan and Alloa. A year later she moved south to St Mary's, Monkseaton, in Newcastle diocese, and in 1984 to London to become Adult Education Officer in the Kensington Episcopal Area. In the following year she married Derek Watson, Vicar of St Luke's and Christ Church, Chelsea, and left her training post in 1987 to share in his ministry as an honorary curate of the parish. Thus began a long partnership in ministry, facilitated by the availability of complementary posts and, sadly for them both, no children.

In 1992 Sheila became a Selection Secretary at the Advisory Board of Ministry at Church House, Westminster, and immediately challenged the assumption that she would deal only with women ordination candidates. The appointment of Derek as Dean of Salisbury in 1996 provided new opportunities for extending her own ministry in the diocese, first as Adviser in Continuing Ministerial Education, then as Director of Ministry.

She became an Honorary Canon of the cathedral in 2000, and two years later Derek retired slightly early, which enabled her to accept the post of Archdeacon of Buckingham. He is now Preacher of Lincoln's Inn. After five years of involvement in the leadership of Oxford diocese, Sheila moved to Canterbury at the request of the Archbishop.

Lucy Winkett

When Lucy Winkett left St Paul's Cathedral in 2010 to become Rector of St James's, Piccadilly, the Bishop of London, Richard Chartres, who has always opposed the ordination of women to the priesthood on ecumenical grounds, described her as 'among the best priests of her generation'. There was ample evidence to support his affirmation. Before going to Selwyn College, Cambridge, to read History in 1987, she spent a year in Australia teaching music. Cambridge was followed by a variety of activities, including more teaching, residence in a L'Arche community, working as a barmaid and training a beautiful soprano voice at the Royal College of Music where she earned an ARCM in 1992. In the same year she went to prepare for the diaconate at the Queen's College, Birmingham, where she took a BD.

By this time, ordination to the priesthood was possible, and from 1995 to 1997 Lucy was a curate at Manor Park in Ilford. The combination of pastoral and musical gifts then took her to St Paul's Cathedral as a Minor Canon, with shared responsibility for the ordering and leading of the cathedral's worship. Joy in this post was, however, diluted considerably for a time by the refusal of the senior Canon Residentiary to attend Eucharists over which she presided. These were also boycotted by other members of the cathedral community.

Strongly supported by the Dean, Eric Evans, and other colleagues, she accepted the deep pain of the situation and battled on valiantly until relief came with the retirement of the aggrieved Canon. So impressive did her ministry become that, when the Canon Precentor moved in 2003, she was appointed in his place with full responsibility for the cathedral's music and liturgy – a considerable undertaking.

Other developments in her ministry led to Lucy becoming a much sought-after preacher, lecturer and broadcaster. *Our Sound is Our Wound: A Contemplative Listening to our Noisy World* was the Archbishop of Canterbury's 2010 Lent Book and sold widely. St James's, Piccadilly, one of the country's most dynamic parishes, is making good use of her gifts.

Cherry Vann

Cherry Vann, who became Archdeacon of Rochdale after wide diocesan consultation in 2008, could hardly have anticipated such an appointment during the four years she was studying piano and violin at the Royal College of Music. But, having taught music for a time, she felt drawn to ordination and spent three years at Westcott House, Cambridge, before becoming a deaconess in 1989.

A curacy in the parish of Flixton marked the beginning of her ministry in Manchester diocese and, always concerned with frontier ministry and those on the fringes of the Church's life, she was from 1992 to 1998 chaplain of Bolton Institute of Further and Higher Education, with a base at St Peter's, Bolton. She was among those ordained to the priesthood in 1994.

Remaining in frontier ministry, Cherry then spent six years with the Deaf Church, based now on the large parish of East Farnworth and Kearsley, also in Bolton, where she was a Team Vicar. This was, she says, 'a life-changing experience'. The need to meet people where they are and to communicate with them in a language they understood helped her to see how God might be at work in the world in new and exciting ways. She also took the opportunity to reflect on the tension between the mainstream Church and 'the Church on the margins'.

This did not, however, discourage her from becoming and remaining a member of the General Synod, nor from leaving her work with the deaf in 2004 in order to take over her parish as Team Rector – this providing the challenge to lead a group of ministerial and lay colleagues in seeking new opportunities of ministry both within and outside the church community. Appointment as Area Dean a year later led her to explore new ways in which clergy and parishes can work together and share resources. As an archdeacon she is able to do this on a wider scale.

Cherry was Bishop's Adviser on Women's Ministry from 2004 to 2009, became an Honorary Canon of Manchester Cathedral in 2007, and in 2008 was elected to the chair of the diocesan synod's House of Clergy. It is fair to presume that she is the only Archdeacon who is also conductor of a chamber orchestra – that of Bolton – taking since 1998 its weekly rehearsals and giving three concerts a year.

Janet Fife

Janet Fife, who became Vicar of Marske-by-the-Sea in 2010, arrived there after one of the toughest experiences of Christian ministry that any priest might have. After gaining an Honours degree in English Literature at Sussex University, she worked in publishing and bookselling before going to Wycliffe Hall, Oxford, in 1984 to prepare for ordination.

The stimulating experience of this turned out to be poor preparation for her role as a deacon chaplain at Bradford Cathedral where she was expected to confine herself to pasturing the congregation but have no opinions about other related aspects of the cathedral's life. Her position was no better when, after two years, she moved to St Michael-le-Belfry in York – one of the leading charismatic evangelical churches in the country. Again part of a large team, her contributions to discussions were usually passed over, and objections were raised to her wearing a clerical collar.

Two senior laymen ripped this from her shirt. Reflection on all this led to a book *To Be Honest* (1993) on the importance of honesty in spirituality.

Movement to Salford University as a chaplain in 1992 brought welcome relief. The bishop told her that it was 'the most difficult job in the diocese', but the opportunity to work on the margins of church life and to create one's own role without an already established status suited Janet well. Apart from the attitudes of some ecumenical colleagues, the issue of her being a woman priest did not arise and she flourished. During the next eight years she came to believe that serving without power on the margins is the authentic path of Christian mission, for this is where the love of God meets human need. Interest in the use and abuse of power in the Church encouraged her to take an MPhil on the pastoral care of sexual abuse survivors.

In 2000 she moved back into parish ministry as Vicar of Upton Priory, Macclesfield – an overspill new housing area from Manchester. Apart from the many routine problems that communities of this sort produce, she fought a ten-year battle against drug barons and was their only enemy who refused to be driven off the estate. She was also able to encourage demoralized residents to have more confidence in themselves and make a difference. An uncaring establishment had in the end to sit up and take notice.

Marske-by-the-Sea is a large North Yorkshire village with a distinct identity that has had a church since Saxon times and was probably visited by St Hilda. It has a solid church life and many of the congregation have a deep spirituality. The contrast with what has gone before in Janet's ministry could hardly be greater, but she sees the pain of the earliest years as an important part of her training and says that she has experienced God's love wherever she has ministered.

Fiona Stewart-Darling

There can be no more important a task in Christian mission in London than that now being exercised by Fiona Stewart-Darling, who has since 2004 been leading the Canary Wharf Chaplaincy. Built on the site of the former West India Docks on the Isle of Dogs, Canary Wharf has some of the tallest buildings in the United Kingdom. It is one of London's two main financial centres, housing the headquarters of major banks and international corporations. Some 90,000 people work there and are served by over 200 shops, boutiques, bars and restaurants.

Fiona has for colleagues another Anglican (male) priest and a Roman Catholic priest, and they recognize the need to be joined by a Muslim and Jewish chaplains, as well as representatives of other faiths. The chaplaincy serves all, regardless of faith or background, and its mission statement outlines the objectives:

> We are here to help people to live as if their beliefs matter in the way they do business.
> We are here to support those who promote honesty, integrity and trust in their business and personal lives.
> We believe that everybody lives by a set of values, whether or not they are aware of it.
> We are here to help people discover and explore how beliefs can inform or give meaning to their values.
> We support people in making the changes they want to make in their professional and personal lives.
> We help people integrate their values and beliefs into every part of their lives.
> We believe everyone should live life to the full.

Given the scope and magnitude of this task, and the fact that London's other main financial centre is served by upwards of 50 priests, the case for some re-deployment of the clergy would not be difficult to argue.

Fiona brought considerable experience to her role. After graduating in Chemistry from Kingston Polytechnic, she completed a PhD in Chemistry at Birkbeck College, London and became a Senior Research Scientist with the Gas Board. Ordination as a deacon in 1991 took her to the Cotswold parish of Cirencester for three years, but she spent another three years as chaplain of the Cheltenham and Gloucester College of Higher Education before moving to the chaplaincy of Portsmouth University from 1997–2004. During this time she was also an honorary chaplain of Portsmouth Cathedral and took an MA at King's College, London.

In her teens she had sometimes thought of full-time Christian work, but was not excited by the prospects of overseas missionary work or any of the other ministries then open to women. It was not until she was working with the Gas Board that she 'discovered' the office of deaconess and, although this offered possibilities that eventually became for her a vocation, she enjoyed her work as a scientist and wanted to achieve as much as possible in this field before turning to ordained ministry.

A gap year spent working at the Lee Abbey Conference Centre in Devon and reflecting and praying about her vocation, changed this. She went to Trinity College, Bristol, and by this time the diaconate was open to women. Initially the call to the priesthood created some problems since it had never entered her head that this might be God's purpose for her, and she struggled with how God could be so cruel as to call her to something which was in conflict with the Church. But she was in the basement café of Church House, Westminster, when the 1992 decision was made and when the result was announced joined in what she described as 'an eruption of sheer joy, an overwhelming moment'.

Besides her demanding responsibilities at Canary Wharf, she is on the staff of All Hallows-by-the-Tower, a member of the London Diocesan Synod, on the editorial board of *Faith in Business Quarterly*, and a Council member of Mission in London's Economy.

Christine Farrington

Christine Farrington, then a deacon, was a member of the General Synod in 1992 when the decision was made to ordain women priests, and it was appropriate that she should be among the first to be ordained. She had in fact felt drawn to ordination at the time of leaving school but, since that was not then possible, went to London and Nottingham Universities before joining the Probation Service at Hemel Hempstead in 1966. She saw this as an alternative way of exercising care and compassion.

She then spent seven years as a Social Work tutor and lecturer at Enfield College (now Middlesex University) before returning to the Probation Service in a senior post.

In 1982 Christine was ordained as a self-supporting deaconess at Redbourn in St Albans diocese and was soon elected to the General Synod. While still a deaconess she was in Lincoln from 1986 to 1987 as Director of Pastoral Studies at the theological college and as assistant chaplain at the prison. Next came seven years at Salisbury as director of a new ecumenical study centre and cathedral deacon. Then, from 1993 to 2002, at Ely as Co-Director of Ordinands and Director of Women's Ministry; a year before becoming a priest she was made an Honorary Canon of the cathedral.

These responsibilities were combined with those of a curacy at Great St Mary's, the university church, at Cambridge, followed by six years as Vicar of St Mark's, Cambridge and chaplain of Wolfson College. Sheila was made a Chaplain to the Queen in 1998 and, having returned to Redbourn for retirement in 2002, has been kept busy, assisting in local parishes and for a time serving as Rural Dean.

Jane Tillier

Jane Tillier was also on the steps of Church House, Westminster, when the historic decision was made in 1992. A deacon at the time and serving at St Mark's, Broomhill in Sheffield, she was among the first to be ordained to the priesthood two years later. Soon afterwards she moved to Gloucester to be cathedral chaplain.

This was followed by six years (1997–2003) as priest-in-charge of the Staffordshire parish of Madeley, to which Betley was added in 2002. Then came four years in the part-time post of Chaplaincy Team Leader at the Douglas Macmillan Hospice in Stoke on Trent. Since 2008 she has been priest-in-charge of St John Baptist, Barlaston, and also Ministry Development Adviser for the Stafford Episcopal Area. She was made a Prebendary of Lichfield Cathedral in 2011.

Jane was educated at New Hall, Cambridge, and, after completing a doctorate in late-medieval Spanish poetry, taught Spanish in the university, as well as serving as a lay chaplain of Jesus College. She was ordained to the diaconate in 1991 after training at Ripon College, Cuddesdon.

Owing much to the friendship and supportive counsel of Una Kroll, Jane is one of the many women priests who have struggled to combine their ministries with the care of a family. Three miscarriages, followed by the birth of Clare, then three more miscarriages cannot be typical, but meeting the needs of one or more toddlers is common enough and inevitably leads to conflicts of duty in a parish.

At this time Janet was fortunate to have the support of her area bishop, but this was limited by the fact that in an entirely new situation the church was, and remains, without the imagination and flexibility necessary to deal adequately with the financial and housing issues arising from the part-time ministries of incumbents.

Nonetheless, Jane believes that her costly experience during the first ten years has informed her priestly ministry in creative ways that she could not have foreseen, and which she can now share with a new generation of women priests.

Jane Hedges

When she became the first-ever female Canon of Westminster in 2006, Jane Hedges entered the Chapter of the most traditional of England's churches, and since then has carried the feminine flag in what remains a largely male-dominated Royal Peculiar. Besides sharing in the Abbey's worship and preaching, and in the considerable administrative burden that falls on the Dean and Chapter, she has a particular responsibility, as Steward, for the reception of the multitude of visitors.

This is no easy task. Trying to ensure that the million or so people who enter the building each year for a variety of reasons are made to feel welcome, rather than a troublesome imposition, and leave with a better understanding of its essentially religious purpose, is obviously of vital importance. Less onerous is the office of Archdeacon of Westminster, into which she entered in 2011, since there is no archdeaconry.

Jane was not born to the Royal scarlet. Nurtured in a family in which children were expected to leave school at 16, her early education was poor, but she felt called to ordination when only 17 and was fortunate enough to live in a parish where the Vicar, who had previously worked with deaconesses, gave her much encouragement.

A degree at St John's College, Durham, followed by vocational training at nearby Cranmer Hall, led to ordination as a deaconess in 1980 and service at Holy Trinity, Fareham in Hampshire. She next widened her experience as a member of the Southampton City Centre Team Ministry from 1983 to 1987 before returning to Portsmouth diocese as Stewardship Adviser, then, a year before her ordination as a priest in 1994, as a Canon Residentiary of the cathedral.

Eight years later she returned to parish ministry as Team Rector, and subsequently Rural Dean, of Honiton in Devon, with its associated rural parishes. It was from there that she moved to Westminster. She is married and has two grown-up sons.

23

Women in the New Theology

The rapid development of the feminist movement in the Western world during the latter part of the twentieth century is now seen to have sprung from the Civil Rights movement in the United States which raised fundamental questions concerning racial justice and freedom. The related emergence of Black Theology then led a new breed of women theologians to question the patriarchal basis of the Judaeo-Christian religion and to investigate the degree to which this religion has over many centuries reinforced, rather than challenged, orderings of an unjust, unequal society in which women are ruled by men.

This questioning largely escaped the attention of those involved in the British theological ferment of the 1960s, as did the rise of Black Theology and Liberation Theology. It was not until the 1970s that feminism began to be taken seriously in Britain. Meanwhile, in the Roman Catholic Church, the Second Vatican Council created an atmosphere in which some of its women members, mainly nuns, felt free to challenge the inferior place accorded to them in the life of their Church, and the theological basis of a clerically dominated hierarchical order.

These stirrings eventually spread worldwide. Thus there are now African, Indian and Oriental forms of feminist theology, relating to particular cultures and traditions, and significant though these are, they cannot be discussed in a book about the Church of England. Within the Western world also, feminine theology has taken on a variety of forms and appears in a number of different guises. These can be roughly divided into two main categories.

Within orthodox Christianity feminists see themselves as in the prophetic tradition, recalling believers back to the authentic faith. The scholars among them examine the New Testament more closely in order to discern more clearly the part played by women in Christianity's origins. The presumption here is that their part has been obscured. Equally, the development of Christian theology during the early formative centuries, and subsequently during the medieval years, is believed to have been deeply compromised by the patriarchal culture the Church embraced.

These fields of study provide considerable scope for reconstruction and reinterpretation. Questions are raised about the use of the Bible and the nature of its inspiration, since almost all of it has for many centuries been used to justify the oppression of women. More questions are raised about the use of exclusively masculine symbols and metaphors in respect of God and other fundamentals of the faith. How can women incorporate these into their own spirituality without adopting potentially disabling contortions?

Questions of this sort lead inevitably to issues relating to the Church's worship, the form of its ordained ministry, the role and responsibilities of the laity, and the broad religious culture that informs the Christian community's life. The exclusive use of masculine terminology in prayer and hymnody should, it is argued, not be taken for granted. Neither should the exclusion of women from any part of the Church's leadership and the assumption that the structure of its organization, devised by men, is necessarily the best for every time and situation.

Therein lies the material of the early debate concerning Christian feminism – a debate of fundamental importance which many in the Church still find disturbing, but which others find stimulating and illuminating. More recently, however, there has been a move by many scholars to go beyond analysis and debate to a consideration of how feminine insights and concerns can be used constructively by both women and men seeking to live the Christian life within and without the faith community.

Feminist theologians are often prolific writers, and a considerable number of books have been produced on, for example, inclusive theologies of God, suggesting the relationships of Friend and Mother – 'She who is'; re-interpretations of the Trinity, expressed as Creator, Redeemer, Sustainer, rather than as Father, Son and Holy Spirit; the use of the title Christa as an alternative to Christ. A new and stronger emphasis on the activity of the Holy Spirit is seen as a key element in this new theology, as also are innovative expressions of spirituality – now emerging on a considerable scale. The calling of women to apply their faith and insights to major social problems that adversely affect women and children is seen as another imperative.

There remains, however, another category of feminist theology, which is far more radical and poses even more serious questions that challenge the very authenticity of the Christian faith itself. Gerda Lerner, a historian, has summarized the challenge succinctly:

> Our whole culture, including the Christian tradition, is infused with a conceptual error of vast proportion – the androcentric fallacy. All human thought has been communicated from the male point of view and is thus skewed. We cannot just add women to thinking and institutions. What is needed is a radical restructuring of all thought from the feminine perspective.

A number of the pioneering feminist theologians were led by their studies and their experience in the Church to embrace positions not far removed from this. They concluded that Christianity is so sexist and so hopelessly compromised that the only solution is to leave what they call patriarchal religion and to accept older 'goddess' traditions of pre-Jewish–Christian paganism.

Others have sought post-Christian solutions in which contemporary feminine experience is accorded priority over what they regard as dubious or unbelievable revelations from the past. This leaves open the possibility of faith in a God who is not other than the world, but connected to everything that is, and commitment to a way of life directed towards the creation of a human society in which all may flourish. The formation of communities of kindred spirits is not ruled out, neither is the awareness of a supernatural power that is responsive to prayer, but most of what has been defined as Christianity is definitely rejected. It is significant, however, that none has embraced atheism.

Joyce Caine (1921–96)

Before turning to some of the chief contributors to the ongoing debate about feminist theology, space must be allocated to a biblical scholar who, though little known outside the evangelical circles of her own Church of England, nonetheless played a significant role in preparing women for ordination and securing the changes necessary for them to become priests.

During her time as Principal of Dalton House, Bristol, and later as

Dean of Women at Trinity College, Bristol, Joyce Caine persuaded many evangelicals that, contrary to their previously held beliefs, there was nothing in the Bible to preclude women from being ordained. Nor, she argued, did the doctrine of the Headship of Christ exclude women from positions of leadership in the Church. She played a vigorous part in the Movement for the Ordination of Women's campaign.

Known throughout her professional life as Joyce Baldwin (she did not marry until 1983, the year after her retirement), Joyce took a degree at Nottingham University and the Cambridge Certificate in Education, before teaching religious education and modern languages in Lancashire. She then offered for service with the China Inland Mission and during her training for overseas work took the London University Diploma in Theology.

She went to China in 1949, but her missionary efforts were severely restricted when the People's Liberation Army took control, and after two years she returned to England. Her hope to be able to take up CIM work in Malaya was dashed by the recurrence of health problems contracted in China, so she went instead as a lecturer to Dalton House, Bristol, where women were trained for missionary work and for parish work in Britain.

She took the external London BD and taught philosophy and ethics and the Old Testament, and when in 1971 Dalton House was merged with Tyndale Hall and Clifton Theological College to form Trinity College, Bristol, she concentrated on teaching Old Testament. She was then one of the few female Old Testament scholars whose knowledge of the Bible was enriched by active interest in the archaeology of the ancient Near East. She wrote six well-received commentaries on books of the Old Testament.

Joyce's concern for the ordination of women was aroused by her acquaintance with women bearing heavy missionary responsibilities in China – as well as by her own experience of male domination in evangelical circles. She was ordained deacon in 1987, but decided not to proceed to the priesthood when that became possible, just two years before her death, since her vocation remained that of a scholar.

Mary Daly (1928–2010)

Mary Daly is an iconic figure among the radicals. Born of working-class Irish–Catholic parents in upstate New York, she described herself as a 'radical lesbian feminist'. Denied, because she was a woman, the opportunity to take a higher degree in any American Catholic institution, she took doctorates in philosophy and theology at the University of Fribourg in Switzerland and taught for 33 years in the Jesuit-run Boston College in the USA.

Frustrated by the failure of attempts to get greater equality for women in her Church, she wrote *The Church and the Second Sex*, which caused a considerable furore in America and condemnation by the Vatican. As a consequence, she was dismissed from her teaching post, though later reinstated. There were other problems over her refusal to accept male students into her classes, maintaining that they would only confuse discussion. A colourful personality, much of her life was spent challenging church authorities, and she wrote many books, in one of which she described 'the eight deadly sins of the fathers' as processions, professions, possessions, aggression, obsession, assimilation, elimination and fragment- ation. She concluded that patriarchy was not only the root of women's oppression, but also of all social ills in which people are treated as objects.

Eventually she called it a day and in *Beyond God the Father* declared her rejection of mainstream Christianity and her belief that the concept of Father God is no more than a speculation in the human imagination. Worship is not, she said, 'kneeling in front of so-and-so but swirling in energy' and she advised women to throw their lives as far as they would go. Daphne Hampson, a British feminist theologian and in some ways a parallel figure, also rejected what she believed to be the Christian faith and explained the consequences of this for her in *After Christianity* (1996 and 2002).

Rosemary Radford Ruether (b. 1936)

Rosemary Radford Ruether is more widely known than Mary Daly is in England where her books have been widely noticed and some become influential. Born of a Roman Catholic mother and an Episcopalian father, she took the Catholic road, though her distinguished academic career has been spent in Protestant colleges and universities. Her initial pioneering work was concerned with the relationship between feminist and liberal theology, and in particular its ethical dimension. In this she was influenced by early experience of working in the Delta Ministry in Mississippi and in a black University Divinity School.

She describes herself as an 'eco-feminist' and has always been an outspoken critic of racism, poverty and war and a campaigner for civil rights for African-Americans, all of which she regards as part of the struggle for liberation in which women are also involved. The Israeli–Palestinian conflict is another of her concerns, as also are the theological roots of anti-Semitism, and she expressed her beliefs powerfully in *Integrating Eco-Feminism, Globalization and World Religions*.

It did not take her long to discern that 'Christianity is riddled by hierarchy and patriarchy', and her first book, *Sexism and God-talk*, now a classic, is a systematic feminist treatment of symbols. *Goddesses and the Divine Feminine* was a clear indication of her disenchantment with the institutional Church, and she has called on women to form 'Women Church', small feminist communities within the traditional Church where women can explore their own spirituality without patriarchal interference. This should have its own theology and practice and incorporate goddess worship into its liturgy, making use of the mythology of the ancient Near East. It not easy to see, however, how this might meet the needs of modern Western women who are seeking to express their religious faith in the context of personal experience.

Elisabeth Schüssler Fiorenza (b. 1938)

Elisabeth Schüssler Fiorenza made a major contribution to biblical studies with her substantial volume *In Memory of Her: A Feminist Theological Reconstruction of Christian Origins* which first appeared in 1983, was translated into several languages, and was provided with a new introduction for a 1994 edition. Her approach to the Bible has a fourfold method in its interpretation.

1 Suspicion of the biblical writers' interpretations, particularly those involving the status of women; 2 The affirmation and proclamation of those parts of the Bible which affirm liberation, and the rejection of the rest; 3 The remembrance, reclamation and honouring of the biblical women who suffered as victims of patriarchy; 4 Rewriting the biblical text to 'put back' the forgotten women.

Born in Romania in 1938, Elisabeth fled with her parents to Germany during the war and afterwards had the ambition to become a professional theologian in her Roman Catholic church. Ordination to the priesthood being impossible, she nonetheless became the first woman to gain admission to the theological course for future priests at the University of Wurzburg.

Her thesis for the Licentiate in Theology was published in 1964 as *Forgotten Partners: Foundations, Facts and Possibilities of the Professional Ministry of Women in the Church*, this being somewhat ahead of the Second Vatican Council meeting at the time, but not beyond its spirit. A doctoral thesis for the Catholic Theological Faculty in the University of Münster produced *Priest for God: A Study of the Motif of the Kingdom and Priesthood in the Apocalypse*. This was a series of Bible studies and the early history of the Church, which provided the foundations for her magnum opus.

More books and articles enhanced her reputation and she moved to a series of academic appointments in America, first at the University of Notre Dame in Indiana, then at the Episcopal Divinity School at Cambridge, Massachusetts, and finally to a Chair in Divinity at the Harvard Divinity School. Her husband also has a Chair, in Catholic Theology, there, and they have a daughter.

Bread Not a Stone: The Challenge of Feminist Interpretation (1984) was a further development of *In Memory of Her* and offered a comprehensive model of biblical interpretation based on feminist insights and scholarship. Liberation is fundamental to human flourishing.

Although some, even among her admirers, find her somewhat Germanic academic style a hindrance to comprehension, her teaching methods involved workshops in which students were asked to retell biblical stories in a variety of media and settings, with a particular emphasis on the sufferings, struggles and dreams of women. This approach was offered more widely in *But She Said: Feminist Practices of Biblical Interpretation* (1992).

Although aware that her work has aroused widespread interest, not least in academic circles, she is naturally disappointed that it has made little difference to the traditional ways in which the study of theology is pursued. Nonetheless, she has remained in the Christian camp.

Ursula King (b. 1938)

Ursula King, a Roman Catholic of German origin, is a scholar of international reputation and, from 1989 until her retirement in 2002, was Professor of Theology and Religious Studies at Bristol University and

Director of its Centre for Contemporary Studies in Religion and Gender. Still busy, she is a Senior Research Fellow at Bristol's Institute of Advanced Studies and a Professorial Research Associate at the London School of Oriental and African Studies Centre for Gender and Religious Research.

Educated at Bonn, Munich, Paris and Delhi before completing a London doctorate, and, prior to her appointment to Bristol, she taught at Delhi, Leeds and Cambridge. She has been President of the European Society of Women in Theological Research and of the British Association for the Study of Religion, and lectured extensively worldwide. In Britain she has delivered the Hibbert and Bampton Lectures and in Norway been a Visiting Professor of Feminist Theology at Oslo University.

Ursula was an early entrant into the field of feminist theology with a special concern for its relation to spirituality.

Grace M. Jantzen (1948–2006)

Grace Jantzen was an innovative philosopher of religion and highly regarded in the academic world, where she was Professor of Religion, Culture and Gender at Manchester, but she is more widely known for her biography of Julian of Norwich, published in 1987. This remains easily the best introduction to the fourteenth-century mystic and contains a scholarly and perceptive evaluation of Julian's spirituality and theology. Of special interest is her discussion of the importance of the use of the Mother metaphor for God and Christ, though she warns against the co-option of Julian into modern feminism.

Grace explained her interest in Julian as arising from 'a conviction that if one is going to do philosophy of religion one ought to know something about religion, not least about the life of prayer, and about giving and receiving love of God and neighbour'. This refreshing approach distinguishes her writing from the dry, detached character of much philosophy of religion, and she challenged her students to explore the social and political relevance of their thinking and to ask – Who benefits from such thinking?

Her *Becoming Divine: Towards a Feminist Philosophy of Religion* (1998) was a major new contribution to the study of religion. Its basic thesis, in outline, is:

Much of traditional philosophy of religion (and Western culture generally) is preoccupied with violence, sacrifice and death and built upon mortality, not only as a human fact but as a fundamental philosophical category. This is essentially a masculine approach. But what if we were to begin with birth and with hope and possibility and wonder implicit in it? How if we were to treat natality and the emergence of this life and this world with the same philosophical seriousness and respect which has traditionally been paid to mortality and the striving for other worlds?

The masculine approach she challenges is not, however, to be seen as an unfortunate philosophical mistake but the devising of the now classical theism 'which validates power, mastery, eternity, utter independence, spirit rather than body, another world rather than this world, maleness rather than femaleness'. More than this, 'It seeks to repress and veil an anxiety of the material body and of female sexuality.' Thus the scriptures portray God as Lord, King, Father, Judge and Warrior, and salvation implies an act of rescue coming from an outside world, rather than the imaging of flourishing in this world.

Beneath the Judaeo-Christian preoccupation with death, there are, however, traces of an alternative world of beauty and life, and the question to be asked of all images of God concerns their ethical adequacy and whether or not they facilitate human beings becoming divine, the underlying belief being that God is to be located in the whole of creation and that human beings must therefore come to recognize and express the divinity that is within them. It is no surprise that she became a Quaker.

An important chapter in the books challenges the belief held by Ruether, Fiorenza, Hampson and other feminists that religious faith must be based on personal experience rather than on revelation or inherited tradition. Whose experience? What experience? she asks, and how is subjective experience of this sort to be shared in such a way that it constitutes an effective challenge to injustice, inequality, repression and the other social and economic ills of the world?

Grace Jantzen was born into a Mennonite family in northern Saskatchewan and remembered travelling to school by horse, cart and sledge. After completing a doctorate in Philosophy and Theology at the University of Calgary she did the same at Oxford and in 1980 took up a teaching post at King's College, London. Her first book, *God's World, God's*

Body (1984) was a clear indication of the way her thought was developing, and in *Power, Gender and Christian Mysticism* (1995) she brought together feminist philosophy and a history of mysticism.

The taking up of a research fellowship at Manchester University led to the creation there of a Centre for Religion, Culture and Gender and to her appointment to a professorship in this combination of subjects. *Becoming Divine* was the framework for a projected six-volume study of Death and the Displacement of Beauty in Western Philosophy, and the first volume, *Foundations of Violence* (2004), was completed before cancer led to her premature death. Colleagues edited *Violence to Eternity* and *A Place of Springs* which were published posthumously in 2008 and 2009. The closing years of her life were spent in a fulfilling partnership with Tina, who survived her.

Ann Loades (b. 1938)

Ann Loades is a philosophical as well as a feminist theologian, and during a distinguished academic career extended her study and teaching to an even wider field of theology. Born in Stockport, Cheshire, she went from a girls' grammar school in Oldham to Durham University to read Theology, following in the footsteps of two brothers who had done the same in preparation for ordination.

It was not her original intention to pursue an academic career and, after taking a teaching diploma, taught in Newbury Grammar School for two years. But the opportunity to undertake postgraduate study took her to McMaster University in Canada and Chicago University, and on her return she was appointed to a tutorship at her former Durham College – St Mary's.

Completion of a PhD equipped her for a university lectureship in 1975 and the beginning of an involvement in Durham's Faculty of Theology, which extended over the next 28 years. During this time she became a prominent figure in Durham's life, was the first scholar to be appointed to a personal chair in the university, was chair of the Board of Studies in Theology, and became the first woman Lay Canon of the cathedral. It seems safe to say that she is the only professional theologian in the world who also taught ballet – a lifelong passion.

Further afield, Ann was editor of *Theology* from 1991 to 1997, President of the Society for the Study of Theology in 2005 and 2006, and Scholar

Consultant of the Christian–Muslim Forum. In 2001 she was appointed CBE – a very rare honour for an academic theologian.

An early interest in philosophical theology, which owed something to the writing of Austin Farrer, found expression in an important study of suffering, *Kant and Job's Comforters* (1985), but an invitation to deliver the Scott Holland Lectures on some aspect of the Incarnation steered her in another direction and the publishing of a book with the engaging title *Searching for Lost Coins* (1987). Thereafter she ranged very widely and came to believe, and teach, that the study of theology should not be restricted to narrow fields but extended to embrace liturgy, spirituality, the arts and social and political realities.

In the realm of feminist theology, of which she has an encyclopaedic knowledge, Ann has been influential, especially in Britain, because of her balanced approach and acute analysis of its very varied international developments. *Feminist Theology: A Reader* (1990) was, and remains, an invaluable source book, providing judiciously chosen extracts from the writings of 22 of the leading exponents at that time. Its usefulness required the printing of several impressions.

Apart from the expression of her feminist outlook in books on other subjects, and in contributions to symposia and learned journals, her most important book on the subject, so far, has been *Feminist Theology: Voices from the Past* (2001). This consists of a study of the lives and works of Mary Wollstonecraft, Josephine Butler and Dorothy L. Sayers. with particular emphasis on the moral and social issues they grappled with. She interweaves with these some contemporary issues such as abortion, child abuse and women's work, and offers her own theological appraisal of them.

In all this, she is sharply critical of some of the early, more radical feminist theologians whom she accuses of paying little attention to the nature of history and the way in which all human thought is socially conditioned, that of women as well as men, and the present as well as the past. She concludes trenchantly that the danger inherent in feminist theology is that in its rightly proper concern with improving the status of women it becomes narcissistic and self-absorbed. A new elite is thereby produced that fails to show due concern and compassion to those who continue to fall foul of existing social structures or who are victims of new situations. Twenty-three pages of references and further reading suggestions follow.

A brief, paperback introduction to the life and thought of Evelyn Underhill (1997) emphasizes, again, the importance of integrating theology and spirituality and suggests that her subject still has things to teach and challenge Christians today.

Jane Shaw (b. 1963)

Jane Shaw, the daughter of a feminist churchwarden, has combined the work of a distinguished church historian with active participation in the life of the Church and much campaigning for the admission of women to the priesthood and the episcopate. In 2010 she left Oxford, where she was Reader in Church History, to become Dean of Grace Cathedral in San Francisco – the most dynamic and probably best known of America's cathedrals. Her nomination by the Bishop of California, after an 18-month global search for a new Dean, was welcomed by the cathedral's trustees 'unanimously and enthusiastically'.

Jane first felt called to ordination when only 16, but it was not until she was reading History at Oxford and MOW was formed, that the possibility of responding came alive. She was among the first to join, was enthused by the American women priests visiting England, and began her own research into the history of women in the Church. Her move to Harvard to take a Master of Divinity degree expanded her vision of possibilities further and she moved on to California to teach at the Church Divinity School of the Pacific and complete a PhD at the University of California at Berkeley.

Returning to England in 1994, she became Tutorial Fellow in Church History at Regent's Park College, Oxford, serving also as Dean until her appointment in 2001 as Fellow, Chaplain and Dean of New College, Oxford. Meanwhile she had prepared for ordination on the St Albans and Oxford Ministerial Course, been made deacon, then priest, serving as a Self-Supporting Minister at the University Church and as an honorary chaplain at Christ Church Cathedral.

At New College she led the college's welfare and pastoral team and also worked with the choir school. Although she taught both theology and church history, she lectured primarily on nineteenth-century Christian thought and directed a research project on modern prophecy movements. She also ran the Oxford Theology Summer School.

She served as vice-chair of WATCH and has used her considerable skill as a writer to promote the cause of an inclusive Church, with regular contributions to the *Guardian* and the *Church Times* and through broadcasting. In a *Guardian* article she strongly opposed the proposed Anglican Covenant, designed as a solution to the division over homosexuality, arguing that baptism already provides the only covenant needed, and 'We should awake to our relationship with a loving God, bathed in the knowledge of God's love for each and every one of us.'

Jane has been a theological consultant to the House of Bishops and a conference consultant to the Lesbian and Gay Christian Movement, as well as Canon Theologian of Salisbury Cathedral and an Honorary Canon of Christ Church, Oxford. Her long and deep connections with the Episcopal Church in the United States have taken her to Visiting Professorships at Berkeley and other American universities. Valued as a preacher and liturgist as well as a theologian, she said at the time of her appointment to Grace Cathedral, 'My vision is of a Church that engages deeply with the world.'

Her writings include *Miracles in Enlightenment England* (2006) and *Octavia, Daughter of God* (2011), and she was joint editor of *The Call for Women Bishops* (2004).

Judith Maltby (b. 1938)

Judith Maltby is also a church historian and an American. After studying at the University of Illinois she came to England in 1979 for doctoral studies at Wolfson College, Cambridge, then a Research Fellowship at Newnham College. From 1987 to 1993 she taught Church History at Salisbury/Wells Theological College, serving also as a parish deacon at Wilton and in two associated parishes. She then moved to Oxford to become Chaplain and Fellow of Corpus Christi College and was ordained to the priesthood in 1994.

Judith specializes in the political and religious history of England in the sixteenth and seventeenth centuries and, in addition to a number of smaller historical studies, has published *The Prayer Book in Elizabethan and Early Stuart England* (1998). She is now Reader in Church History at Oxford and Canon Theologian of Leicester and Winchester Cathedrals. Active in MOW, she a member of WATCH and also of the official Church of England/Methodist Conversations.

Among the many other feminist theologians, one of the most exciting, who died far too young in 2009, was **Marcella Althaus-Reid**, an Argentinian Methodist schooled in Latin American Liberation Theology and the radical pedagogical insights of Paulo Freire. At the time of her appointment as Professor of Contextual Theology at New College, Edinburgh in 2006, she was the only woman Professor of Theology in a Scottish university. She wrote on Liberation Theology, Feminist Theology and what she called Queer Theology.

Janet Martin Soskice is a Canadian Roman Catholic and now Professor of Philosophical Theology and a Fellow of Jesus College, Cambridge. Before this she taught at Ripon College, Cuddesdon, Heythrop College, London and Oxford, and is a former Visiting Professor at the Gregorian University in Rome. She is President of the Society for the Study of Theology and has written on *Metaphor and Religious Language* (1987) and *The Kindness of God* (2007).

Elaine Graham is a Research Professor at Chester University, having spent several years as Professor of Social and Pastoral Theology at Manchester University. She has drawn attention to the lack of female insight and experience in the study and teaching of pastoral theology. *Life Cycles: Women and Pastoral Care* (1993), which she co-edited with Margaret Halsey, broke new ground and has been followed by *Making the Difference: Gender, Personhood and Theology* (1995), and *Transforming Practice: Pastoral Theology in an Age of Uncertainty* (1996). She is a Lay Canon of Manchester Cathedral.

Paula Gooder is a freelance biblical scholar who teaches as a Visiting Lecturer at King's College, London and an Honorary Lecturer at Birmingham University. A Reader, she is Canon Theologian of Birmingham and Guildford Cathedrals and is a member of the General Synod.

Charlotte Methuen is an Anglican priest who lectures in Church History at Glasgow University. Before this she taught in several major German universities, as well as at Oxford, and is a Lay Canon of Gloucester Cathedral. Earlier still, she was a community worker in the East End of London.

Nicola Slee is a Research Fellow at the Queen's Foundation, Birmingham, and has drawn attention to the fact that little, if any, attempt has been made to differentiate between the needs and experience of women and men in the development of religious faith. *Women's Faith Development: Patterns and Processes* (2004) indicates how much work is needed in this field. Her study of the place (usually beneath the surface) of women in the parables is particularly illuminating. She has also written many children's books.

In spite of these and other encouraging examples, there remains, however, little sign of feminist theology, as such, becoming a major subject for serious study in university theology departments. That it should inform and influence study across the whole field of theology is obviously of the greatest importance, but it also requires particular, specialist attention. For those who are preparing for service in the churches, a much clearer focus on the insights of feminist theology and their implications for life in communities of faith is also urgently needed.

24

The End of the Beginning

Viewed historically, the reform of the Church of England's life that has opened the priesthood and the episcopate to women has proceeded remarkably quickly. Not quickly enough for some (including the present author), and recent delays have been lamentable, but on the time-scale of other reforms, and this has easily been the most radical, it is hard to believe, realistically, that it could have been achieved very much sooner.

Just how radical it will prove to be has yet to be discovered and must await the advance of women into substantial, influential positions of leadership. Even then, it will be some time before, to use a common analogy, so large and ancient a vessel as the Church of England can be steered onto a very different course. The fact that it is already adrift in dangerous waters does, however, demand urgent action and, without succumbing to panic, wider vision, different experience, greater courage and new energy are required on the bridge.

Although in the short term it impinges less directly on the Church's life, the challenge posited by feminist theological insights is far more fundamental – more so than any other theological movement of the last century, and arguably more than any of the previous centuries of the Christian era. Much significant pioneering work has already been done in this many-sided enterprise, and its importance needs to be more widely recognized. At the same time, however, feminist theology's challenge has to be seen as one part of the major reconstruction required in other theological domains.

The contextual factors which help to explain why, for so many centuries, theological interpretations reinforced the oppression of women, as well as the victims of slavery and racism, and also assist in understanding why many traditional expressions of the Christian faith are not credible to inhabitants of the modern world. This is only to be expected, though not complacently tolerated.

St John's Gospel attributes to Jesus a promise which is of singular importance at the present time – 'When the Spirit of truth comes, he will guide you into all the truth' (John 16.13). While recognizing and being grateful for those insights into the truth disclosed by devout thinkers across the centuries, belief in the ceaseless activity of the Holy Spirit does not permit an absolute attachment to the disclosures that took place in the worlds of Augustine of Hippo, Thomas Aquinas, Martin Luther, John Calvin, Richard Hooker or even Karl Barth. More exploration is needed by both women and men theologians, and the fear of heresy subdued by deeper trust in the God whose love is always open-ended.

Meanwhile, the consecration of women bishops, completing the admission of women to the priesthood, should open the door to church reform – a task requiring the closest collaboration between women and men. First, however, it will be necessary for men in positions of leadership to listen carefully, humbly and positively to what their women colleagues may propose. The days when women's opinions were heard only to be stifled are now ended.

That acknowledged, I feel bold enough, as a retired, octogenarian Dean with 60 years of varied ministerial experience, to suggest a few areas in which the insights, experience and methods would bring significant benefits. Given the magnitude of the reforms required it is, however, important that new women church leaders should not be burdened with unreasonable expectations.

Consecration will incorporate them into an institution with long and deep historical roots which is highly resistant to change and highly skilled in coaxing new entrants into conformity. It will therefore be necessary to appoint several women to diocesan bishoprics quickly. Lone voices are soon subdued, and the suffragan bishopric route to diocesan responsibility, with its inhibition of initiative, is certainly undesirable.

The Church will be served well if women raise the question: 'What are bishops for?' The ordinal used at the consecration of bishops indicates with fearful clarity what they are expected to do, and the episcopal office has been exercised in different ways by individual bishops at different times in the Church's history. Recent developments have driven it much too far in the direction of management, with the result that the volume of e-mails, faxes, letters and meetings has created a burden of duty that can be carried only by workaholics. In most cases, space for reflection, strategic thinking and adequate pastoral care is entirely lacking. It is not to be expected that such a ministry will appeal to women, and perhaps they alone, with different priorities and a stronger sense of the need for collaborative ministry, will be capable of transforming it into something more apostolic.

Closely related to this are questions concerning the future of the thousand-years-old parochial system which is creaking badly for want of clergy, money and imagination. In spite of the major social changes of the last hundred years, particularly those affecting rural areas, there undoubtedly remains a place for ministry in local, residential communities; but not for that of single-handed priests entrusted with responsibility for an ever-increasing number of parishes. This no longer offers a solution and must be replaced by carefully designed forms of collaborative ministry involving stipendiary, self-supporting and local ordained priests, as well as a mobilized and trained laity. Male leadership has failed to devise this, and in some ways the recent ordination of a large number of women priests has helped to prop up something in need of reform. A fresh approach is needed.

At the same time, much wider recognition is needed of the fact that local residential communities are not the only, or even the most important, places where the Church's ministry is needed. Non-parochial ministries have already attracted a large number of women priests, and this for a variety of reasons. A substantial body of experience is being added to that of those male priests who have for many more years been involved in similar ministries, and the time has come, indeed is long overdue, for this to be assessed with a view to expansion.

This raises immediate questions related to the Church's deployment of its money and ministerial resources. Important research carried out by Teresa Morgan, Fellow and Tutor in Ancient History at Oriel College, Oxford, and a Self-Supporting Minister in the parish of Littlemore, revealed in 2011 that there is nothing approaching a system of effective deployment of the 3,100 Self-Supporting Ministers (1,586 of them women) who now constitute 27 per cent of the Church's ordained ministry. This was not altogether surprising since there is no system of deployment of the stipendiary ministry either – the long-standing *ad hoc* method has been recently reinforced by the advertising of many posts to which individuals from far and wide may or may not respond.

It goes without saying, though it had better be reaffirmed, that organizational change will not fulfil its true purpose unless it is grounded in and sustained by a deep spirituality, expressed in worship and prayer of different kinds. Spirituality I take to be that openness to God which characterized the life of Jesus and which enables his followers to discern, through openness also to the Christian tradition, including the Bible, what the Holy Spirit is saying today about life's opportunities and demands. This is no less necessary for communities of believers.

Women – priests and laity – have, as is only to be expected, already demonstrated what distinctive and creative insights they have to share in this vital area of Christian discipleship, and this needs to be shared more widely. The access of women to more positions of leadership in the Church will, it may confidentially be assumed, lead to a much stronger emphasis on the centrality of spirituality and a widening of its expressions.

During the last 50 years the Church of England has experienced more changes in its forms of worship than at any other time since the Reformation. More recently, several women have served on the Liturgical Commission responsible for initiating and formulating these changes. The once sacrosanct concept of a single Book of Common Prayer, designed to secure uniformity of worship in England's parish churches and cathedrals, has given way to a doctrine of variety expressed in a multiplicity of books and as wide a choice of liturgical material as most worshippers care to imagine.

In these circumstances it would be unwise to assume that proposals for further, more radical, liturgical change would be widely welcomed, even by the most flexible and forward-looking congregations. But within the existing arrangements there is, in preaching, leading of prayers, use of inclusive or non-gender language, presidency at the Eucharist and the ordering of ceremonial, as well as freedom to engage in extra-liturgical worship, much scope for significant change in the atmosphere of corporate prayer – much of which is already being experienced in parishes where women priests are influential.

Having themselves been excluded from ordained ministry for so long, and having often endured painful experiences of rejection when admitted to the priesthood, women are well placed to help the Church become a more inclusive community. That anyone should feel excluded from full participation on the Church's life by reason of their ethnicity, sexual orientation, social status or firmly held beliefs is always a denial of the gospel the Church exists to proclaim and exemplify. There is a long way to go before failure in this fundamental area of its life is remedied.

The infusion of new life and changed outlook in these, and doubtless other, parts of the Church's life and witness is an exciting prospect and one that engenders hope. The Church, being a community of sinners, will still have many weaknesses and never be 'without spot or wrinkle'. Men will not find it easy to relinquish power, and the challenge of presenting the Christian faith in terms that are both credible and attractive in the modern world will be as formidable as ever. But the Church will, by God's grace, move decisively towards that wholeness of life in the Spirit to which it is called and which is essential to a dynamic contribution to the longed-for greater unity of the whole human race.

Further Reading

The most comprehensive history of women in the Christian tradition is *Women and Christianity* (Columba Press, 3 volumes, 2000, 2001 and 2003) by Mary T. Malone, formerly Professor of Theology at Toronto School of Theology and now retired to her native Ireland.

The Women's Movement in the Church of England, 1850–1930 (Clarendon Press, 1988) is a classic study by Brian Heeney, a notable Canadian scholar, who left the manuscript when he died in 1983.

A New Strength, A New Song by Margaret Webster (Mowbray, 1994) is a first-hand account, with some background, of the part played by the Movement for the Ordination of Women in the campaign that brought success in 1992. Essential reading.

Had space and time permitted I would have written about the ordination of women in the main Free Churches. Unhindered by papal threats or untenable interpretations of apostolic succession, the Congregationalists began to ordain women in 1917, the Baptists in 1922, the Presbyterians in 1956 and the Methodists in 1974. These encouraging developments are, however, more than adequately described and evaluated in *This is Our Story: Free Church Women's Ministry*, edited by Janet Wootton (Epworth, 2007).

Most of the lay women who exercised outstanding ministries in the nineteenth and early twentieth centuries have their biographies, of varying quality. Among the best are: *Florence Nightingale* by Mark Bostridge (Viking, 2008, Penguin Books, 2009); *Josephine Butler* by Jane Jordan (John Murray, 2001); *Maude Royden* by Sheila Fletcher (Basil Blackwell, 1989).

Feminist Theology: Voices from the Past by Ann Loades (Polity, 2001) is a valuable study from a feminist perspective of the lives of Mary Wollstonecraft, Josephine Butler and Dorothy L. Sayers.

A History of the Mothers' Union: Women, Anglicanism and Globalisation,

1876–2008 by Cordelia Moyse (The Boydell Press, 2009) is a scholarly and perceptive history of the most influential lay movement in the Anglican Communion.

Bird of Paradise: *Glimpses of a Living Myth* by Monica Furlong (Mowbray, 1995) is the revealing autobiography of one of the radical leaders of the Movement for the Ordination of Women.

Feminist Theology by Natalie K. Watson (Eerdmans, 2003) is the most useful introduction to its subject, and the 54-page annotated bibliography indicates how prolific is the work now being undertaken in this domain.

Feminist Theology: A Reader edited by Ann Loades (SPCK, 1990) provides a selection of material representing the work some of the most influential scholars of its time.

The Cambridge Companion to Feminist Theology edited by Susan Frank Parsons (Cambridge University Press, 2002, third impression 2008) contains 13 articles of considerable erudition and depth.

Index